Algorithmic Market Making

Strategies for Liquidity and Profitability

William Johnson

For permissions and other inquiries, write to:
P.O. Box 3132, Framingham, MA 01701. USA

Contents

1 **Introduction to Algorithmic Market Making**   **7**

  1.1   Understanding Market Making 7

  1.2   Historical Context and Evolution 10

  1.3   The Role of a Market Maker 13

  1.4   Key Terms and Concepts 16

  1.5   Benefits and Challenges 20

  1.6   Overview of Algorithmic Strategies 23

  1.7   Impact of Technology and Innovation 26

2 **Basics of Financial Markets and Liquidity**   **31**

  2.1   Structure of Financial Markets 31

  2.2   Market Participants 34

  2.3   Liquidity and Market Depth 36

  2.4   Price Formation and Discovery 39

  2.5   Factors Affecting Market Liquidity 41

  2.6   Types of Orders and Their Impact 44

  2.7   Measuring and Analyzing Liquidity 47

3 **Market Microstructure and Price Dynamics**   **51**

  3.1   Understanding Market Microstructure 51

  3.2   Order Types and Matching Mechanisms 55

  3.3   Role of Information in Price Dynamics 59

3.4   Order Flow and Liquidity Provision   62

3.5   Market Impact and Transaction Costs   66

3.6   Price Volatility and its Drivers   70

3.7   High-Frequency Trading and Market Dynamics   74

4   Mathematics for Market Making Strategies   79

4.1   Probability and Statistics in Financial Markets   79

4.2   Stochastic Processes and Random Walks   83

4.3   Time Series Analysis   86

4.4   Mathematical Models of Market Making   89

4.5   Game Theory and Strategic Interaction   92

4.6   Optimization Techniques for Strategy Development . . .   94

4.7   Risk Measurement and Statistical Models   97

5   Risk Management in Market Making   101

5.1   Identifying Risks in Market Making   101

5.2   Risk Assessment and Measurement   104

5.3   Capital Allocation and Risk Limits   106

5.4   Hedging Strategies for Risk Mitigation   109

5.5   Portfolio Diversification   112

5.6   Adaptive Risk Management Strategies   115

5.7   Regulatory Compliance and Reporting   118

6   Statistical Arbitrage and Mean Reversion   123

6.1   Concept of Statistical Arbitrage   123

6.2   Mean Reversion Theory   126

6.3   Pairs Trading Strategies   129

6.4   Quantitative Models for Arbitrage   132

6.5   Risk and Reward in Statistical Arbitrage   134

6.6   Implementation Challenges   137

6.7   Performance Evaluation and Optimization   140

7 Machine Learning Techniques for Market Prediction   **145**

  7.1 Overview of Machine Learning in Finance 145

  7.2 Data Preprocessing and Feature Engineering 149

  7.3 Supervised Learning Algorithms 152

  7.4 Unsupervised Learning and Clustering 155

  7.5 Time Series Forecasting with ML 158

  7.6 Model Evaluation and Validation 161

  7.7 Advanced Techniques and Deep Learning 164

8 Algorithm Design and Backtesting   **169**

  8.1 Principles of Algorithm Design 169

  8.2 Data Collection and Processing 172

  8.3 Strategy Development and Testing 175

  8.4 Backtesting Frameworks 177

  8.5 Performance Metrics and Evaluation 180

  8.6 Optimization and Parameter Tuning 183

  8.7 Deployment and Monitoring 185

9 Implementing Market Making Algorithms   **189**

  9.1 Choosing the Right Tools and Platforms 189

  9.2 Designing Algorithmic Trading Logic 192

  9.3 Coding and Implementation Practices 195

  9.4 Order Execution and Management 198

  9.5 Monitoring and Surveillance Systems 200

  9.6 Handling Market Data in Real-Time 203

  9.7 Integration with Brokerage and Clearing Systems 206

10 Regulatory Considerations and Ethical Implications   **209**

  10.1 Regulatory Frameworks for Market Making 209

  10.2 Licensing and Registration Requirements 212

  10.3 Market Manipulation and Anti-Fraud Rules 215

10.4 Data Privacy and Security Considerations 218

10.5 Ethical Trading Practices 221

10.6 Impact of Regulation on Innovation 223

10.7 Global Harmonization of Regulations 226

11 Performance Evaluation and Optimization   231

11.1 Defining Performance Metrics 231

11.2 Analyzing Trading Performance 234

11.3 Benchmarking Against Market Standards 237

11.4 Identifying Areas for Improvement 240

11.5 Algorithm Optimization Techniques 242

11.6 Risk-Adjusted Performance Evaluation 245

11.7 Continuous Improvement and Adaptation 248

12 Technological Infrastructure for Market Making   253

12.1 High-Performance Computing for Trading 253

12.2 Data Management Systems 256

12.3 Network and Connectivity Solutions 259

12.4 Cloud Computing and Virtualization 261

12.5 Security and Cyber-Resilience 264

12.6 Algorithmic Trading Platforms 267

12.7 Maintenance and Technical Support 270

13 Case Studies and Real-World Applications   273

13.1 Historical Market Making Successes 273

13.2 Algorithmic Trading Firms and Their Models 276

13.3 Failures and Lessons Learned 279

13.4 Innovative Strategies in Emerging Markets 282

13.5 Ethical Challenges in Real-World Scenarios 285

13.6 Technology-Driven Transformations 287

13.7 Future Trends and Developments 290

Preface

In the intricate tapestry of global finance, where fractions of a second can sway fortunes, the art and science of market making stand as a beacon of opportunity and innovation. Algorithmic Market Making, once the preserve of elite financial institutions, has now moved to the forefront of trading strategies, redefining the landscape of liquidity provision and profitability. This book endeavors to demystify the complexities of algorithmic market making and arm you with the knowledge to navigate and thrive in the world of automated trading.

At its core, this book is an exploration of how technology and sophisticated models empower traders to capture value from market inefficiencies. As financial markets continue to evolve at a staggering pace, understanding how algorithms operate within this framework is crucial. This text is not merely theoretical; it bridges the gap between abstract mathematical concepts and practical trading tools.

Readers will embark on a detailed study of financial markets, delving into the mechanics of liquidity and exploring how pricing dynamics shape trading opportunities. Through comprehensive analysis of market microstructure and the strategic use of data, we uncover the fundamental processes that underlie effective algorithmic market making.

The synthesis of risk management practices with market making strategies is a pivotal theme throughout this book. Mastery of risk is the cornerstone of any successful trading enterprise, and you will learn how to quantify, assess, and strategically mitigate risks inherent in market making. By leveraging statistical models and machine learning techniques, traders can transcend traditional methods, achieving an astute understanding of market patterns and predictive analytics.

This book offers you the tools and insights needed to design, implement, and optimize robust market making algorithms. Through a blend of case studies and real-world applications, you will witness the transformative impact of these strategies across diverse market conditions. Emphasizing ethical and regulatory considerations, it ensures you are not only equipped to succeed but also attuned to the responsibilities of digital trading.

The journey through Algorithmic Market Making: Strategies for Liquidity and Profitability is both an intellectual and practical engagement with the cutting-edge of financial technology. Whether you are a nascent trader, a seasoned professional, or simply curious about the intersection of finance and automation, this book promises to be an invaluable companion, guiding you through the age of algorithms with clarity and precision. As you turn the pages, expect to gain not only knowledge but also a strategic advantage that reflects the elegance and expertise this field demands.

Chapter 1

Introduction to Algorithmic Market Making

Algorithmic market making represents a profound shift in the dynamics of financial markets, facilitating increased liquidity and efficiency through the use of automated trading systems. By understanding the historical evolution of market making and the contemporary role of algorithms in financial transactions, this section establishes the foundational knowledge necessary to grasp the intricacies of this field. Key concepts such as bid-ask spread, order book, and liquidity are introduced, providing the essential terminology for beginners. The benefits, challenges, and impact of technological innovations are also explored, setting the stage for a deeper analysis of algorithmic strategies in the subsequent chapters.

1.1 Understanding Market Making

Market making plays a vital role in the financial ecosystem, primarily by providing liquidity and ensuring efficient market operations. In essence, market makers serve as intermediaries that facilitate trading by continuously providing buy and sell quotes for various financial instruments.

By being ready to trade at publicly quoted prices, market makers help reduce the transaction costs and enhance the overall liquidity in the market. This section delves into the intricate details of market making, shedding light on its importance, mechanics, and implications in today's financial markets.

The essence of market making lies in liquidity provision. Liquidity, in this context, refers to the ease with which securities can be bought or sold without causing significant price changes. Market makers contribute significantly to liquidity by maintaining a continuous presence in the market, ready to buy or sell at certain prices. This presence ensures that investors, regardless of size, can execute trades promptly and at predictable prices. Without such liquidity, markets could become illiquid, where buying or selling significant volumes might lead to substantial price swings. These swings can introduce volatility and discourage market participation, particularly from retail investors or smaller institutional players.

Market makers profit from the bid-ask spread, which is the difference between the price at which they are willing to buy a security (bid price) and the price at which they are willing to sell (ask price). This spread compensates the market maker for the risk they undertake by providing liquidity. The narrower the spread, the more efficient the market is considered to be. In deep and liquid markets, competitive forces often drive spreads to be very tight, reflecting high efficiency and low transaction costs for traders.

A key aspect of market making is managing the inventory. Unlike traditional brokers who may just execute trades, market makers hold an inventory of stocks, currencies, or other financial instruments. This inventory management requires careful analysis and strategy to mitigate risks associated with price volatility. Market makers aim to maintain a balanced inventory, so they don't become overly exposed to market movements in one direction. If a market maker accumulates too large a position, they might adjust prices to incentivize traders to take the opposite side, thereby rebalancing their position.

Market making is not without its challenges. Market makers face substantial risks, primarily from adverse selection and market volatility. Adverse selection occurs when market makers trade with informed traders, who have superior information about the true value of an asset. To mitigate this risk, market makers often rely on sophisticated models and real-time data analysis to adjust prices dynamically based on perceived information asymmetry. Additionally, during periods of high volatility, managing risk becomes more complex as price swings can significantly impact the value of their inventory.

The importance of market makers becomes particularly evident during periods of financial stress or uncertainty. In such times, the role of market making in providing liquidity can be the difference between orderly and disorderly market functioning. Market makers help stabilize the market by absorbing shock trades and providing a buffer against rapid price movements. Consequently, regulatory frameworks often emphasize the need for robust market making as a pillar of market integrity.

The advent of electronic trading platforms and algorithmic trading has transformed the landscape of market making. Traditional human-led market making has increasingly been replaced by automated systems capable of executing trades at unprecedented speeds. These systems employ advanced algorithms that continually assess market conditions and adjust quotes in real-time. This shift towards automation has enhanced market efficiency but has also introduced new complexity in understanding market dynamics.

Algorithmic market makers leverage vast datasets and computational power to remain competitive. They utilize algorithms programmed to operate on predefined sets of rules and statistical correlations. These algorithms continuously monitor order flows and market indicators, updating bid and ask prices to manage risk and capture profit opportunities. The integration of machine learning techniques further enhances the capability of such systems to predict market trends and optimize decision-making.

A classic example of market making can be observed in the foreign exchange (FX) market. Forex market makers provide liquidity by quoting continuous buy and sell prices on currency pairs. Their operations are crucial for ensuring that currencies remain accessible for transactions globally, supporting international trade and investment activities. An efficient FX market promotes economic stability by facilitating cross-border trade and helping in currency risk management.

While market making is largely conducted by large financial institutions or specialized trading firms, technological advancements have democratized access to these activities. Retail traders now have access to platforms that offer market making services, allowing them to simulate providing liquidity with digital assets, particularly within the expanding realm of cryptocurrencies. In these cases, market making involves strategically placing orders to benefit from the bid-ask spread while providing liquidity to the asset class.

In modern financial markets, the significance of market making extends beyond traditional assets to commodities, derivatives, and even cryptocurrencies. Each market has its own set of dynamics and challenges for market makers to consider. For instance, in commodity markets, factors such as seasonality, geopolitical tensions, and supply chain disruptions can affect liquidity and price stability. Market makers operating in these markets must account for these unique characteristics in their strategies.

Within the domain of cryptocurrency trading, market making assumes additional complexity due to the inherently volatile nature of digital assets. The nascent state of many cryptocurrency exchanges and the relative lack of regulation further contribute to challenges in providing liquidity consistently. Nonetheless, the growing interest in digital currencies has seen market makers adapting their models to accommodate crypto assets, thereby contributing to the maturation of these markets.

Understanding market making involves appreciating its multifaceted nature and acknowledging the broader economic implications. Market makers not only enhance liquidity and reduce transaction costs but also play a crucial role in price discovery, enabling markets to function more effectively. However, the complexities inherent in their operations demand a comprehensive understanding of both market conditions and the regulatory environment.

In today's interconnected and digitalized markets, the role of a market maker is indispensable. Their ability to provide liquidity, facilitate trades, and manage risks ensures that markets remain viable and efficient over time. As financial markets continue to evolve, driven by technological innovations and regulatory changes, market making will likely undergo further transformations, emphasizing the need for ongoing learning and adaptation within this essential market function.

1.2   Historical Context and Evolution

The concept of market making has evolved dramatically over time, reflecting shifts in technology, economic paradigms, and regulatory environments. Understanding this evolution offers a window into how financial markets themselves have transformed and provides a foundation for appreciating the sophisticated nature of modern algorithmic market making. This section explores the historical trajectory of market making, tracing its origins from the earliest forms of trade to the advanced digital platforms of the present era.

In its most rudimentary form, market making can be traced back to ancient times when merchant traders facilitated commerce by matching buyers with sellers, thus providing liquidity in localized markets. These early market facilitators were pivotal in fostering trade routes across continents, such as the Silk Road, connecting diverse economies and laying the groundwork for more organized exchanges.

During the Middle Ages, as trading hubs like Venice and Amsterdam gained prominence, the role of market makers began to formalize. The Amsterdam Stock Exchange, established in the early 17th century, is often cited as the world's first official stock exchange. Here, brokers and money changers acted as early market makers, quoting prices for shares of the Dutch East India Company, which dominated maritime trade. Their presence not only facilitated transactions but also helped in the establishment of reliable pricing mechanisms and the expansion of financial instruments.

The 19th century witnessed significant advancements in market making as financial markets became more structured with the rise of stock exchanges in London, New York, and other major cities. The London Stock Exchange, for instance, saw the emergence of 'jobbers,' who specialized in creating liquidity by buying and selling shares from brokers. These jobbers were the predecessors to modern market makers, utilizing their capital to hold inventory and manage the spread between their buying and selling prices.

Parallel developments occurred in the New York Stock Exchange (NYSE) where specialists performed similar roles, maintaining an orderly market by providing liquidity and continuity for designated stocks. The specialist system was a defining feature of the NYSE for much of its history, with specialists acting as both auctioneers and market makers, balancing supply and demand while managing their inventory positions.

As the 20th century progressed, market making began to undergo significant transformations driven by technological advancements and regulatory developments. The introduction of electronic trading came about in the latter half of the century, revolutionizing how market making was conducted. The advent of computerized systems enabled the automation of many facets of trading, leading to increased speed, efficiency, and transparency in executing orders.

The shift towards electronic trading was marked by the establishment of

NASDAQ, which began operations in 1971 as the first electronic stock market. Unlike the NYSE, which was still heavily reliant on face-to-face trading and a specialist system, NASDAQ allowed for multiple competing market makers, each quoting prices in a decentralized manner. This openness attracted smaller firms to participate in market making, vastly increasing the liquidity available.

Increased competition among market makers, as facilitated by electronic markets, led to tighter spreads and improved market efficiency. Regulatory changes, such as the Securities Acts Amendments of 1975, further encouraged the development of a National Market System (NMS) in the United States. This system sought to integrate disparate markets, ensure fair competition, and enhance the ease of trade execution, thus democratizing access to market making.

The late 20th and early 21st centuries saw the rapid advancement of computing technology and data analytics, which revolutionized market making once again. Algorithmic trading emerged, allowing market makers to deploy sophisticated algorithms that could analyze large datasets in real time and execute trades with minimal latency. Such technology proved instrumental in handling the growing volumes and complexities of modern financial markets.

Algorithmic market making systems use mathematical models to assess risk, manage inventory, and adjust pricing strategies dynamically. These algorithms enable market makers to operate in various asset classes, including equities, fixed income, commodities, and foreign exchange, with high efficiency. Unlike traditional market makers, who rely on manual decision-making, algorithmic systems can process information and execute trades at a speed far beyond human capability.

One of the pinnacle achievements in the evolution of market making is the development and application of artificial intelligence (AI) and machine learning in trading algorithms. These technologies have empowered market makers with predictive capabilities, allowing them to forecast price movements and optimize liquidity provision strategies. AI-driven market makers analyze vast quantities of historical and real-time data to adapt their models continuously, thus improving their decision-making process.

However, the evolution of market making has not been without challenges. The 2010 Flash Crash, where the US stock market temporarily fell dramatically before recovering within minutes, underscored the potential risks associated with high-speed electronic trading. It highlighted the importance of effective controls and oversight in preventing market

14

disruptions caused by algorithmic anomalies or erroneous trades.

Regulators worldwide have since bolstered their frameworks to ensure the stability and transparency of financial markets, acknowledging the critical role market makers play. Measures such as circuit breakers, tighter scrutiny of high-frequency trading, and enhanced reporting requirements have been introduced to safeguard against systemic risks.

Today, market making is an intricate blending of human expertise and technological prowess. Firms involved in market making leverage state-of-the-art technology to conduct trading across global markets, employing teams of quantitative analysts, programmers, and traders to develop and refine their strategies. The integration of blockchain technology and distributed ledger systems is also beginning to change the future landscape, promising greater transparency and security in trading operations.

The historical evolution of market making elucidates the transformative power of innovation in shaping financial markets. From the bustling trade routes of the ancient world to the high-frequency algorithms of today, market makers have continuously evolved to meet the changing needs of market participants. This evolution reflects broader themes in economic history, technological progress, and regulatory adaptation, and it highlights the enduring importance of liquidity provision as a cornerstone of efficient market operations.

As global markets continue to innovate and adapt, understanding the journey of market making is essential for anyone wishing to comprehend its role and impact comprehensively. The lessons learned from past developments guide present practices and future innovations, ensuring that market making remains a dynamic and vital component of the financial ecosystem.

1.3   The Role of a Market Maker

In the intricate tapestry of financial markets, market makers occupy a pivotal position, ensuring smooth and efficient trade execution. Their role extends beyond mere participation; they are architects of liquidity, shaping the market landscape with their continuous presence. This section delves into the multifaceted responsibilities and objectives of market makers, exploring how they balance inventory management, risk minimization, and profit generation. Through a deeper understanding of these dynamics, one can appreciate the vital contribution market makers make to market stability and efficiency.

At the core of a market maker's role is the provision of liquidity. By continuously quoting both bid and ask prices for financial instruments, market makers ensure that other market participants can buy or sell assets with minimal friction. This perpetual quoting acts as a lubricant in the financial system, facilitating trading activities and enabling price discovery. The liquidity provided by market makers reduces the transaction costs for investors and minimizes the impact of large orders on market prices.

A market maker's profitability is closely tied to the bid-ask spread, the difference between the price a market maker is willing to buy a security (bid) and the price it is willing to sell (ask). This spread compensates the market maker for the risks involved in holding inventory and the capital committed to market making activities. However, the spread must be carefully managed to balance competitiveness and risk. In highly liquid markets, spreads tend to be narrower due to intense competition among market makers, leading to lower transaction costs and enhanced market efficiency.

Inventory management is a defining responsibility for market makers. Unlike brokers who simply facilitate transactions, market makers actively trade and hold positions. Effective inventory management requires a delicate balance between having enough inventory to provide liquidity and limiting exposure to market price fluctuations. Market makers continuously assess their inventory positions, using sophisticated models and real-time data to adjust their portfolios dynamically.

They may employ hedging strategies, using derivatives or other financial instruments, to mitigate the risk arising from holding large positions in volatile markets. For example, a market maker in the equities market might use options or futures contracts to hedge against adverse price movements. This allows them to maintain liquidity while protecting their profitability from market downturns.

Another essential aspect of a market maker's role is risk management. Market makers are exposed to various risks, including market risk, credit risk, and operational risk. Market risk arises from changes in asset prices, which can affect the value of their inventory. To manage this risk, market makers use real-time analytics and trading algorithms to adjust their quotes and inventory in response to market conditions. They employ risk models to quantify and control potential losses, ensuring that their risk exposure remains within acceptable limits.

Credit risk is another concern, particularly when market makers engage in bilateral trading agreements. Counterparties may default on their obligations, exposing the market maker to potential losses. To mitigate this risk, market makers perform rigorous credit assessments and may require collateral to secure trades. Operational risk, stemming from system failures or errors, is mitigated by implementing robust trading infrastructures, conducting regular system audits, and maintaining rigorous compliance protocols.

The technological transformation of market making has introduced advanced algorithms and electronic trading platforms that have redefined how market makers operate. Algorithmic trading has enabled market makers to execute large volumes of transactions at high speeds with precision. These algorithms factor in numerous variables, including order flow, market depth, and volatility patterns, to optimize quoting strategies and respond to market changes instantaneously.

Market makers also play a crucial role in price discovery, the process by which the fair market value of an asset is determined. By providing continuous quotes, they help integrate diverse market information, reflecting supply and demand dynamics in asset prices. Price discovery is particularly vital in less liquid markets where the flow of information is not as robust as it is in highly liquid markets. In these settings, market makers' quotes can significantly influence the perceived value of assets, impacting investment decisions and market trends.

Market makers must also adhere to a complex web of regulations governing market conduct and operational standards. These regulations, designed to protect market integrity and ensure fair trading practices, encompass various aspects of market making, from capital requirements to reporting obligations. Regulators require that market makers maintain adequate capital reserves to withstand market shocks and continue providing liquidity during periods of stress. Compliance with these regulations is critical, as violations can lead to severe penalties and reputational damage.

An illustrative example of the critical role of market makers can be seen in the options and futures markets, which involve complex derivative instruments. In these markets, market makers facilitate trading by providing liquidity, enabling hedging, and arbitrage strategies for other market participants. Their presence supports the efficient functioning of the derivatives market, where the lack of liquidity can lead to heightened volatility and increased transaction costs.

Crypto markets present a modern and compelling instance of market

17

making's evolution. Given the decentralized and often fragmented nature of cryptocurrency exchanges, market makers are vital for providing liquidity and stability across various digital coins. They deploy advanced algorithms to manage the high volatility and rapid trading dynamics characteristic of this emerging asset class. Through their operations, crypto market makers contribute to the maturation and legitimization of these markets, attracting institutional investors and fostering broader adoption.

To summarize the role of a market maker without employing explicit concluding phrases, it is evident that their operations are indispensable to the health and efficiency of financial markets. By providing liquidity and facilitating smoother trade execution, they help stabilize prices and reduce costs for all participants. The evolution of market making reflects broader trends in financial innovation, technological advancement, and regulatory developments, ensuring that markets function effectively in an ever-changing landscape. Consequently, the role of market makers remains crucial, underscoring their importance in safeguarding market integrity and fostering economic growth.

1.4   Key Terms and Concepts

In market making, a firm grasp of essential terminology is fundamental to understanding how these financial activities operate in various contexts. This section elucidates key terms and concepts that underpin market making, offering detailed explanations and examples to illustrate their practical significance. By mastering these concepts, readers can navigate the intricacies of market making with confidence, whether they are novice traders or seasoned investors looking to deepen their expertise.

The **bid-ask spread** is one of the foundational concepts in market making. It represents the difference between the bid price, which is the highest price a buyer is willing to pay for a security, and the ask price, the lowest price a seller is willing to accept. The spread is a critical indicator of market liquidity and efficiency. A narrow spread generally suggests a liquid market with high trading activity and competition among market makers, thereby indicating lower transaction costs for investors. Conversely, a wider spread often points to less liquidity, potentially increasing the cost for traders to execute their orders.

Consider the stock of a well-known company like Apple Inc. In a highly liquid market, the bid-ask spread for Apple's shares might be just a few cents, reflecting intense competition among market makers and the high trading volume. In contrast, a smaller company with limited trading volumes might experience a bid-ask spread of several dollars, indicating less liquidity and greater market maker risk in holding inventory.

The **order book** is another vital concept, serving as a repository of all buy and sell orders for a specific asset within a market. It provides a real-time snapshot of market supply and demand, listing all outstanding orders arranged by price level. The order book is routinely displayed in two columns: bids on one side and asks on the other, along with the number of shares or contracts available at each price. This tool is indispensable for market makers as it helps them assess the depth of the market and the likely impact of large transactions. Monitoring the order book allows market makers to make informed pricing and risk management decisions.

Liquidity refers to the ease with which an asset can be converted into cash without significantly affecting its market price. Market makers are integral to maintaining liquidity by continuously providing buy and sell quotes, enabling swift and smooth transactions. High liquidity is desirable in financial markets as it facilitates rapid order execution, tightens spreads, and reduces the price impact of trades. Illiquid markets, on the other hand, can lead to higher spreads and increased volatility, posing risks to both investors and market makers.

Liquidity is essential across asset classes, including equities, fixed income, foreign exchange, and commodities. For instance, U.S. Treasuries are often hailed as highly liquid due to their vast market depth and frequent trading, whereas a micro-cap stock may suffer from illiquidity, resulting in larger bid-ask spreads and more pronounced price swings.

Volatility is a measure of the frequency and magnitude of price movements for a given security. It signifies how much the price of an asset fluctuates over a specified period. For market makers, volatility is a double-edged sword. While it can present opportunities to profit from price fluctuations, it also introduces heightened risk to holding inventory. High volatility can widen the bid-ask spread as market makers adjust their prices to account for uncertainty and protect against rapid adverse movements.

To manage increased volatility, market makers may employ various risk mitigation strategies, such as diversifying their asset holdings or utilizing derivatives to hedge their exposures. During periods of intense market activity, like earnings announcements or geopolitical events, volatility tends to rise, challenging market makers to balance competitive pricing with prudent risk management.

Market depth is a related concept that refers to a market's ability to absorb large orders without having a substantial impact on the asset's price. A market with considerable depth is one where significant buy and sell orders can be processed with minimal price disruption. Market depth is closely linked with liquidity, and a deep market usually exhibits tight spreads and reduced volatility. The order book is a direct reflection of market depth, displaying the volume of outstanding bid and ask offers at various price levels.

Understanding market depth is critical for market makers as it informs them of the potential liquidity available for large trades. Visual representations of market depth charts enable market makers to visualize supply and demand concentrations, which can guide them in setting bid and ask quotes and managing inventory levels effectively.

Market depth analysis is particularly important in scenarios involving large institutional trades, where the void left by massive order volumes can create liquidity vacuums. To prevent significant adverse price effects, market makers may stagger trade execution across different times or price levels, leveraging their understanding of available market depth.

Adverse selection is a concept that defines the scenario where market makers might incur losses due to trading with counterparties who possess superior information about the value of an asset. These informed traders may capitalize on market makers' lack of access to the same level of insights, executing trades that benefit the well-informed counterparties at the expense of the market maker. To mitigate adverse selection, market makers rely on sophisticated risk models and constantly update their pricing strategies, reflecting changes in market sentiment and information flow.

For instance, if a market maker unknowingly trades with a sophisticated investor ahead of an unexpected earnings announcement, they may end up acquiring inventory that could decline significantly in value, assuming the news is unfavorable. Understanding the risk of adverse selection encourages market makers to leverage technology and algorithms to dynamically adjust quotes, balancing profitability with risk exposure.

Integral to market making is the notion of **inventory risk**, which arises from the market maker's role as a principal in buying and selling financial instruments. Managing this risk requires a strategic balance between inventory levels and market conditions, as excessive exposure in one direction may amplify losses during market downturns. Effective inventory risk management entails continuous assessment of market trends, diversification, and hedging activities to stabilize potential impacts on the portfolio.

Inventory risk can manifest in rapidly moving markets where executing hedging strategies become challenging due to increased volatility and widening spreads. Market makers might deploy dynamic hedging techniques, such as delta-hedging options positions, to keep portfolios balanced and mitigate directional market risks.

Stop loss orders and their proper management represent another critical aspect for market makers seeking to manage their risk. These orders trigger an automatic sale of a security when its price reaches a predetermined level, acting as a safeguard against excessive losses. Market makers must anticipate and manage potential market reactions to clusters of stop-loss orders, as these can lead to cascading price movements during periods of high volatility.

Finally, the rise of **algorithmic trading** has significantly shaped the landscape of market making by introducing efficiency and precision. Algorithms programmed to execute trades based on specific criteria can optimize the execution of market makers' strategies, continuously adjusting to the market environment. Algorithmic systems enhance the ability of market makers to manage spreads, optimize liquidity provision, and implement rapid hedging maneuvers in response to evolving market conditions.

These key terms and concepts form the vocabulary of market making and provide the analytical tools required to understand this essential market function. By mastering them, participants can navigate the complexities of financial trading environments with a clearer perspective, enhancing their capabilities to strategize and make well-informed decisions. As market conditions and technologies continue to evolve, these foundational concepts remain critical to understanding and engaging effectively in market making.

1.5   Benefits and Challenges

The dual nature of benefits and challenges encapsulates the essence of market making in the financial markets. Market making stands as a keystone, fostering liquidity and facilitating fair price discovery while also confronting inherent operational risks and regulatory hurdles. This section comprehensively explores both the advantages enjoyed by market makers and the challenges they must navigate, detailing the complex yet rewarding landscape of market making.

One of the most significant benefits of market making is the provision of liquidity, which is crucial for the smooth functioning of financial markets. Market makers consistently quote buy and sell prices, enabling other market participants to execute trades efficiently at nearly any moment. This process reduces transaction costs and minimizes slippage, thus allowing for the fluid movement of capital within the financial system. By bridging the gap between buyers and sellers, market makers enhance market efficiency, leading to tighter bid-ask spreads and improved volume turnover.

Liquidity provision, particularly in less liquid asset classes, such as certain corporate bonds or emerging market stocks, is a notable contribution that market makers provide. Without these entities, accessing or exiting a position could become costly and slow, hampering market participation and potentially deterring investors. This liquidity ensures that even during periods of market stress, market makers can help stabilize the system by continuing to provide quotes and execute trades.

The role of market makers extends to facilitating price discovery, a core function of the market. Through their continuous quotations and willingness to engage in trades, market makers gather and reflect vast amounts of information about buyer and seller intentions, ecosystem-wide demand, and supply characteristics. The aggregation of such data into actionable price points aids in painting an accurate picture of an asset's fair market value, benefitting the entirety of market participants by reducing information asymmetry and promoting transparency.

Additionally, market making offers economic incentives to the entities involved. By profiting from the bid-ask spread, market makers can generate substantial revenue streams, particularly in high-volume markets where transaction frequency offsets typically narrow spreads. In algorithmic trading setups, this revenue model benefits further from the ability to operate at exceptional speeds, capturing small profit margins on a massive scale through high-frequency trading.

Market making firms also benefit from advanced technology and data analytics, providing them with the ability to leverage artificial intelligence, machine learning, and predictive modeling. These technological tools enable faster decision-making processes, improved risk management, and more precise order execution. As a result, technology not only acts as an enabler of efficiency and profit maximization but also as a differentiator in gaining competitive advantages over other market participants.

Despite these considerable benefits, market making is accompanied by an array of challenges, primarily rooted in risk exposure. Market makers carry inventory, exposing themselves to market risk associated with price fluctuations of held assets. In highly volatile markets, these risks are amplified, necessitating robust risk management strategies, such as hedging, to mitigate exposure to sudden price movements. Hedging requires the use of financial derivatives or corresponding offsetting positions that can limit potential losses.

Operational risk is another concern, particularly in the context of algorithmic trading and high-frequency environments. The rapid display and execution of quotes demand that trading platforms be robust, reliable, and capable of processing vast quantities of data with minimal latency. The risk of system failure or software glitches can lead to significant financial consequences, as seen in historical "flash crashes" resulting from erroneous algorithmic trades. To counteract these risks, market makers must invest in resilient technological infrastructures, conduct routine audits, and institute failsafe mechanisms such as kill-switches to immediately halt trading activities if anomalies are detected.

Adverse selection poses another layer of complexity challenging market makers. It refers to the situation where market makers may inadvertently trade with informed counterparties who possess superior information, potentially leading to unfavorable outcomes. When market makers engage in transactions without access to full information, they may find themselves on the losing side of trades as informed traders capitalize on knowledgeable insights about asset valuations. To mitigate adverse selection, market makers leverage sophisticated real-time data analytics and employ algorithms with adaptive pricing models that can detect discrepancies and adjust strategies accordingly.

One of the nuanced challenges for market makers operating within highly regulated environments is the constantly evolving regulatory landscape. Regulations aim to ensure market stability and fairness, requiring market makers to adhere to strict guidelines surrounding cap-

ital requirements, reporting obligations, and risk management practices. However, adapting to these regulations can entail considerable
costs and resource commitments, demanding that market makers keep
abreast of legal developments and remain compliant. The ability to navigate these changes agilely while maintaining operational efficiency is
crucial for sustained success.

Geopolitical factors offer additional layers of challenge to market makers, often introducing unpredictable risks into the financial environments within which they operate. Political tensions, trade policies, and
economic sanctions can disrupt capital flows and market sentiment,
leading to volatility spikes that affect the liquidity and pricing strategies
maintained by market makers. For instance, uncertainty around major
market events, such as Brexit or international trade negotiations, can
necessitate the reevaluation of risk exposures and preemptive adjustments to limit vulnerability.

Market makers in the cryptocurrency domain, an emerging and rapidly
evolving area, experience additional distinct challenges. The inherent volatility of digital asset markets and their nascent regulatory
contexts create unique conditions that market makers must navigate.
Crypto market makers must contend with fragmented liquidity across
exchanges and rapidly changing market structures, requiring technologically adaptive strategies and a deep understanding of cryptographic
principles and blockchain technology.

The esteemed duality of the benefits and challenges of market making
reflects the complex landscape within which these entities operate. The
liquidity provision, enhanced market efficiency, and price discovery facilitated by market makers are indispensable to sound and transparent
markets. However, the inherent risks, operational complexities, regulatory dynamics, and technological demands render market making as
a domain necessitating expert analysis, robust strategies, and continuous adaptability.

As markets evolve with technological innovation and regulatory developments, market makers must remain agile, balancing their drive for
profitability with a cognizance of the challenges underpinning their operations. Embracing advancements in artificial intelligence, data analytics, and high-frequency trading will continue to redefine the capabilities
and roles of market makers, firmly rooting them as integral components
of the global financial landscape.

1.6   Overview of Algorithmic Strategies

Algorithmic trading has emerged as a cornerstone in the realm of market making, significantly enhancing the ability of market makers to provide liquidity efficiently, manage risks, and optimize trading strategies. This section offers a comprehensive examination of various algorithmic strategies employed by market makers, delving into their mechanisms, objectives, and the technological advancements that drive them. By exploring these strategies, readers will gain insight into how algorithmic tools have revolutionized trading, enabling market makers to thrive amidst today's dynamic financial landscapes.

At the heart of algorithmic strategies is the deployment of advanced computational algorithms that automate trading decisions and execution processes. By utilizing computer programs designed to operate based on pre-defined rules and logic, market makers can analyze vast datasets in real-time, execute trades at lightning speeds, and manage positions with precision. The sophistication of these algorithms allows market makers to navigate complex market environments, capitalize on arbitrage opportunities, and mitigate exposure to risks.

One of the primary algorithmic strategies employed in market making is **statistical arbitrage**, which involves exploiting price inefficiencies between different financial instruments or markets. This strategy relies on sophisticated mathematical and statistical models to identify temporary mispricings and execute trades that profit from the eventual correction of these anomalies. By performing minor yet high-frequency transactions, market makers can capture differential valuations and enhance trade profitability.

Statistical arbitrage requires a deep understanding of market relationships, as well as the ability to construct and continuously update models that predict pricing discrepancies. For example, a statistical arbitrage strategy in the equities market might involve simultaneously buying and selling correlated stocks whose prices have diverged from their historical spread, betting on a reversion to the mean. The success of such strategies lies in accurate model calibration, robust backtesting, and effective real-time execution.

Market making algorithms are a direct evolution of traditional market making practices, focused on providing liquidity by continuously quoting bid and ask prices across different financial instruments. These algorithms are designed to optimize the bid-ask spread, balancing the need for competitive pricing against the requirement to maintain prof-

25

itability. They adaptively adjust quotes based on prevailing market conditions, ensuring that market makers can respond swiftly to changes in market depth, volatility, and order flow.

In crafting effective market making algorithms, market makers employ techniques such as reinforcement learning and machine learning to enhance decision-making processes. These technologies enable the algorithm to learn from historical data, improving its ability to predict future market movements and dynamically adjust its strategies. As the market evolves, these learnings are incorporated into the algorithm, allowing it to refine its quoting behavior continually, thereby maximizing competitive advantage.

Another key algorithmic strategy is **trend following**, which aims to capitalize on the momentum of asset prices by identifying and following prevailing price trends. Unlike strategies that seek market inefficiencies, trend following algorithms monitor price patterns, volume indicators, and technical analysis signals to identify trending assets, executing trades aligned with these movements. This strategy is employed across asset classes, from equities and commodities to foreign exchange and cryptocurrencies, taking advantage of the momentum effect that often characterizes trending markets.

Successful trend following relies on the careful calibration of entry and exit points to ensure trades align with the trend effectively. Algorithms used in this strategy often incorporate technical indicators, such as moving averages, relative strength index (RSI), or Bollinger Bands, to quantify market trends and trigger trading actions when predefined conditions are met. One of the greatest challenges in trend following is balancing responsiveness to short-term fluctuations with the ability to capture long-term trends without frequent whipsaws.

In contrast to trend following, **mean reversion** strategies bet on the temporary deviation of an asset's price from its historical average, assuming that prices will eventually revert to the mean. This algorithmic strategy involves identifying asset prices that are overextended relative to historical norms and executing contrarian trades to profit from their eventual correction. Mean reversion is grounded in the statistical properties of prices, leveraging historical volatility measures, and regression analysis to identify opportunities.

Market makers use mean reversion in conjunction with other algorithms to manage inventory risks and preserve profitability in volatile market conditions. For instance, a market maker observing that a particular stock has deviated significantly from its average price might increase inventory levels on the assumption of a price correction, thereby capitalizing on the anticipated reversion.

Further enhancing algorithmic trading capabilities are **execution algorithms**, which are designed to minimize market impact when executing large orders. These algorithms strategically break down large orders into smaller trades, spacing them out over a period of time to avoid unfavorable price distortions. Utilizing techniques such as Volume-Weighted Average Price (VWAP) or Time-Weighted Average Price (TWAP), execution algorithms aim to achieve the best possible average execution price without disrupting market equilibrium.

Market makers employ execution algorithms to fulfill large institutional orders or manage sizable inventory positions, mitigating risks associated with liquidity constraints and price slippage. These algorithms incorporate market depth analysis, expected order book dynamics, and historical trading patterns to determine optimal trade schedules and execution paths.

High-frequency trading (HFT) represents a pinnacle of algorithmic trading, characterized by ultra-fast order executions measured in microseconds. HFT algorithms conduct a vast number of trades in rapid succession, capitalizing on minute price discrepancies and market inefficiencies. The goal of HFT strategies is to secure consistent, albeit small, profit margins over a high volume of transactions, resulting in substantial cumulative returns.

HFT is driven by state-of-the-art technologies that ensure low-latency trading and co-location of servers near exchange platforms. Market makers utilizing HFT strategies must maintain cutting-edge infrastructure, employ real-time data feeds, and possess exceptional risk management protocols to succeed in this highly competitive space. The high speeds and complexity inherent to HFT also introduce unique challenges, such as the risk of algorithmic errors or inadvertent market disruptions, necessitating rigorous oversight and fail-safes.

In recent years, **artificial intelligence (AI) and machine learning** have further propelled the evolution of algorithmic strategies, enabling greater predictive capabilities and enhanced adaptability. By ingesting and analyzing large datasets, machine learning algorithms can uncover complex patterns and nonlinear relationships, optimizing trading models and refining decision-making processes.

For example, deep learning algorithms can identify latent features in market data, improving the ability to predict price movement, trend reversals, and volatility spikes. By integrating AI with traditional strategies such as statistical arbitrage or trend following, market makers can enhance their capability to respond to evolving market conditions in an adaptive and automated manner.

The overview of algorithmic strategies highlights the transformative impact of technology and innovation in market making, showcasing how these strategies equip market makers to thrive in today's fast-paced and data-driven environment. By leveraging the power of algorithmic tools, market makers can improve liquidity provision, manage risks, and maximize profitability, thereby reinforcing their standing as key players in the global financial markets. As technology continues to advance, the development of more sophisticated algorithms and the integration of emerging technologies, such as blockchain, promise further enhancements in the evolution of market making strategies.

1.7   Impact of Technology and Innovation

The financial markets have undergone profound transformations due to the relentless advancement of technology and the continuous wave of innovation. This evolution has radically changed the landscape of market making, enabling market makers to operate with unprecedented speed and efficiency while empowering them with new tools for risk management and strategic decision-making. This section delves into the multifaceted impact of technology and innovation on market making, illustrating how these developments have reshaped trading practices and enhanced the functioning of financial markets.

One of the most significant impacts of technology on market making is the automation of trading processes. The transition from manual trading floors to electronic trading platforms has revolutionized the way market makers interact with the market. Electronic trading enables near-instantaneous execution of trades, dramatically improving speed and reducing transaction costs. This shift has enhanced liquidity provision and market efficiency, as market makers can now respond to market changes with heightened agility and precision.

Automated trading systems, built upon algorithmic foundations, allow market makers to process and analyze vast quantities of market data in real time. These systems utilize sophisticated algorithms to generate buy and sell signals based on a variety of inputs, including historical price data, order flow, and market sentiment. This capability not only increases the speed at which market makers can execute trades but also enhances their capacity for managing inventory and mitigating risk exposure. For example, when a market maker detects a sudden increase in selling pressure on a particular asset, algorithms can automatically adjust asking prices or hedge positions to offset potential losses.

Algorithmic trading has also facilitated the rise of high-frequency trading (HFT), a strategy that leverages low-latency infrastructure and rapid order execution to capture small price discrepancies across highly liquid markets. HFT firms often co-locate their servers near exchange data centers to minimize latency and gain a competitive edge. The automation and speed of HFT enable market makers to execute thousands of trades per second, providing liquidity at an unprecedented scale and tightening bid-ask spreads across multiple asset classes.

Furthermore, advancements in data analytics and machine learning have enabled market makers to employ predictive models that improve decision-making processes. Machine learning algorithms can analyze complex datasets and identify patterns or correlations that might elude human analysis. These models can forecast price movements, detect anomalies, and optimize trading strategies based on evolving market conditions. By integrating machine learning with traditional market making strategies, firms enhance their ability to adapt to new information and adjust their trading tactics accordingly.

For instance, deep learning models can process historical data to identify latent features indicative of future price behavior. Such insights can inform market makers about likely trend reversals or volatility spikes, allowing them to adjust their inventory positions proactively. As machine learning technology continues to evolve, its integration into market making strategies promises to further refine these predictive capabilities and foster more intelligent trading systems.

The introduction of blockchain technology and distributed ledger systems represents another groundbreaking innovation with significant implications for market making. Blockchain's transparent, decentralized nature enhances transaction security and reduces the risk of fraud or manipulation, providing greater confidence to market participants. The immutable records maintained by blockchain technology also facilitate more efficient settlement processes, reducing counterparty and operational risks associated with traditional clearing and settlement mechanisms.

Market makers in cryptocurrency markets already leverage blockchain-powered exchanges to navigate the decentralized and fragmented landscape of digital assets. These platforms offer unique challenges and opportunities for liquidity provision, demanding that market makers develop specialized algorithms and trading strategies tailored to the volatility and complexity of cryptocurrency markets. The emergence of decentralized finance (DeFi) platforms further highlights the potential for innovative market making practices that can operate outside conventional centralized systems.

Technological innovation has led to the democratization of market making, lowering barriers to entry for smaller firms and enabling retail investors to participate in liquidity provision activities. Advances in cloud computing and software as a service (SaaS) have made it cost-effective for smaller players to access powerful algorithmic trading platforms, which were traditionally confined to large institutions. This democratization has increased competition among market makers, driving tighter spreads and enhancing overall market efficiency.

Yet, the rise of technology in market making is not without its challenges. The complexity of algorithmic systems and HFT requires rigorous technical infrastructure and sophisticated risk management protocols. Market makers must continuously monitor and optimize their systems to prevent potential malfunctions or unintended consequences, such as flash crashes, triggered by erroneous algorithmic behaviors. Robust cybersecurity measures are essential to protect sensitive data and trading strategies from external threats.

Moreover, technological advancements have prompted regulatory bodies to enhance oversight and ensure fair market practices. Regulators have introduced measures such as circuit breakers to curb wild price swings, stricter reporting requirements for algorithmic trading activities, and controls on HFT practices to maintain market integrity. Market makers must navigate an evolving regulatory landscape, balancing compliance with innovation to remain competitive while fulfilling their obligations to market stability and transparency.

In addition, technological innovation within market making prompts a reevaluation of talent requirements within trading firms. The integration of advanced technology mandates a workforce that is adept in both financial analysis and software development. Quantitative analysts, data scientists, and software engineers are increasingly collaborating with traders to develop, test, and refine sophisticated trading algorithms. This multidisciplinary approach is vital for extracting maximum value from technological advancements and achieving operational excellence.

The impact of technology and innovation on market making resonates beyond operational efficiencies, influencing broader market dynamics and investor behavior. As markets evolve with technological progression, market makers are instrumental in ensuring that these changes translate into more liquid, transparent, and accessible financial environments. By embracing continuous innovation, market makers contribute to the sustained growth and development of global capital markets, reinforcing their role as pivotal pillars of the financial system.

In the face of burgeoning technology, market makers are poised to benefit from emerging innovations such as quantum computing and artificial intelligence advancements. The potential of these nascent technologies to reshape data processing, modeling accuracy, and trading speed promises to open new frontiers in market making practices, offering tools that further hone the effectiveness and adaptability of market makers in a rapidly shifting global landscape.

Ultimately, the relentless march of technology and innovation stands as both a catalyst for advancement and a source of challenge within market making. By harnessing the transformative power of technology, market makers will continue to drive market evolution, playing a crucial role in crafting efficient, resilient, and inclusive financial markets of the future.

Chapter 2

Basics of Financial Markets and Liquidity

This chapter delves into the essential structure and function of financial markets, highlighting the roles of various participants, from institutional to retail investors. A comprehensive examination of liquidity concepts, including market depth and price formation, is provided to underscore their importance in maintaining market stability and efficiency. The discussion extends to factors influencing market liquidity and the impact different types of orders have on it. By analyzing the metrics used to measure and analyze liquidity, readers are equipped with the foundational understanding needed to navigate and assess financial markets effectively.

2.1   Structure of Financial Markets

Financial markets are the backbone of economic activities in a globalized world, serving as platforms where financial instruments, assets, and securities are exchanged between willing buyers and sellers. Understanding their structure is crucial for anyone engaged in trading and investing, as it provides insights into how these markets operate and how they can be harnessed for strategic financial decision-making.

The complex ecosystem of financial markets can broadly be categorized into several types: equity, fixed income, forex, and derivatives markets. Each type of market has a unique structure, purpose, and function that caters to different financial needs and objectives.

The equity market, often known as the stock market, is where shares of publicly-held companies are bought and sold. This market allows corporations to raise capital by distributing ownership of the company to the public through shares. It is characterized by exchanges such as the New York Stock Exchange (NYSE) and NASDAQ where transactions are centralized. Equity markets are governed by stringent regulatory frameworks to protect investors and ensure market integrity. The success of equity markets hinges on factors like corporate earnings, investor sentiment, and macroeconomic indicators.

Conversely, the fixed income market comprises markets for debt instruments, including government bonds, municipal bonds, and corporate bonds. Unlike equities, bonds confer no ownership rights but are loans made by investors to borrowers (typically corporations or governments) in exchange for periodic interest payments plus the return of the bond's face value when it reaches maturity. The bond market's structure allows for the valuation of instruments based on interest rates, credit quality, and duration. Notably, this market is pivotal for governments and companies looking to finance large projects or manage cash flows. The bond market is often utilized as an indicator of economic health, primarily driven by interest rate movements and inflation expectations.

The foreign exchange (forex) market is the arena for currency trading on an international scale. It operates on a decentralized platform, distinct from the centralized exchanges of equity markets, and is considered the largest financial market in the world by trading volume. The forex market enables currency conversion essential for international trade and investments, catering to businesses, governments, investors, and speculators. It is highly sensitive to geopolitical events, economic indicators, and central bank policies. Forex trading involves currency pairs, and the market operates 24 hours a day due to the various time zones across the globe, making it an attractive choice for traders seeking high liquidity and leverage.

Derivatives markets, another critical component, allow trading of contracts whose value is linked to underlying assets like stocks, bonds, commodities, or indices. These contracts include futures, options, swaps, and forwards. Derivatives are versatile tools used for hedging risk, speculative opportunities, and arbitrage. The structure of the derivatives market facilitates price discovery and risk management, with implications across the entire financial system. Exchanges such as the Chicago Mercantile Exchange (CME) and the Intercontinental Exchange (ICE) are pivotal in providing regulated environments for trading derivatives.

Each of these markets is integral to the global economy, with a network of intermediate institutions, technological platforms, legal frameworks, and regulatory bodies ensuring their smooth operation. Market participants in these arenas include institutional investors, retail investors, central banks, and more, each playing roles tailored to their investment strategies and risk appetites.

Technological innovations have significantly influenced the structure of financial markets. The rise of algorithmic trading, high-frequency trading (HFT), and online brokerage platforms have reshaped traditional market dynamics, enhancing market efficiency while also introducing new risks and regulatory considerations. The integration of blockchain technology and cryptocurrencies further pushes the boundaries, presenting both challenges and opportunities in market structure evolution.

Furthermore, the interconnection between these markets contributes to systemic stability while also posing risks. For instance, the equity and derivatives markets are closely linked, with movements in one influencing the other significantly. The 2008 financial crisis underscored the interconnected nature of markets, highlighting how detrimental cross-market contagion can be.

Within this context, the structure of financial markets is not static but adaptive, converging with global economic shifts, regulatory overhauls, and technological advancements. An understanding of this structure is instrumental in navigating the intricate world of financial trading and investing, equipping market participants with the knowledge to exploit opportunities while mitigating risks effectively.

In essence, the structure of financial markets serves as the intricate architecture that underpins the global financial system. Its influence extends across economic growth, wealth distribution, and financial stability, making its comprehension indispensable for anyone seeking to participate effectively in the economic landscape. The intricacies of how these markets are organized and function exemplify their critical role in enabling economic exchanges, providing a fertile ground for investment opportunities, and safeguarding the financial ecosystem's overall health.

2.2   Market Participants

Market participants are the diverse entities and individuals who engage in trading activities within financial markets, contributing to their dynamic and ever-evolving nature. Understanding the roles and motivations of these participants is crucial for grasping how markets operate and influence asset pricing, liquidity, and volatility. Each category of participant brings unique perspectives and strategies that shape the financial landscape.

Institutional investors are some of the most influential participants in financial markets due to the large volumes of capital they manage. These entities include pension funds, mutual funds, insurance companies, endowments, and hedge funds. Institutional investors play a pivotal role in price discovery and liquidity provision as their large-scale transactions contribute significantly to market movements. For example, mutual funds pool funds from numerous investors to purchase diversified portfolios of stocks and bonds, providing individual investors with access to professional management and diversified investment options. Pension funds, managing retirement savings on behalf of beneficiaries, focus on long-term performance and stable returns, often balancing their portfolios between equities, fixed income, and alternative investments.

Hedge funds, known for their aggressive investment strategies, participate in a variety of markets, utilizing techniques such as leverage, short selling, derivatives, and arbitrage to achieve alpha—returns beyond that of the market benchmark. The strategies employed by hedge funds can range from global macroeconomic plays, exploiting economic trends across countries, to highly specialized approaches like event-driven strategies, which capitalize on corporate actions such as mergers or restructurings. The significant influence of institutional investors necessitates stringent regulatory oversight to protect market integrity and ensure investor protection.

Retail investors, individuals who buy and sell securities for personal accounts, constitute another vital group of market participants. With the democratization of market access, facilitated by online brokerage platforms and the reduction of commission fees, retail investors have amassed considerable influence. The rise of investment apps and social media platforms has also empowered retail investors, evidenced by their substantial role in movements such as the GameStop short squeeze, wherein coordinated trading efforts led to unprecedented volatility and attention from larger market stakeholders.

Retail investors typically invest for a variety of reasons, ranging from building retirement savings and funding education to achieving financial independence. Their strategies may vary extensively, from passive investing through index funds to active trading and speculative investments. Retail investors bring diversity to the market, and while their orders are generally smaller, the cumulative effects of their activities can be significant, particularly in less liquid stocks where retail interest can drive price swings.

Speculators are market participants who seek to profit from anticipated price changes, operating on short to medium-term horizons. Their activities are inherently risky as they often involve leveraging capital in markets with high volatility, including equities, commodities, forex, and derivatives. Speculators serve as essential liquidity providers, especially in times of minimal market activity, facilitating price discovery. For instance, in the futures market, speculators take positions on the direction of price movements in commodities such as oil or agricultural products, absorbing risks that farmers and producers wish to hedge against.

Hedgers operate with the primary objective of mitigating risk exposure related to price fluctuations of underlying assets. These participants include corporations, financial institutions, and producers who engage in hedging to safeguard their operations or investments from adverse price movements. For example, a company with substantial exposure to foreign exchange risk may use currency futures or options to lock in exchange rates and stabilize cash flows, thereby reducing uncertainty in financial projections.

Arbitrageurs capitalize on price discrepancies across different markets or instruments by simultaneously buying and selling similar assets to lock in risk-free profits. Their actions help ensure market efficiency by aligning prices across different exchanges and reducing disparities. High-frequency trading (HFT) firms are a modern iteration of arbitrageurs, employing sophisticated algorithms to execute trades at lightning speeds, capturing minuscule price differences that human traders cannot exploit. By doing so, arbitrageurs contribute to liquidity and price stability, though the ethical and regulatory implications of practices like HFT remain a subject of debate.

Market makers are specialized participants providing liquidity by quoting buy and sell prices for a range of securities, profiting from the spread between the bid and ask prices. They ensure that orders can be executed swiftly even during periods of low demand or supply, thus maintaining an orderly market. While traditionally constituted by brokerage firms or banks, technological advancements have allowed electronic market makers to increasingly dominate the landscape, particularly in electronic trading platforms.

Central banks also play an influential role in financial markets, though they do not participate for profit. Through monetary policy maneuvers, such as interest rate adjustments and open market operations, central banks regulate money supply and stabilize currencies. Their actions have profound impacts on financial markets, influencing borrowing costs, investor sentiment, and overall economic activity. The communication of policy changes can move markets significantly, highlighting the importance of central bank transparency in guiding market expectations.

Together, these diverse market participants form a complex web of interactions that facilitate the functioning of financial markets. Each group has distinct motivations and strategies, but collectively they contribute to liquidity, depth, and efficiency. Understanding the behavior and objectives of market participants is essential for trading and investing success, as it influences market trends, asset prices, and volatility. The intricate interplay among these actors underscores the dynamic and multifaceted nature of financial markets, where continuous adaptation and analysis are key to thriving in an ever-changing environment.

2.3   Liquidity and Market Depth

Liquidity and market depth are cornerstone concepts in the realm of financial markets, playing a critical role in the execution of trades and the overall health of the market. They underpin the ability of market participants to buy and sell assets without causing significant price changes, thus affecting price stability and market efficiency. A comprehensive understanding of these concepts enables investors and traders to make informed decisions about entering or exiting positions and managing risk effectively.

Liquidity refers to the ease with which an asset can be converted into cash or another asset without significantly affecting its price. High liquidity implies that an asset can be traded swiftly and with minimal price impact, whereas low liquidity suggests that significant price changes may occur with relatively small trading volumes. Liquidity is not a static attribute; it can vary over time and across different market conditions.

Several factors influence market liquidity. Firstly, trading volume is a direct indicator of liquidity; higher volumes usually mean greater liquidity, as more investors are participating in buying and selling the asset. For example, blue-chip stocks such as Apple or Microsoft typically exhibit high levels of liquidity due to their popularity among a broad base of investors, including institutional funds and retail traders. In contrast, small-cap stocks or those of lesser-known companies may suffer from low liquidity, leading to higher bid-ask spreads and increased volatility.

Another crucial aspect of liquidity is the bid-ask spread, the difference between the prices quoted for an immediate sale (bid) and an immediate purchase (ask). Narrower spreads indicate more liquidity, as they reflect a higher level of agreement between buyers' and sellers' valuations of the asset. Market-makers often step in to provide liquidity by narrowing these spreads in exchange for the profit made through the spread itself.

The existence of varied types of orders also impacts liquidity. Limit orders contribute to a more stable and liquid market by providing a queue of transactions that must be fulfilled at predetermined prices, thus preventing drastic swings in one direction. Conversely, market orders, executed immediately at the best available price, can move prices more significantly, especially in less liquid markets.

Market depth, often considered an extension of liquidity, measures the market's capacity to absorb large trade volumes without experiencing substantial price movements. It is depicted by the order book, which displays all the pending buy and sell orders at different price levels. A deep market is characterized by a large number of orders distributed across a range of price levels, indicating that large trades can be executed with minimal impact on the asset's price.

For example, in the forex market, pairs like EUR/USD typically demonstrate significant depth due to active participation from central banks, corporations, institutional investors, and retail clients, allowing considerable transactions to occur with little effect on the exchange rate. By contrast, trading in exotic currency pairs with less depth might result in greater price volatility upon execution of substantial trades.

Liquidity and market depth are vital for ensuring price stability. They help maintain orderliness in the market, allowing for accurate price discovery, where the current market prices reflect available information and the consensus of valuations by market participants. The ability to execute trades without affecting the market price significantly is essential for avoiding slippage—the difference between the expected price of a trade and the actual price paid or received after execution.

The liquidity of financial markets can also serve as a barometer for gauging overall market confidence and economic stability. In crisis situations, liquidity can dry up quickly, exacerbating market downturns and leading to cascading effects across financial systems. The 2008 financial crisis is a notable example where liquidity shortages triggered a vicious cycle of asset sell-offs and price plummeting across global markets, leading to systemic illiquidity and financial failures.

Efficient liquidity management is therefore paramount for maintaining market health and supporting functional economies. Regulators and central banks monitor liquidity levels closely, employing measures such as open market operations and policy rate adjustments to ensure liquidity sufficiency. The introduction of quantitative easing in the wake of the 2008 crisis, for example, demonstrated a decisive intervention aimed at injecting liquidity into the markets to promote borrowing and investment.

Lastly, technological advancements and innovations in trading platforms have ushered in significant changes to liquidity and market depth. The rise of algorithmic and high-frequency trading (HFT) has enhanced liquidity provision by allowing rapid execution and integration of vast volumes of data, ensuring tighter bid-ask spreads and more competitive pricing. However, these technologies also pose challenges, as they can contribute to market volatility through flash crashes or exacerbated price swings under certain conditions.

Understanding liquidity and market depth enables traders to formulate strategies aligning with their risk tolerance and investment goals. For instance, entering highly liquid markets allows for ease of entry and exit, appealing to short-term traders seeking to capitalize on frequent price movements. Conversely, long-term investors might consider less liquid assets for potential upside, recognizing the inherent risks associated with such positions.

In essence, liquidity and market depth are indispensable facets of financial markets. Their influence extends beyond individual trades, affecting market stability, participant confidence, and systemic financial health. Mastery of these concepts offers a competitive advantage in navigating the complexities of market dynamics and crafting effective investment strategies in a rapidly evolving financial landscape. Their intricate relationship with trade execution, price formation, and market efficiency underscores the necessity for continual engagement and analysis by market practitioners.

2.4 Price Formation and Discovery

Price formation and discovery are central components of financial markets, reflecting the complex interplay of demand and supply dynamics, information flow, and market participant behavior. These processes determine the prices at which securities are bought and sold, providing crucial signals for the allocation of resources in an economy. Understanding how prices are formed and discovered is essential for investors, traders, and policymakers, as it shapes their strategic decisions and policy interventions.

Price formation refers to the mechanism through which market prices are set, considering the various factors that influence demand and supply. It begins with individual buyers and sellers placing orders in a market, which aggregate into a collective expression of buying and selling pressures. The interactions between these orders create a dynamic pricing environment where prices fluctuate in response to changing market conditions.

Supply and demand are fundamental determinants of price formation. When demand for a security exceeds supply, prices tend to rise, attracting additional sellers into the market. Conversely, when supply surpasses demand, prices fall, encouraging more buyers to enter. This equilibrium-seeking behavior ensures that prices reflect the current consensus valuation among market participants.

Market information plays a pivotal role in price formation, as it shapes participants' perceptions and expectations. Information ranges from macroeconomic indicators, corporate earnings reports, and geopolitical events to market rumors and analyst forecasts. The efficient market hypothesis suggests that securities prices fully reflect all available information, ensuring that prices are an unbiased estimate of their intrinsic value. However, due to information asymmetries and behavioral biases, prices may deviate from their true value, creating opportunities for active investors to capitalize on mispricings.

Price discovery, a closely related concept, involves the process through which market participants determine the price of a security through their trading activities. It is the continuous search and negotiation process where buyers and sellers exert their preferences and knowledge, cul-

41

minating in an agreed-upon transaction price. Price discovery is an ongoing mechanism that adapts to new information and evolving market conditions.

Trading venues, such as stock exchanges and electronic communication networks (ECNs), facilitate price discovery by providing platforms for transparent, real-time transactions. These venues aggregate orders, match buyers with sellers, and disseminate price information to the wider market. The increasing adoption of algorithmic trading and high-frequency trading (HFT) has transformed the landscape of price discovery, enabling rapid processing and integration of vast datasets to establish more efficient prices.

Market makers, crucial participants in the price discovery process, provide liquidity by standing ready to buy or sell securities at quoted bid and ask prices. By narrowing bid-ask spreads and executing orders quickly, market makers ensure that prices evolve smoothly and reflect current market conditions. Their presence helps mitigate short-term price volatility and facilitates a more accurate discovery process.

Auction markets, characterized by open outcry or electronic bidding systems, offer another model for price discovery. In these settings, traders submit competitive bids and offers, with prices adjusting until supply matches demand. This process can occur in discrete sessions, such as opening or closing auctions on stock exchanges, where concentrated trading volumes provide significant insights into equilibrium pricing levels.

Futures and options markets introduce unique dynamics to price formation and discovery, allowing participants to express expectations about future price movements. These derivative instruments derive value from underlying assets, enabling hedging, speculation, and arbitrage activities that influence spot market prices. For instance, futures prices often incorporate expectations about interest rates, supply constraints, or geopolitical risks, providing predictive insights for spot prices.

Price formation and discovery are not just mechanical processes but are susceptible to behavioral factors that affect market efficiency. Investor sentiment, cognitive biases, and herd behavior can lead to deviations from rational pricing models, creating temporary inefficiencies. Behavioral finance studies these anomalies, uncovering patterns such as overreaction, mental accounting, and loss aversion, which contribute to market volatility and mispricing.

The price discovery process can also reflect market power imbalances, where certain participants exert disproportionate influence over pricing. For example, in thinly traded markets, large institutional orders can cause significant price movements, distorting the discovery process. Regulatory frameworks aim to address these imbalances, ensuring fair and transparent markets through rules on insider trading, disclosure requirements, and circuit breakers designed to curb excessive volatility.

Technological advancements and the proliferation of data sources have further transformed price formation and discovery. The rise of big data analytics, machine learning, and artificial intelligence enables market participants to process vast amounts of information and identify pricing patterns more effectively. These technologies facilitate more informed decision-making, enhance risk management, and improve forecasting accuracy, contributing to more efficient market dynamics.

Emerging markets and less-developed regions often present unique challenges and opportunities in price formation and discovery. Factors such as limited market infrastructure, regulatory uncertainty, and lower liquidity can lead to inefficient pricing and heightened volatility. However, these conditions also offer potential for growth and development, as improvements in market access, transparency, and regulatory frameworks can attract capital and enhance efficiency.

Ultimately, price formation and discovery are integral to the health and functionality of financial markets. By reflecting the collective judgment of market participants, these processes guide the allocation of capital, inform policy decisions, and influence global economic development. A robust understanding of these mechanisms equips investors and traders with the analytical tools necessary to navigate markets effectively, capitalize on investment opportunities, and manage risks prudently. In an ever-evolving financial landscape, continuous engagement with and adaptation to new information and technological innovations are essential for maintaining market efficiency and fostering sustainable economic growth.

2.5   Factors Affecting Market Liquidity

Market liquidity, a crucial feature of financial markets, denotes the ability to buy or sell assets quickly without causing significant price changes. A liquid market is characterized by tight bid-ask spreads, high trading volumes, and robust market depth, enabling participants to transact efficiently. Various factors influence liquidity, encompassing microeconomic elements related to specific markets or securities and broader macroeconomic conditions.

One fundamental factor that impacts market liquidity is trading volume. High trading volumes typically signify greater liquidity since more participants are actively buying and selling assets. Liquid markets benefit from numerous transactions, facilitating easy entry and exit and contributing to narrower bid-ask spreads. A quintessential example is the foreign exchange market, the largest and most liquid market globally, where currency pairs like EUR/USD enjoy substantial trading volumes, allowing for rapid order execution with minimal price impact.

Market structure, including the presence of exchanges and alternative trading systems like electronic communication networks (ECNs), plays a vital role in enhancing liquidity. Exchanges provide centralized platforms where buyers and sellers converge, promoting transparency and competition. ECNs and dark pools, for instance, offer venues for discreet transactions outside traditional exchanges, often impacting liquidity by allowing large trades with reduced immediate market impact.

The number and diversity of market participants also significantly affect liquidity levels. Institutional investors, retail traders, market makers, and arbitrageurs collectively contribute to providing liquidity. The presence of market makers, in particular, is instrumental, as they continuously offer buy and sell quotes, facilitating trade execution and smoothing price volatility. During periods of market stress or reduced participation, liquidity can dry up, leading to erratic price movements and increased transaction costs.

A critical driver of market liquidity is the cost associated with trading, encompassing both explicit expenses, such as brokerage fees and taxes, and implicit costs, such as the bid-ask spread and market impact. Lower transaction costs encourage trading activity by reducing the barriers for entry and exit, thereby enhancing liquidity. Financial innovation and technological advancements, exemplified by algorithmic trading and low-latency infrastructures, have contributed to diminishing transaction costs, fostering greater liquidity.

Information transparency and asymmetry influence liquidity by affecting the confidence and willingness of participants to engage in markets. Transparent markets, where relevant information about securities and economic indicators is readily available, attract more participants due to reduced uncertainty, enhancing liquidity. However, information asymmetries, where certain participants possess superior knowledge, can deter others from trading, compressing liquidity. Regulatory requirements mandating disclosure and trading transparency are vital in addressing these asymmetries and bolstering market confidence.

Macroeconomic conditions, including monetary policy, interest rates, and economic indicators, exert profound effects on market liquidity. Central banks, through monetary policy tools such as interest rate adjustments and open market operations, influence the availability of financial resources, shaping liquidity conditions across markets. In environments of low interest rates, liquidity tends to increase as borrowing costs decrease, encouraging asset purchases and stimulating trading activities. Conversely, in tight monetary conditions, liquidity can contract, reflecting increased aversion to risk and higher funding costs.

Economic stability and growth prospects are closely linked to liquidity levels. During periods of economic expansion and stable growth, market participants exhibit confidence, increasing their willingness to engage in trading, which bolsters liquidity. Alternatively, economic recessions or geopolitical uncertainties can lead to market participants withdrawing to safe havens or holding cash equivalents, reducing liquidity and heightening volatility.

Regulatory and geopolitical events can impact liquidity by altering the risk landscape for market participants. Regulatory changes that affect market structure, such as transaction taxes or capital requirements, influence the incentives and participation of market agents. Geopolitical events, including wars, sanctions, or political instability, can disrupt trading conditions, diminish investor confidence, and lead to liquidity squeezes. For instance, the Brexit referendum introduced uncertainty to financial markets, affecting the liquidity of UK equities and currencies as traders adjusted to changing risk perceptions.

Technological innovations and disruptions also shape liquidity dynamics. The proliferation of high-frequency trading (HFT) and algorithmic strategies has redefined liquidity provision, enabling rapid execution and enhanced market efficiency. However, these advancements are not without challenges; instances like the 2010 Flash Crash underline the potential for technological systems to exacerbate liquidity crises under certain conditions. Technological resilience, robust infrastructure, and risk management protocols are crucial in mitigating disruptions and sustaining liquidity.

Liquidity varies across asset classes, influenced by inherent characteristics such as market size, regulation, and the nature of the underlying asset. Equities of major corporations tend to exhibit higher liquidity due to broader investor interest and established markets, while bonds,

45

particularly corporate and high-yield debt, might have varying liquidity contingent on issuer credit quality and market conditions. Commodity markets exhibit unique liquidity patterns tied to seasonality, supply chains, and geopolitical factors impacting supply-demand balances.

The time dimension is another crucial factor, as liquidity levels can fluctuate throughout trading sessions due to varying participant activity and operational hours across global markets. The opening and closing of exchanges often witness heightened liquidity due to concentrated order flows and the convergence of various market participants during these peak times. Conversely, after-hours or thinly traded sessions might exhibit lower liquidity, causing wider spreads and increased volatility.

Understanding the myriad factors affecting market liquidity enables traders and investors to devise informed strategies, anticipate market conditions, and manage risks effectively. Liquidity assessment forms a vital component of portfolio management, asset allocation, and risk mitigation, guiding decisions on market entry, position sizing, and exit strategies. In ever-evolving financial landscapes, maintaining a keen awareness of liquidity dynamics and adapting to shifts is essential for sustainable success and resilience in market participation. The intricate interdependencies and influences on liquidity render it a multifaceted determinant of market functionality, with far-reaching implications for participants and the broader economic environment.

2.6   Types of Orders and Their Impact

Financial markets are multifaceted arenas where investors and traders execute transactions through various types of orders. Understanding the different order types is crucial as they directly influence trading outcomes, market liquidity, and price volatility. Each order type serves specific strategic purposes, tailored to the objectives and risk tolerance of market participants, and their effective deployment is pivotal for optimizing trading operations.

A market order is the most straightforward type of order used by traders to buy or sell a security immediately at the best available price. This order type prioritizes execution speed over price precision, making it suitable for highly liquid markets where spreads are narrow, and voluminous trading ensures minimal market impact. Market orders are often favored by traders requiring immediate execution, such as in high-frequency trading environments or during volatile market conditions, where locking in a position is prioritized over achieving a specific price.

However, market orders carry the risk of slippage, wherein the final executed price deviates from the expected price due to rapid market movements or insufficient liquidity. Slippage can be particularly pronounced in less liquid markets or during periods of heightened volatility around economic data releases or geopolitical events. As such, traders must weigh the need for immediacy against potential cost implications when deploying market orders.

In contrast, limit orders allow traders to specify the maximum or minimum price at which they are willing to buy or sell a security. This order type provides price control and mitigates the risk of slippage, ensuring that trades are executed only at predetermined acceptable levels. Limit orders contribute to market liquidity by increasing the depth of the order book, providing a queue of pending transactions that stabilize prices during market fluctuations.

Limit orders are instrumental for traders seeking particular entry or exit points, allowing them to capitalize on price retracements or breakout levels identified through technical analysis. For example, an investor anticipating a stock's rise might set a limit order to buy shares at a targeted support level, capturing favorable price conditions without constant market monitoring. However, the caveat with limit orders is that they remain unexecuted if the market price fails to reach the specified level, leaving potential opportunities unrealized.

Stop orders, also known as stop-loss orders, are designed to limit potential losses by triggering a market or limit order once a predetermined price is breached. This order type is an essential risk management tool, especially in volatile markets where rapid price changes can lead to significant losses. For instance, an investor holding a long stock position might place a stop-loss order below the current price to protect against a downside move.

Stop orders can also be employed to secure profits, such as a stop-limit order placed above the market price in a short-selling strategy, automatically locking in gains when prices decline to a favorable level. While these orders provide crucial safeguards, they are subject to execution risk during sharp market moves or gaps, where triggered orders may fill at less advantageous prices.

Stop-limit orders introduce a combination of stop and limit orders, specifying both a trigger price and a limit price. This configuration allows traders to exert greater control over execution, ensuring that positions are only opened or closed within acceptable price ranges. However, stop-limit orders carry the risk of non-execution if the market price surpasses the limit price post-trigger, potentially leaving positions exposed in adverse market scenarios.

Fill or kill (FOK) orders are specialized instructions requiring immediate, complete execution, or else they are canceled. These orders are often employed by institutional traders needing to transact large positions without partial fills that might expose trading intentions or distort market sentiment. While beneficial for high-volume transactions, FOK orders are less suitable for thin liquid assets due to the likelihood of non-execution.

Good-'til-canceled (GTC) orders remain active until executed or deliberately canceled by the trader, permitting ongoing engagement in the market without constant input. GTC orders provide convenience for traders with longer-term perspectives, enabling execution at desired price points over extended periods. However, market conditions, corporate actions, and regulatory changes may necessitate periodic review and adjustment of GTC orders to align with evolving strategic objectives.

Advanced order types, such as iceberg orders, offer discretion for large traders by revealing only a portion of the total order size to the market. Iceberg orders mitigate market impact and prevent front-running by concealing trading intentions, preserving anonymity while facilitating gradual position building or unwinding. Similarly, bracket orders encapsulate a primary order alongside predefined exit strategies, combining profit targets and stop-losses to automate sophisticated trading tactics.

Order type selection profoundly affects market liquidity and volatility. Market orders boost liquidity by facilitating immediate trade execution; however, they can exacerbate volatility if executed in bulk or during periods of limited trading activity, often leading to transient price spikes or drops. Limit and stop orders enhance order book depth, stabilizing prices by providing structured pricing frameworks and queuing mechanisms essential for orderly market function.

Regulators and exchanges impose stringent guidelines on order types to ensure fair and transparent market operations. This includes monitoring for potential abuses, such as manipulative practices or improper order routing that might distort price discovery or disadvantage investors. Compliance protocols and technological oversight, including surveillance systems and risk management tools, are critical in maintaining market integrity while accommodating diverse trading strategies.

Market participants, from individual retail investors to seasoned institutional players, leverage distinct order types to achieve tailored investment goals, manage risks, and respond adaptively to market fluctuations. Mastery of these order types, and the nuanced implications of their application, enables informed decision-making and strategic agility in an evolving financial landscape. The ability to precisely execute trades, align with market conditions, and optimize trading costs through advanced order type utilization is indispensable for achieving sustainable success and competitive advantage within financial markets. As innovation and complexity in market structures intensify, the continued evolution and adaptation of order execution strategies remain pivotal in navigating the intricate web of modern trading environments.

2.7 Measuring and Analyzing Liquidity

Liquidity is a fundamental attribute of financial markets, reflecting the ease with which assets can be traded without causing significant price changes. Accurately measuring and analyzing liquidity is essential for investors, traders, and policymakers, as it provides insights into market efficiency, risk management, and the overall health of financial systems. A comprehensive approach to assessing liquidity involves various quantitative metrics and analytical techniques that capture different dimensions of market liquidity.

One of the primary measures of liquidity is the bid-ask spread, which represents the difference between the prices quoted for an immediate sale (bid) and an immediate purchase (ask) of an asset. A narrower bid-ask spread indicates higher liquidity, as it reflects better agreement between buyers and sellers on the asset's value. The bid-ask spread is influenced by factors such as trading volume, market volatility, and the presence of market makers. For instance, highly liquid stocks like those in major indices often exhibit tight spreads, whereas the spreads for small-cap stocks or illiquid securities tend to be wider.

Trading volume is another key indicator of liquidity, measuring the number of shares or contracts traded over a specific period. High trading volumes suggest an active market with numerous participants willing to buy and sell, enhancing liquidity by facilitating easier transaction execution. Conversely, thin trading volumes may indicate limited liquidity, leading to increased price volatility and transaction costs. Analyzing changes in trading volumes can also provide insights into market sentiment and investor behavior, such as identifying accumulation or distribution phases.

The turnover ratio, calculated as the total trading volume divided by the average number of shares outstanding, offers a liquidity metric reflecting the frequency at which a security is traded relative to its quantity available in the market. A high turnover ratio signifies an active and liquid market, while a low ratio implies that a security is held for longer periods with fewer transactions occurring. Turnover ratios can be used to compare liquidity across different securities or market segments, helping investors assess relative marketability.

Depth of market (DOM), often visualized through an order book, provides a detailed view of the volume of buy and sell orders at various price levels. Market depth indicates the capacity of the market to sustain large orders without substantial price impacts. Analyzing market depth allows traders to assess the balance of supply and demand across the price spectrum, informing trade execution strategies and risk assessments. For example, a deep and balanced order book suggests stable liquidity, whereas a skewed order book may forecast potential price movements or volatility.

Price impact measures the effect of trade size on the security's price, capturing the market's ability to absorb transactions. A small price impact for large trades implies high liquidity, whereas a substantial impact indicates limited liquidity. The price impact is particularly relevant for institutional investors executing large orders, as it reflects the trade-off between order size and market price alterations. Advanced execution algorithms often incorporate price impact estimates to optimize order slicing and minimize market disruption.

Another important liquidity metric is the Amihud illiquidity ratio, which measures the price response associated with trading volumes. It is defined as the absolute value of the stock return divided by the stock's dollar trading volume. Higher values of the Amihud ratio indicate lower liquidity, as price changes are more sensitive to trading volumes. This ratio effectively captures the cost of trading on a security and is used extensively in empirical finance studies to assess liquidity's role in asset pricing.

For a more comprehensive liquidity assessment, the Composite Liquidity Index (CLI) combines multiple liquidity dimensions, including spreads, depth, volume, and price impact, into a single measure. The CLI provides a holistic view of liquidity conditions and can be customized to reflect specific market or asset characteristics. By integrating various metrics, the CLI aids in identifying systemic liquidity trends and anomalies, enabling informed portfolio management and risk evaluation.

On an aggregate level, systemic liquidity in financial markets is often assessed through broader indicators, such as money supply measures (e.g., M1, M2), interbank lending rates (e.g., LIBOR, SOFR), and central bank policy reports. These indicators offer insights into the overall monetary environment, highlighting changes in liquidity availability across financial systems. During periods of financial stress or market dislocation, such as the 2008 financial crisis, monitoring systemic liquidity becomes crucial for predicting market responses and implementing appropriate policy interventions.

Liquidity analysis also extends to identifying liquidity risk, the risk that an entity will be unable to meet its obligations due to insufficient liquidity. This risk is a vital consideration for both market participants and regulators, as it can lead to forced asset sales, margin calls, and solvency challenges during market downturns. Stress testing, scenario analysis, and liquidity planning are common tools used by financial institutions to manage liquidity risk, ensuring adequate contingency measures are in place under adverse conditions.

Technological advancements have revolutionized liquidity measurement and analysis, with big data analytics, machine learning, and artificial intelligence offering new perspectives. These technologies enable real-time processing and analysis of large datasets, enhancing liquidity modeling and forecasting capabilities. For instance, machine learning algorithms can identify liquidity patterns, predict order flow dynamics, and optimize trading strategies by uncovering non-linear correlations within market data.

Understanding liquidity metrics equips investors and market participants with the knowledge to tailor their strategies to current market conditions, optimize execution, and manage risk effectively. By continually analyzing liquidity, stakeholders can adjust asset allocations, evaluate counterparty risks, and engage in proactive decision-making, fostering resilience in the face of market fluctuations. Liquidity, a linchpin of market integrity and functionality, remains a central focus in both financial research and practice, reflecting its essential role in sustaining thriving and efficient markets.

Chapter 3

Market Microstructure and Price Dynamics

This chapter provides an in-depth analysis of market microstructure, illuminating how the organization of trading venues and order types influences price formation and discovery. Key elements such as information flow, order matching mechanisms, and liquidity provision are examined to reveal their roles in shaping price dynamics. The chapter also explores the implications of market impact and transaction costs on trading efficiency. High-frequency trading and its effect on volatility and market behavior are discussed, equipping readers with a comprehensive understanding of the forces driving modern financial markets.

3.1 Understanding Market Microstructure

In the intricate world of financial markets, understanding market microstructure is akin to unlocking the mechanisms that dictate how trading and price formation truly occur. Market microstructure examines the processes and systems that facilitate trading, as well as the factors influencing the price discovery process. It extends beyond merely observing price changes and delves into how these prices are formed, manipulated, and influenced by various market participants.

Market microstructure is crucial because it directly impacts trading

costs, liquidity, and efficiency. Traders and investors need to comprehend these elements to make informed decisions and optimize their
strategies. Delving into the details of market microstructure enables
one to appreciate how subtle differences in market mechanisms can
lead to significant variations in trading outcomes.

At its core, market microstructure studies how particular trading rules
and features of different market structures affect trading activity, price
formation, and informational efficiency. The relevance of this field is
evident in today's financial world, where lightning-fast transactions and
complex market systems abound.

- Order Driven vs. Quote Driven Markets

Understanding the framework of different markets often begins with
distinguishing between order-driven and quote-driven markets. Order-
driven markets, like most stock exchanges, rely on investors placing
buy and sell orders into a central limit order book. Prices are determined purely by market demand and supply mechanics. The auction-
like nature of these markets ensures that prices are transparent and
formed dynamically, fostering efficient price discovery.

In contrast, quote-driven markets, such as the foreign exchange market, involve dealers who continuously quote bid and ask prices. These
dealers or market makers are ready to buy or sell at these quoted
prices, ensuring continual liquidity. Here, price discovery is closely tied
to dealer behavior, with spreads reflecting not just demand and supply
but also the risk appetite and competitive landscape among dealers.

- The Role of Auction Markets

Auction markets play a pivotal role in price discovery by facilitating interactions among numerous buyers and sellers. Consider the NYSE,
where an open auction system determines the opening price. These
auctions absorb vast amounts of trading information and compress it
into a single opening price, setting the stage for subsequent trading
sessions.

In an auction, the price is established at a level where the quantity supplied equals the quantity demanded. Different auction formats, like the
Dutch auction or sealed-bid auction, offer nuanced approaches to this
process. Understanding these formats is essential for traders and investors, especially those involved in initial public offerings (IPOs) or

government bond auctions, where auction mechanics significantly impact outcomes.

- Information and Its Dissemination

Information plays a fundamental role in market microstructure. The availability and distribution of information can significantly impact price changes and volatility. Timely and accurate information enables market participants to update their valuations, fueling trading activity that, in turn, drives prices toward their true intrinsic value.

An important component of market microstructure concerns itself with how information is incorporated into prices. Markets are often categorized by their level of informational efficiency. In a perfectly efficient market, prices fully reflect all available information. However, practical markets are rarely perfectly efficient, leading to opportunities — and challenges — for traders as price adjustments occur in response to new information.

Asymmetric information, where some participants have access to more or better information than others, further complicates this landscape. This asymmetry can lead to adverse selection, where traders with less information are disadvantaged, often resulting in widened spreads and increased transaction costs.

- The Importance of Liquidity

Liquidity is a cornerstone of market microstructure and a critical factor for any trader or investor to consider. It refers to the ability to quickly buy or sell an asset without causing a significant change in its price. Liquid markets are typically characterized by smaller bid-ask spreads, greater depth, and higher volume.

The complexity of liquidity extends to its measurement and perception, often being dynamic and temporal. For example, a stock may be highly liquid during regular trading hours but become illiquid after hours or during periods of market stress.

Liquidity provision typically comes from market makers, who are pivotal in ensuring that markets remain efficient by facilitating trades at tight spreads. However, market makers also face risks, such as inventory risk and the potential for profit erosion from informed traders. Understanding these dynamics can aid traders in appreciating how liquidity is priced and how it affects their trading strategies.

- Impact of Technology on Market Microstructure

The advent of technology has dramatically transformed market microstructure over the past few decades. Algorithmic trading, which employs complex mathematical models to make transaction decisions in milliseconds, has reshaped how liquidity is sourced and how prices are formed.

With the rise of electronic trading platforms, trading speed, execution, and strategies have evolved, leading to increased market integration and more transparent price discovery processes. However, this technological advancement also raises challenges, such as the possibility of systemic risk events caused by high-frequency trading algorithms and flash crashes.

- Practical Implications for Traders and Investors

Traders and investors can greatly benefit from understanding market microstructure. Grasping the intricacies of how markets operate enables them to develop more effective trading strategies tailored to specific market conditions. For instance, knowing when markets have the least liquidity can allow traders to avoid executing large orders during these times, thereby minimizing market impact and execution costs.

Market microstructure also influences risk management. Traders have to accommodate the microstructural elements — such as market impact and slippage — into risk models, ensuring that strategies are robust across various market conditions.

- Conclusion

The comprehension of market microstructure is indispensable for modern traders and investors. By exploring the nuances of how financial markets operate, one can gain a competitive edge in price discovery and trade execution. The systematic study of order types, liquidity provision, and the influence of technology provides a deep well of knowledge to draw from in a landscape marked by rapid change and innovation. Immersing oneself in market microstructure not only enhances trading acumen but also shapes a more thorough understanding of the complex forces orchestrating the symphony of financial markets.

3.2 Order Types and Matching Mechanisms

Navigating the labyrinthine structure of financial markets requires a comprehensive understanding of how orders are placed, executed, and matched. Different order types and matching mechanisms form the bedrock of financial trading, influencing how trades are executed and what prices are set. These functions are vital for optimizing trading strategies, minimizing transaction costs, and ensuring execution quality.

The diversity of order types available to traders provides the flexibility needed to tailor trading strategies to specific goals and market conditions. Similarly, understanding the matching mechanisms employed by various exchanges is crucial, as these directly impact the speed and efficiency with which orders are filled.

- **Common Order Types**

The array of order types available in modern financial markets caters to a wide spectrum of trading strategies and risk appetites. Some of the fundamental order types include:

- **Market Orders**: A market order is one of the most straightforward order types, where an investor instructs to buy or sell a security immediately at the current market price. The primary advantage of a market order is the high likelihood of execution, as it does not specify a price limit. However, this also means that the final executed price could be less favorable, especially in volatile markets or illiquid securities.

- **Limit Orders**: A limit order specifies the maximum or minimum price at which an investor is willing to buy or sell a security. This control over the execution price is particularly beneficial in volatile markets, where price protection is paramount. Limit orders remain on the order book until they are filled, providing traders with enhanced control over their trading strategies.

- **Stop Orders**: Stop orders, often referred to as stop-loss orders, are designed to limit an investor's loss or to lock in a profit on an existing position. A stop order becomes a market order once a predetermined stop price is reached. This order type is indispensable for risk management, enabling traders to automatically exit a position when the market moves against them.

- **Stop-Limit Orders**: Combining features of both stop and limit orders, a stop-limit order will be triggered at a specified stop price, but the subsequent trade will only be executed at a predetermined limit price. This dual-condition order type offers traders more precise control over execution conditions, though it carries the risk of non-execution if the market moves away from the limit price.

- **Trailing Stop Orders**: A trailing stop order is dynamic, with the stop price automatically adjusting according to market movements at a predetermined distance from the market price. This order type allows traders to lock in profits as prices move favorably while protecting against downside risks.

- **Fill or Kill (FOK) Orders**: A fill or kill order must be executed immediately in its entirety or not at all. Typically used in high-precision strategies, FOK orders ensure that large orders do not fragment, thereby reducing slippage and adverse market impact.

- **Good Til Cancelled (GTC) Orders**: A GTC order remains active until the trader decides to cancel it or it gets filled. This order type is ideal for long-term trading strategies where timely execution is not critical.

- **Advanced Order Types**

Beyond conventional order types, traders employ advanced orders to implement complex strategies that require precise execution conditions. These include:

- **Iceberg Orders**: In large volume trades, revealing the full size of an order may adversely affect market prices. Iceberg orders display only a portion of the trade size in the order book, concealing the full size to minimize market impact. As each displayed portion is filled, a new portion becomes visible until the entire order is executed.

- **Bracket Orders**: A bracket order allows traders to set a target profit level and a stop-loss level simultaneously. This limits passively to both maximize potential gains and minimize risks, automating much of the risk management process.

- **One Cancels Other (OCO) Orders**: OCO orders involve placing two orders simultaneously where the execution of one automatically cancels the other. This conditional strategy ensures traders maximize potential price movements while protecting against unfavorable outcomes.

- **Matching Mechanisms**

Matching mechanisms determine how buy and sell orders are paired in financial markets. Their efficiency and design significantly impact execution quality, market liquidity, and price discovery.

- **Continuous Trading and Auction Markets**

- **Order Matching in Continuous Markets**: In continuous trading, orders are continuously matched and executed as they arrive. Market liquidity and price fluctuations define the efficiency of these mechanisms. Matching typically follows a price-time priority, wherein orders are filled based on the best available prices and, for identical prices, on a first-come, first-served basis.

  The immediacy of continuous markets provides traders flexibility and speed, which are critical in fast-moving markets. However, during periods of thin liquidity or extreme volatility, such rapid execution can also exacerbate price fluctuations.

- **Periodic Auction Markets**: Unlike continuous markets, periodic auctions gather orders over a set time and execute them at a singular point, usually yielding a single clearing price. This batching mechanism can minimize market impact, providing a fair price by aggregating demand and supply evidence.

  Auction markets, such as the opening and closing auctions in major stock exchanges, offer traders a venue to transact significant volumes efficiently. They act as focal points for rebalancing portfolios, particularly critical for institutional investors requiring substantial liquidity.

- **Alternative Trading Systems (ATS) and Dark Pools**

Alternative trading systems, including dark pools, have gained prominence as venues offering liquidity outside traditional exchanges. Dark pools enable block trading by large players without their orders being visible to the broader market, reducing the likelihood of adverse price movements.

While dark pools can offer price improvements and reduced transaction costs, they face criticism for the lack of transparency and potential for information asymmetry. Regulators closely scrutinize these systems to ensure fair and orderly markets.

- **Technological Implications and the Evolution of Order Matching**

The evolution of order matching mechanisms is intrinsically linked to technological advancements. Algorithms have revolutionized trading strategies, enabling high-speed and low-latency execution that outpaces human capabilities.

High-frequency trading (HFT) represents one of the apexes of algorithm-driven order matching, leveraging advanced technological infrastructures to facilitate large volumes of orders at unprecedented speeds. While HFT enhances market efficiency and liquidity, it also introduces new risks, such as market manipulation and systemic failures like flash crashes, necessitating robust regulatory frameworks.

- **Practical Strategy Implementation**

Understanding the range of order types and the mechanics of matching systems empowers traders to fine-tune their trading strategies. For instance, an investor aiming to capture a profitable swing without emotional biases might employ bracket orders to automate take-profit and stop-loss conditions.

Similarly, an astute market participant, aware of thin liquidity periods, might leverage iceberg orders to manage order visibility, ensuring minimal market impact.

Traders must also weigh the costs and benefits of trading in continuous versus auction markets, tailoring their strategies to balance execution speed with transaction cost efficiencies. This calculus becomes even more significant in high-volume or volatile markets, where careful order type selection can dramatically alter profitability.

- **Strategic Insights for Traders**

Ultimately, mastering the intricacies of order types and matching mechanisms provides traders with a toolkit to navigate financial markets' complexities with precision and confidence. By aligning these components with one's broader trading goals, potential market participants can make informed decisions that enhance their positioning, improve execution quality, and optimize returns.

Appropriately leveraging order types while applying sophisticated matching mechanisms can result in a significant competitive edge, enabling traders to exploit nuanced market movements with surgical precision. This informed blend of strategy and execution is foundational for sustained success in the ever-evolving landscape of financial markets.

3.3 Role of Information in Price Dynamics

Information serves as the critical engine that powers price dynamics within financial markets. It is the availability, flow, and interpretation of information that catalyzes changes in asset prices, influences volatility, and affects trading decisions. Understanding how information underpins market movements and forms prices is essential for investors and traders aiming to navigate the financial landscape effectively.

The complexity of financial markets arises from the diverse sources of information and the varying speeds at which they are absorbed and acted upon by market participants. From macroeconomic indicators and corporate announcements to geopolitical events and market rumors, the spectrum of information influencing price dynamics is vast. Each participant in the market, from individual retail investors to sophisticated institutional traders, interprets this information distinctively, impacting demand and supply forces that, in turn, drive prices.

Information is a fundamental driver of market activity. When new information becomes available, it prompts market participants to reassess their expectations and valuations, leading to trades that influence price formations. This information can take many forms:

- Economic Data Releases: Economic indicators such as GDP growth rates, employment figures, and inflation statistics wield tremendous influence over market expectations and, by extension, asset prices. For instance, a better-than-expected employment report can lead investors to anticipate stronger economic growth, prompting a rally in equity markets.

- Corporate Announcements: Information from corporations,

including earnings releases, mergers and acquisitions, and changes in management, provides signals about a company's financial health and prospects. Positive earnings surprises can lead to upward revisions in stock valuations as investors adjust their net worth calculations.

- Geopolitical Events: Political developments, international conflicts, and policy decisions often lead to market volatility as participants reassess the risks associated with certain assets or geographies. For example, a geopolitical conflict could trigger an immediate flight-to-safety pattern, where investors shift capital to less risky assets such as gold or government bonds.

- Market Rumors and Speculation: Not all market-moving information is factual; rumors and speculative reports can also cause significant price fluctuations. Traders might react to market hearsay on anticipated regulatory changes or acquisitions, despite the lack of confirmed information.

The reaction of prices to new information is an ongoing process in financial markets, making information dissemination and accessibility crucial components of market efficiency.

Information asymmetry occurs when some market participants possess more or better information than others. This imbalance can significantly influence trade outcomes and market efficiency.

- Adverse Selection: When one party in a transaction is at an informational disadvantage, it may result in adverse selection. In securities markets, informed traders may exploit their knowledge to trade against less-informed participants, leading to suboptimal decisions and wider bid-ask spreads.

- Moral Hazard: This situation arises when one party takes on riskier behavior because the adverse effects are not borne by them, often stemming from an informational imbalance. For instance, a financial advisor might engage in riskier investments on behalf of clients without fully disclosing the risks.

- Liquidity Impact: Information asymmetry directly impacts market liquidity. When traders suspect they might be at an informational disadvantage, they may demand larger compensation for trading, resulting in higher volatility and lower liquidity.

To mitigate these impacts, regulatory bodies mandate timely and accurate disclosure of relevant information, and efforts have been made to democratize access to information through technological advancements such as high-speed data feeds and public dissemination platforms.

The efficient market hypothesis (EMH) postulates that at any given time, asset prices fully reflect all available information. There are three forms of EMH, varying based on the scope of the information encompassed:

- Weak Form Efficiency: Implies that current prices incorporate all historical price and volume data, rendering technical analysis ineffective in predicting future price movements.

- Semi-Strong Form Efficiency: This form asserts that securities quickly adjust to publicly available new information, suggesting that neither fundamental nor technical analysis can consistently achieve excess returns.

- Strong Form Efficiency: Proposes that prices reflect all information, both public and private. This implies that even insider information is already imbedded into current prices and cannot offer any predictive advantage.

Though the EMH provides a theoretical framework for understanding how information integrates into prices, critiques point to instances of market inefficiency and systematic patterns—phenomena like behavioral biases and anomalies often challenge its assumptions.

The way information is processed and acted upon by different market participants gives rise to various trading strategies. Investors and traders design strategies to leverage the movement of prices resulting from new information:

- News-Based Trading: Strategies predicated on reacting swiftly to market-moving news serve a cornerstone in many trading approaches. Traders employing news-based strategies exploit rapidly disseminated information to capitalize on the ensuing price adjustments. Algorithmic trading systems often automate this process, scanning news feeds and executing orders at needle-sharp speeds when certain information is detected.

- Event-Driven Strategies: These strategies focus on exploiting price movements that occur before or after specific events. Corporate earnings announcements, dividends, product launches, or geopolitical developments are monitored closely, as these can trigger substantial market reactions.

- Statistical and Sentiment Analysis: Quantitative strategies might employ statistical models to discern informational patterns and correlations that indicate mispricing, while sentiment analysis scours social media data and news sentiment to anticipate market responses to prevailing narratives.

Given the vital role of information in influencing price dynamics, the integrity of how information is disseminated is paramount to fair trading environments. Regulatory measures seek to safeguard the integrity of markets by mandating transparency and minimizing the potential for insider trading, which could create unfair advantages.

The Securities and Exchange Commission (SEC) in the United States, for instance, enforces rules such as Regulation Fair Disclosure (Reg FD) to ensure that all investors have equal access to pertinent company communications.

The inexhaustible flow of information remains the lifeblood of financial markets. As each new piece of information is parsed, assessed, and acted upon by a myriad of market participants, the resulting price dynamics form a reflection of collective market sentiment and expectations.

For traders and investors, understanding how different types of information impact market conditions and prices is fundamental. Strategies that incorporate the ramifications of information dissemination, asymmetry, and processing are often better equipped to harness opportunities and mitigate risks inherent in trading environments.

In a landscape characterized by rapid innovation, globalization, and instant information flow, remaining attuned to the nuances of information as a driver of price dynamics becomes not just a necessity but a competitive edge for market participants. By mastering the art of information interpretation, both in its presentation and its hidden depths, traders can navigate markets with heightened acuity and insight.

3.4   Order Flow and Liquidity Provision

Order flow and liquidity provision are two interlinked components that interact to ensure that financial markets operate efficiently, allowing participants to transact at prices that reflect true market conditions. The movement of orders in the market, known as order flow, significantly impacts liquidity provision — the ability of the market to absorb large orders without significant price fluctuations. Understanding these concepts is crucial for market participants, including traders, investors, and liquidity providers, as they seek to engage in markets efficiently and profitably.

Understanding order flow refers to the sequence and frequency of buy and sell orders submitted to the market. It captures the actions of market participants and provides insights into the underlying demand and supply dynamics. By analyzing order flow, traders can gauge market sentiment, identify potential trends, and make well-informed trading decisions.

- **Types of Order Flow**:

    - **Buy-Side Order Flow**: Consists of buy orders submitted to purchase securities, indicating the demand side of the market.
    - **Sell-Side Order Flow**: Comprises sell orders submitted to offload securities, representing the supply side of the market.

Order flow can either be aggressive or passive. Aggressive order flow involves market orders that demand immediate execution, often crossing the spread to match available counterparties. Passive order flow, on the other hand, consists of limit orders placed in the order book, waiting for the market to come to the desired price level.

The balance of aggressive and passive order flows reflects the liquidity landscape of the market. An increase in aggressive buy orders, for instance, might lead to rising prices as buying interest overcomes the existing sell-side liquidity.

- **Order Flow Analysis**: Analyzing order flow involves tracking the volume and type of orders hitting the market in real time. Traders look for patterns, such as clustering of large orders or imbalances between buy and sell activities, to gauge momentum and predict short-term price movements.

Order flow analysis is integral to intraday trading strategies, where decisions are based on nuanced insights into the actions of other market

65

participants. By dissecting order flow, traders aim to anticipate subsequent price changes and align their trades accordingly.

Liquidity provision refers to the process by which liquidity is supplied to the market, primarily by market makers or liquidity providers. These entities ensure that there's sufficient buy and sell interest to accommodate other participants wishing to enter or exit positions.

- **The Role of Market Makers**: Market makers play a crucial role in enhancing market liquidity. By continuously quoting buy (bid) and sell (ask) prices, market makers facilitate trade execution and help tighten bid-ask spreads. This provision of liquidity ensures that trades can be executed expediently, maintaining orderly market conditions.

Market makers assume the risk of holding an inventory of securities, which becomes particularly challenging during periods of market stress or when dealing with less liquid assets. To manage these risks, market makers often employ sophisticated risk management strategies and models.

- **Automated Liquidity Models**:   With technological advancements, algorithmic trading systems have become prevalent in liquidity provision.   These systems automate the process of quoting prices and managing inventories, optimizing liquidity provision based on real-time data.

Algorithmic liquidity models have enhanced efficiency by ensuring tighter spreads and increasing market depth, benefiting all market participants. However, they also raise challenges, such as the potential for flash crashes or systemic risks when coupled with high-frequency trading.

The dynamics between order flow and liquidity maintain a symbiotic relationship. The nature of incoming order flow influences liquidity conditions, while the availability of liquidity determines how order flow impacts price formation. This interaction is crucial in understanding market microstructure.

- **Impact of Order Flow on Liquidity**:

  Heavy volumes of aggressive order flow can deplete liquidity quickly, especially if market makers or liquidity providers are unable or unwilling to accommodate the volume. Such a scenario can lead to sharp price movements or increased volatility.

Conversely, in markets with abundant liquidity, even large orders may have minimal impact on price, as liquidity providers efficiently absorb the flow, maintaining price stability.

- **Impact of Liquidity on Order Flow**: In liquid markets, the cost of executing large trades is typically lower due to narrow spreads and minimal slippage, encouraging more active trading and consequently higher order flow. On the other hand, in less liquid markets, participants may split large orders into smaller chunks to minimize market impact, leading to slower execution but stabilizing prices over time.

Whole understanding these dynamics helps traders identify optimal times to enter or exit positions, optimizing transaction costs and execution quality.

Traders and investors employ various strategies to leverage insights from order flow and liquidity provisioning mechanisms. These include:

- **Liquidity Seeking Strategies**: These strategies are designed to execute large orders with minimal market impact. Traders using such strategies might break down large orders into several smaller pieces to prevent signaling and avoid revealing full trade intentions.

  Execution algorithms, such as Volume Weighted Average Price (VWAP) or Time Weighted Average Price (TWAP), are often used to distribute orders optimally over time, matching the natural trading rhythm.

- **Order Flow Monitoring**: By continuously monitoring order flow, traders can detect significant shifts in market sentiment. For instance, an unexpected surge in sell-side order flow can indicate weakening market confidence, prompting traders to adjust positions or hedge risk.

- **Spread Capture**: Market makers and passive liquidity providers might focus on spread capture strategies, where they benefit from buying at the bid and selling at the ask. The profitability of such strategies hinges on their ability to manage inventories and minimize adverse selection.

Implementing these strategies effectively demands an acute understanding of the interplay between order dynamics and liquidity, as well as the ability to react swiftly to market changes.

Examination of order flow and liquidity aids in characterizing prevailing market conditions:

- **Bull Markets**: Typically characterized by sustained aggressive buy-side order flow, with liquidity providers facilitating upward price movements as demand persistently outpaces supply.

- **Bear Markets**: Defined by prevalent sell-side order flow, where liquidity provision may become constrained as market makers adjust to heightened selling pressure.

- **Lateral Markets**: In such conditions, order flow is relatively balanced and liquidity robust, resulting in narrow trading ranges as orders efficiently match across the book.

By understanding these paradigms, participants can tailor tactics to capitalize on specific market phases.

Order flow and liquidity provision are fundamental pillars in the architecture of financial markets. They dictate how trades are executed, influencing pricing, volatility, and market efficiency. Market participants, from liquidity providers to active traders, must understand these concepts thoroughly to navigate markets effectively and strategically implement decisions.

The complexity of modern markets continues to evolve, driven by technological advancements and changing economic conditions. Yet, the fundamental relationship between order flow and liquidity remains a cornerstone of market microstructure, providing essential insights and opportunities for those adept at reading and responding to its signals. By mastering these elements, market actors can enhance execution proficiency and fortify their trading strategies amidst an ever-shifting financial landscape.

3.5   Market Impact and Transaction Costs

Market impact and transaction costs are critical considerations for traders and investors, influencing the net profitability of trades and the overall efficiency of capital markets. Understanding these facets is essential for designing effective trading strategies, optimizing execution, and managing risk. These costs can erode potential gains, making it vital for participants to minimize them through sophisticated techniques and informed decision-making.

- **Understanding Market Impact**:

  Market impact refers to the effect that a trade has on the price of a security. When executing large orders, the market impact can become significant, resulting in less favorable prices and increased costs. The impact is most pronounced in less liquid markets or for large orders relative to the typical trading volume of a security.

  - **Causes of Market Impact**:

    Market impact generally arises from supply and demand imbalances created by large orders. When a large buy order is placed, the increased demand can drive up the price, while a large sell order can depress it. This effect occurs because the available liquidity may not be sufficient to absorb the trade at the current price level without adjustment.

  - **Types of Market Impact**:

    * **Temporary Market Impact**: This occurs when the price change due to a trade is short-lived and reverses after the order is executed as liquidity returns to the market.
    * **Permanent Market Impact**: This is characterized by a lasting change in the price level, indicating that the trade potentially relays new information to the market, thereby altering participants' perceptions of the security's value.

- **Analyzing Transaction Costs**:

  Transaction costs encompass all the expenses incurred in the buying and selling of securities. These costs can be explicit, such as broker commissions, or implicit, like the market impact and opportunity costs.

  - **Explicit Costs**:

    * **Brokerage Fees**: The fees paid to brokers for executing trades. These can vary greatly depending on the service level, trading volume, and the type of instruments traded.

69

* **Exchange Fees**: Charges levied by the trading venue, often based on the transaction volume.
* **Taxes**: Various taxes may apply, such as stamp duties or Financial Transaction Taxes (FTTs), which vary by jurisdiction.

- **Implicit Costs**:
    * **Bid-Ask Spread**: The difference between the bid (buy) price and the ask (sell) price represents a cost for traders. Wider spreads increase costs, especially in less liquid markets.
    * **Market Impact Costs**: These are indirect costs incurred when a trade affects the market price, as previously discussed.
    * **Opportunity Costs**: These arise when a trader misses potential gains due to delayed order execution or failure to execute at a desired price level.

Understanding these costs allows traders to better anticipate trade execution outcomes and price trades more accurately.

• **Strategies to Mitigate Market Impact and Transaction Costs**:

Traders employ various strategies to minimize market impact and transaction costs, thereby enhancing trade profitability.

- **Optimal Order Execution**:
    * **Order Splitting**: Rather than executing a large trade in one go, traders might split orders into smaller pieces to reduce market impact. This strategy, however, can increase the time it takes to fully execute a wholesale position.
    * **Algorithmic Trading**: Many institutional traders utilize algorithmic trading to execute orders strategically. Algorithms like TWAP (Time-Weighted Average Price) and VWAP (Volume-Weighted Average Price) distribute orders over a specified timeframe to blend with market liquidity, thereby minimizing impact.
    * **Dark Pools**: These private trading venues offer anonymity and reduced market impact by matching substantial buy and sell orders away from the public eye. However, they carry the risk of adverse selection.

70

- **Liquidity Management**:

    * **Selecting Liquidity Providers**: Collaborating with top-tier liquidity providers ensures access to deep markets, assisting in executing significant trades with minimal impact.
    * **Market Timing**: Executing trades when markets are most liquid (e.g., during primary trading hours or after significant market releases) can reduce both spreads and market impact.

- **Cost Analysis and Benchmarking**:

    By regularly analyzing past trades' transaction costs and comparing them to specific benchmarks, traders can refine their execution strategies. Post-trade cost analysis facilitates improvements in trading strategies and execution policies.

- **Practical Examples of Market Impact and Mitigation**:

    - **High-Volume Equity Purchase**:

        Consider an institutional investor intending to buy a substantial amount of a mid-cap stock. Directly placing a large order might significantly push up the stock price due to insufficient current sell-side depth. By breaking the order into smaller chunks and aligning trades with market liquidity patterns, the investor can minimize the upward price drift and optimize execution costs.

    - **Cross-Asset Strategy**:

        A hedge fund might engage in a cross-asset strategy that involves the simultaneous buying and selling of correlated assets. Proper synchronization and timing are critical to reduce market impact and slippage risks, capturing arbitrage effectively.

- **Broader Implications for the Market**:

    The careful management of market impact and transaction costs has broader implications for market efficiency and the behavior of financial ecosystems.

    - **Enhanced Market Liquidity**:

        By smoothing out the flow of large orders, techniques to mitigate market impact contribute to deeper and more resilient markets, where prices reflect true supply-demand dynamics.

71

- **Informed Price Discovery**:
  Efficient management of transaction costs helps ensure that prices evolve in response to genuine market information rather than distortionary transactional pressures.

- **Regulatory Considerations**:
  Regulators closely monitor transaction costs and market impact to ensure fairness and transparency. The growing reliance on dark pools, for instance, has attracted scrutiny for potentially undermining public price discovery and equity.

Market impact and transaction costs present continual challenges for traders and investors seeking to maximize returns and efficiency. Through strategic order execution, leveraging technological advancements, and careful analysis, participants can significantly reduce these costs, contributing to better market conditions and improved trading outcomes.

In the evolving landscape of financial markets, where technology and regulation continue to influence trading practices, an adept understanding and management of market impact and transaction costs is indispensable. Mastery of these factors enables market participants not only to enhance efficiency and transparency in their trading activities but also to sustainably achieve their investment objectives amidst a backdrop of dynamic and challenging markets.

3.6   Price Volatility and its Drivers

Price volatility is a fundamental characteristic of financial markets, reflecting the degree of variation in asset prices over time. It serves as a crucial indicator of market risk and uncertainty, influencing investment decisions, risk management, and financial model estimation. Understanding the drivers of price volatility is vital for traders, investors, and policymakers alike, as it provides insights into market behavior, systemic risk, and economic conditions.

Defining Price Volatility

Price volatility quantifies the magnitude of price fluctuations for a given asset or market index. It is typically measured by the standard deviation of returns over a specified time period, indicating how much an asset's price can diverge from its expected value.

Volatility is often categorized into different types, including:

- **Historical Volatility**: Calculated using past price data, historical volatility provides a backward-looking measure of how an asset's price has fluctuated over a particular period.

- **Implied Volatility**: Derived from the prices of financial derivatives, such as options, implied volatility represents the market's expectation of future price swings. It reflects investors' perceptions of future uncertainty and demand for hedging.

- **Realized Volatility**: Refers to the actual volatility observed over a specific period, calculated from historical price movements.

Volatility can be high, indicating large price swings, or low, signifying more stable price movements. Both conditions present unique opportunities and challenges for market participants.

Fundamental Drivers of Price Volatility

A variety of factors can drive price volatility, each impacting market dynamics differently. Understanding these drivers helps investors and traders better anticipate market movements and adapt their strategies accordingly.

- **Macroeconomic Factors**: Macroeconomic variables, such as inflation rates, interest rates, and GDP growth, play a significant role in influencing market volatility. Unexpected changes in these indicators can lead to abrupt shifts in asset prices as market participants reassess economic prospects.

  For example, a surprise interest rate hike by a central bank may lead to heightened volatility across bond and equity markets as investors adjust portfolios to new yield expectations and valuations.

- **Geopolitical Events**: Geopolitical developments, including elections, conflicts, trade negotiations, and policy decisions, can introduce substantial volatility. Such events often lead to rapid repricing of risk as investors recalibrate expectations of political stability, regulatory landscapes, and international relations.

  A notable example includes the volatility spikes following Brexit announcements, where uncertainty surrounding trade agreements and economic implications prompted significant price swings in the British pound and UK equities.

73

- **Market Microstructure Factors**: Elements of market microstructure, such as trading volume, liquidity, and order flow imbalances, can generate volatility. In periods of low liquidity, for instance, even modest trades can lead to large price fluctuations, a phenomenon frequently observed in small-cap stocks or in after-hours trading sessions.

   High-frequency trading and algorithmic trading strategies also contribute to volatility by rapidly executing large volumes of trades, sometimes exacerbating short-term price oscillations.

- **Corporate Announcements and Earnings Releases**: Company-specific news, such as earnings announcements, mergers and acquisitions, or changes in corporate guidance, can prompt significant volatility as market participants revise expectations based on new information.

   For example, a tech company releasing better-than-expected quarterly earnings might experience a sharp uptick in its stock price, reflecting heightened investor optimism and trading activity.

- **Speculative Behavior and Market Psychology**: Investor sentiment and speculative behavior often lead to exaggerated price movements, especially in asset classes with pronounced narrative-driven perceptions, such as cryptocurrencies or emerging technology stocks.

   Behavioral biases, such as fear and greed, can result in overreaction to news, driving volatility as traders capitulate to emotional decision-making rather than fundamental analysis.

Measuring and Managing Volatility

Assessing and managing volatility is a critical component of financial market participation, influencing risk assessment, portfolio allocation, and derivative pricing.

- **Volatility Indices**: Indices such as the CBOE Volatility Index (VIX), often referred to as the "fear index," provide investors with a measure of market volatility expectations derived from options pricing on the S&P 500 index. Spikes in the VIX are typically associated with periods of heightened uncertainty and risk aversion.

- **Risk Management Techniques**: Portfolio diversification is a fundamental approach to mitigating the impact of volatility on investment returns by spreading exposure across various asset classes and geographies.

Derivatives, such as options and futures, offer tools for hedging against adverse price movements. For example, a put option provides protection against a decline in stock prices, allowing investors to guard against downside volatility.

Stop-loss orders are another technique, automatically executing trades when an asset reaches a predetermined price level, curbing potential losses in volatile markets.

- **Volatility Modeling and Forecasting**: Financial models, including GARCH (Generalized Autoregressive Conditional Heteroskedasticity) and stochastic volatility models, help forecast future volatility patterns, offering valuable insights for quantitative traders and risk managers in constructing robust trading and hedging strategies.

Practical Examples of Volatility in Different Asset Classes

Volatility impacts various asset classes uniquely, influenced by the factors and forces relevant to their markets.

- **Equities**: Stocks are inherently volatile assets, with prices influenced by broad economic conditions, sector-specific developments, and company-level events. A growth-oriented technology firm may demonstrate higher volatility than a well-established utility company, reflecting different investor perceptions of risk and return.

- **Fixed Income**: Volatility in bond markets often correlates with interest rate changes and economic outlooks. Long-dated bonds typically exhibit greater price sensitivity to interest rate fluctuations than short-dated bonds, due to differences in duration and expected future cash flows.

- **Commodities**: Commodity prices can experience pronounced volatility driven by supply-demand imbalances, geopolitical tensions, and currency fluctuations. For instance, oil prices are susceptible to production decisions by OPEC, geopolitical disputes in oil-rich regions, and shifts in global energy consumption trends.

- **Cryptocurrencies**: The cryptocurrency market is characterized by extreme volatility, often driven by speculative trading, regulatory developments, and technological advancements. The rapid rise and fall of Bitcoin and other cryptocurrencies highlight the substantial price swings within this nascent and rapidly evolving asset class.

Price volatility is an intrinsic aspect of financial markets, offering both risks and opportunities for market participants. By understanding the underlying drivers and dynamics of volatility, traders and investors can better position themselves to navigate and exploit market fluctuations.

Effective volatility management requires a blend of analytical tools, risk mitigation strategies, and a keen awareness of market conditions across different asset classes. Embracing these disciplines supports informed decision-making, enhances portfolio resilience, and contributes to financial success in the ever-changing landscape of global markets.

3.7   High-Frequency Trading and Market Dynamics

High-Frequency Trading (HFT) represents a paradigm shift in the landscape of financial markets, characterized by the execution of a large number of trades at extremely high speeds, often in fractions of a second. This trading methodology relies on sophisticated algorithms and state-of-the-art technology to capitalize on minute price discrepancies that arise momentarily due to market inefficiencies. As a significant driver of modern market dynamics, HFT has transformed liquidity provision, price formation, and volatility, sparking considerable debate among market participants and regulators.

- **Defining High-Frequency Trading:** High-Frequency Trading encompasses a variety of strategies that share commonalities in speed and execution style. These strategies often involve placing and cancelling thousands of orders in a single trading day, seeking to exploit transient arbitrage opportunities and capturing liquidity imbalances.

Key characteristics of HFT include:

- **Speed and Latency:** Speed is the essence of HFT. The systems involved are designed to execute orders in microseconds, requiring minimal latency – the delay between a market event and response time.

- **Algorithmic Nature:** HFT relies on complex algorithms to identify trading opportunities and execute orders automatically without human intervention. These algorithms continuously process vast amounts of data, including order flow, market depth, and price trends, to make decisions.

- **Short Holding Periods:** HFT positions are typically held for very brief periods, ranging from milliseconds to a few seconds, emphasizing the short-term orientation of these strategies.

- **High Order-to-Trade Ratios:** HFT strategies frequently submit numerous orders to the market, many of which are canceled before execution, resulting in a high ratio of order submissions to executed trades.

- **HFT Strategies:**

A myriad of strategies fall under the high-frequency trading umbrella, each designed to exploit specific market conditions and inefficiencies.

- **Market Making:** High-frequency market makers continuously quote buy and sell prices for securities, profiting from the bid-ask spread. These traders play a pivotal role in providing liquidity to the markets, ensuring that orders can be executed efficiently by other participants. Market making stabilizes prices by narrowing spreads and facilitating trade execution.

- **Statistical Arbitrage:** Statistical arbitrage strategies leverage mathematical models to identify pricing inefficiencies between correlated securities or market indices, executing simultaneous long and short positions to exploit discrepancies.

  For example, if Company A and Company B typically trade at a stable relative price ratio, a temporary deviation from this norm presents an arbitrage opportunity, prompting the algorithm to place offsetting trades to capture the price convergence.

- **Latency Arbitrage:** This approach takes advantage of the differences in latency across trading venues. By acting on price information marginally quicker than other market participants, HFT firms can benefit from arbitrage opportunities before prices align across platforms.

- **Event-Driven Strategies:** Algorithms monitor news releases, earnings reports, or macroeconomic data for anomalies that might provoke short-term price movements. HFT systems can react almost instantaneously to such stimuli, placing trades that capitalize on initial market overreactions.

- **Impact on Market Dynamics:**

High-Frequency Trading has profound effects on market dynamics, re-shaping how liquidity, price discovery, and volatility unfold.

- **Liquidity Provision:** HFT firms enhance market liquidity by consistently quoting buy and sell orders, resulting in tighter spreads and more efficient markets. Their contribution to liquidity is particularly pronounced in asset classes or market hours traditionally considered illiquid.

- **Price Discovery:** The rapid execution and sophisticated analytics employed by HFT contribute to more efficient price discovery. By arbitraging discrepancies almost instantaneously, HFT aligns prices across markets and reduces the duration of pricing inefficiencies.

- **Volatility and Stability:** The relationship between HFT and market volatility is complex. On one hand, by contributing liquidity and narrowing spreads, HFT can reduce short-term volatility. Conversely, during periods of market stress or technical disruptions, the same characteristics can exacerbate volatility, as seen in instances like the 2010 Flash Crash, where sudden withdrawal of HFT liquidity amplified price swings.

- **Challenges and Controversies:**

Despite HFT's benefits, it remains a controversial topic, with debates centering on issues of market fairness, systemic risks, and regulatory oversight.

- **Market Fairness:** Critics argue that HFT creates an uneven playing field, where technologically advanced firms benefit at the expense of slower participants. The advantage in speed allows these traders to locate and act on information before others, raising questions about market transparency and fairness.

- **Flash Crashes and Systemic Risks:** High-frequency trading's potential to rapidly withdraw liquidity underlines the risks of system-wide events like flash crashes. Flash crashes occur when markets plummet sharply and then recover within minutes, often exacerbated by the withdrawal or malfunctioning of HFT algorithms during tumultuous conditions.

  Regulators and market participants alike must grapple with balancing the technological advantages of HFT against these systemic vulnerabilities, focusing on implementing safeguards and circuit breakers to mitigate their impact.

- **Market Manipulation:** HFT's high order-to-trade ratio has raised concerns about manipulative practices such as spoofing, where bogus orders are placed to mislead other participants about supply and demand conditions. Regulators increasingly scrutinize such activities to uphold market integrity.

- **Regulatory and Technological Advancements:**

The growing influence of HFT has prompted regulatory bodies to establish frameworks ensuring market stability and integrity without stifling innovation.

- **Regulatory Responses:** Regulatory initiatives, such as MiFID II in Europe, require increased transparency and reporting for trading activities, including HFT. These measures aim to ensure that trading activity is fair and reflective of genuine market interests.

- **Technological Developments:** Advances in trading technology, such as ultra-low latency networks and co-location services, continue to progress, further enhancing the capabilities of HFT. These developments keep pushing the boundaries of transaction speeds and algorithmic sophistication.

  Risk management systems within HFT firms are also evolving to detect and mitigate the potential for unintended consequences such as runaway trades or outages.

High-Frequency Trading is entrenched as a core component of contemporary market dynamics, with its profound influence ranging from bolstering liquidity to enhancing price discovery mechanisms. Despite its contributions, HFT's complexities and potential risks necessitate a vigilant equilibrium of regulatory oversight, technological advancement, and market discipline.

As financial markets continue to innovate, the interplay between human oversight and algorithmic execution shaped by HFT will define the strategies that can harness its potential while safeguarding the stability and integrity of global financial systems. Understanding these dynamics equips market participants to navigate this rapidly evolving landscape with an informed perspective.

Chapter 4

Mathematics for Market Making Strategies

This chapter introduces the mathematical foundations critical to developing effective market making strategies, focusing on probability, statistics, and stochastic processes. Time series analysis and mathematical modeling are examined to provide tools for predicting price movements and optimizing trades. The application of game theory is explored to understand strategic interactions within financial markets, while optimization techniques are discussed to refine market making strategies. Risk measurement and statistical models are also covered, offering essential methodologies for managing and mitigating the inherent risks in market making activities.

4.1 Probability and Statistics in Financial Markets

In financial markets, probability and statistics form the backbone of quantitative analysis. They provide essential tools for modeling uncertainties, evaluating risks, and making informed decisions. Understanding the fundamentals of probability and statistics is crucial for anyone involved in market making, as it aids in developing strategies that can effectively navigate the inherently volatile financial landscape.

At the core of probability theory lies the concept of random variables. A random variable is a quantity whose value is subject to variations due to randomness. In the context of financial markets, stock prices, interest rates, and currency exchange rates can all be viewed as random variables. These variables are characterized by probability distributions, which describe the likelihood of different outcomes.

One of the most commonly used probability distributions in finance is the normal distribution, also known as the Gaussian distribution. It is characterized by its bell-shaped curve and is defined by two parameters: the mean (μ) and the standard deviation (σ). The mean represents the average expected value, while the standard deviation measures the volatility or dispersion around the mean. For a stock price following a normal distribution, the standard deviation can be interpreted as the degree of risk or uncertainty associated with the price.

A significant property of the normal distribution is the 68-95-99.7 rule. This rule states that approximately 68% of the data falls within one standard deviation of the mean, 95% within two standard deviations, and 99.7% within three standard deviations. Financial analysts often use these properties to assess risk and determine the potential for extreme price movements.

In addition to normal distributions, other distributions such as the binomial, Poisson, and exponential distributions are used to model various financial phenomena. For example, the binomial distribution is useful for modeling binary outcomes, such as the up or down movement of a stock price. In contrast, the Poisson distribution can model the number of trades or arrivals of orders in a given time frame, assuming events occur with a known constant mean rate.

Understanding the characteristics of these distributions enables investors to perform hypothesis testing, a statistical method used to infer properties about a population based on a sample. In financial markets, hypothesis testing can be employed to determine if a certain trading strategy is significantly different from random chance or to compare the performance of two different investment portfolios.

One crucial application of hypothesis testing in finance is the usage of p-values. A p-value assesses the strength of evidence against the null hypothesis, which is a default assumption that there is no effect or no difference. A small p-value, typically less than 0.05, indicates strong evidence against the null hypothesis and suggests that the observed effect is statistically significant.

Alongside hypothesis testing, statistical analysis in finance is deeply connected to the concepts of expected value and variance. The expected value ($E[X]$) of a random variable X represents the long-term average or mean outcome, formally defined as:

$$E[X] = \sum_i x_i \cdot P(X = x_i)$$

where x_i denotes the possible outcomes, and $P(X = x_i)$ represents the probabilities of those outcomes. Understanding the expected value is crucial for evaluating the fairness and expected returns of financial instruments and strategies.

Variance ($\mathrm{Var}(X)$), on the other hand, quantifies the extent to which values differ from the expected value. It is given by:

$$\mathrm{Var}(X) = E[(X - E[X])^2]$$

A higher variance indicates a wider spread of possible outcomes, signifying greater risk. In portfolio management, variance is a critical measure for assessing and mitigating risk, enabling investors to construct more balanced and diversified portfolios.

Another fundamental statistical tool employed in financial markets is the concept of correlation. Correlation measures the degree to which two random variables move in relation to each other. The correlation coefficient (ρ) ranges from -1 to 1, where +1 denotes a perfect positive correlation, -1 indicates a perfect negative correlation, and 0 indicates no correlation.

The calculation of correlation is expressed as:

$$\rho = \frac{\mathrm{Cov}(X, Y)}{\sigma_X \sigma_Y}$$

where $\mathrm{Cov}(X, Y)$ is the covariance between X and Y, and σ_X, σ_Y are the standard deviations of X and Y, respectively. In the context of financial markets, investors leverage the concept of correlation to identify asset relationships, optimize portfolio diversification, and improve overall risk-adjusted returns.

Moving towards practical applications, probability and statistics in financial markets facilitate the construction of predictive models through techniques like regression analysis. Regression models help explain the relationship between a dependent variable and one or more independent variables. In finance, regression can be used to forecast future asset prices, evaluate the influence of market indicators, or model returns with factors such as interest rates, economic indicators, or company-specific metrics.

An important regression model commonly utilized is the linear regression model, represented as:

$$Y = \beta_0 + \beta_1 X_1 + \beta_2 X_2 + \cdots + \beta_n X_n + \epsilon$$

where Y is the dependent variable, X_i are the independent variables, β_i are the coefficients, and ϵ is the error term. The coefficients β_i quantify the change in the dependent variable for a one-unit change in the respective independent variable, assuming all other variables are constant.

Advanced statistical models, such as autoregressive integrated moving average (ARIMA) and generalized autoregressive conditional heteroskedasticity (GARCH), take this a step further by incorporating time series data to model market phenomena that exhibit trends and volatility clustering. These models are instrumental in developing complex, data-driven strategies that anticipate market movements with greater accuracy.

In addition to the individual tools and concepts, the integration of probability and statistics in financial markets provides the foundation for risk assessment techniques. Value at Risk (VaR) is one such method that estimates the potential loss in value of an asset or portfolio over a defined period for a given confidence interval. It is a widely-used risk management tool that aids investors in understanding potential downside risks and capital requirements.

Monte Carlo simulation is another powerful statistical technique that uses probability distributions to model and assess the impact of risk and uncertainty in financial forecasts and decision-making processes. By simulating a wide range of possible market conditions, Monte Carlo simulations allow investors to visualize the distribution of potential outcomes and evaluate strategies under various scenarios.

The interplay of probability and statistics within the financial markets creates a robust framework for understanding and navigating uncertainties. It empowers market participants with the quantitative insights required to design, evaluate, and implement trading strategies, enhance risk management protocols, and make informed investment decisions that align with both short-term objectives and long-term financial goals. As with any scientific discipline, mastery of probability and statistics involves continual learning and practical application, ensuring that analysts and investors can adapt to the ever-evolving dynamics of global financial markets.

4.2 Stochastic Processes and Random Walks

The modeling of financial markets often relies on stochastic processes, which provide a framework for understanding and predicting the random variables that represent asset prices over time. In essence, a stochastic process is a collection of random variables indexed by time, capturing the evolution of a system that is subject to inherent randomness. In financial markets, these systems include stock prices, interest rates, and exchange rates, all of which exhibit stochastic behavior.

One of the most fundamental types of stochastic processes used in finance is the random walk. The concept of a random walk was first articulated in the early 20th century as a statistical model of a path that consists of a succession of random steps. In a financial context, a random walk describes the path of an asset price that follows a sequence of changes, each of which is a random deviation from its current state. This model assumes that changes in asset prices are independent and identically distributed, with the implication that past movements or trends cannot predict future prices.

Mathematically, a simple random walk can be expressed as follows:

$$X_t = X_{t-1} + \epsilon_t \tag{4.1}$$

where X_t represents the asset price at time t, and ϵ_t is a random variable representing the price change from time $t-1$ to time t, often modeled as having a mean of zero and a constant standard deviation.

The random walk hypothesis, which underpins the Efficient Market Hypothesis (EMH), suggests that if markets are efficient, all known information is already reflected in current asset prices, and future price changes are determined solely by new information, which is inherently unpredictable. Thus, price movements exhibit a random walk behavior.

While the random walk provides a simplified view of asset price movements, it serves as the basis for more complex stochastic models that capture additional dynamics observed in real-world financial markets. One such extension is the Brownian motion, also known as a Wiener process, named after the botanist Robert Brown who discovered the erratic movement of pollen particles in a fluid.

A standard Brownian motion $B(t)$ is defined by the following properties:

- $B(0) = 0$.

- $B(t)$ has independent increments; the future path of the process is independent of its past.

- For any t, $B(t)$ follows a normal distribution with mean 0 and variance t, i.e., $B(t) \sim N(0, t)$.

- The paths of $B(t)$ are continuous with probability one.

Given these properties, Brownian motion becomes an ideal candidate for modeling continuously varying stock prices in continuous-time finance applications. A notable application of Brownian motion is the Black-Scholes-Merton (BSM) model, which revolutionized options pricing by introducing a differential equation grounded in Brownian motion.

The BSM model prices a European call option as follows:

$$C = S_0 N(d_1) - K e^{-rT} N(d_2) \tag{4.2}$$

where
$$d_1 = \frac{\ln(S_0/K) + (r + \sigma^2/2)T}{\sigma\sqrt{T}} \tag{4.3}$$

$$d_2 = d_1 - \sigma\sqrt{T} \tag{4.4}$$

and $N(\cdot)$ denotes the cumulative distribution function of the standard normal distribution, S_0 is the current stock price, K is the strike price, σ is the volatility, r is the risk-free rate, and T is the time to maturity.

Beyond standard Brownian motion, the financial markets also employ models based on Geometric Brownian Motion (GBM) to address the issue of potentially negative stock prices and capture the observed phenomenon of relative, rather than absolute, price changes. GBM is characterized by the stochastic differential equation:

$$dS_t = \mu S_t \, dt + \sigma S_t \, dB_t \tag{4.5}$$

In this expression, S_t denotes the stock price at time t, μ is the drift coefficient representing the deterministic trend, σ is the volatility coefficient, and dB_t is the increment of a standard Brownian motion. The multiplicative nature of the stochastic and deterministic parts ensures that the stock prices remain strictly positive.

GBM effectively models the exponential growth feature of stock prices and serves as the assumption behind various option pricing and risk management strategies due to its ability to replicate the statistical properties of asset returns.

Another category of stochastic processes prevalent in financial modeling is mean-reverting processes, which are particularly useful for modeling interest rates and stochastic volatility. These processes include the Ornstein-Uhlenbeck process and the Cox-Ingersoll-Ross (CIR) model. A mean-reverting process is characterized by the tendency to revert to a long-term mean value, making it suitable for assets whose prices or indices exhibit cyclical behavior.

The Ornstein-Uhlenbeck process is depicted by the stochastic differential equation:

$$dX_t = \theta(\mu - X_t)\,dt + \sigma\,dB_t \tag{4.6}$$

where θ is the speed of mean reversion, μ is the long-term mean, and σ is the volatility parameter. This process captures assets that display regular oscillations around a historical average.

Stochastic processes play a pivotal role in modeling random phenomena across various domains of finance, including equity valuations, fixed income instruments, and derivatives pricing. Through the exploration of advanced topics such as Levy processes, Jump-Diffusion models, and the Vasicek interest rate model, financial practitioners can capture complex behaviors, such as sudden jumps or spikes, diffusion trends, and reversion tendencies, that arise in contemporary markets.

In practical applications, the real value of stochastic processes and random walks is realized through simulation, such as Monte Carlo methods, which leverage stochastic processes to model the behavior of asset prices over time and quantify risk exposure. Monte Carlo simulations assess future portfolio returns under various stochastic scenarios, enabling investors to evaluate the probability distribution of potential outcomes in a risk-sensitive manner.

While stochastic processes inherently imply unpredictability, they offer a structured method to handle the randomness and uncertainty of financial markets. By equipping traders, analysts, and portfolio managers with quantitative tools to describe and anticipate future price behaviors, stochastic processes form a cornerstone of modern financial theory and empirical practice. They continue to adapt and expand with advancements in computational power and data availability, providing deeper insights into the ever-evolving dynamics of financial systems.

4.3   Time Series Analysis

Time series analysis is a powerful statistical tool used to analyze sequences of data points collected over time. This method is particularly relevant in financial markets, where historical data such as stock prices, interest rates, and trading volumes are key to understanding market dynamics and predicting future movements. As financial markets are inherently temporal, time series analysis provides the scaffolding necessary to model trends, seasonal patterns, and cyclic behaviors, as well as to forecast future values of these financial indicators.

At the heart of time series analysis lies the decomposition of a series into three main components: trend, seasonality, and noise (or random fluctuations).

- **Trend** refers to the long-term progression or movement of the data. In finance, a trend might signify the general direction in which an asset price is moving over a prolonged period.

- **Seasonality** refers to periodic fluctuations that occur at regular intervals, typically seen in quarterly revenue reports of businesses, where certain seasons might yield higher profits. In finance, seasonality can manifest as regular patterns observed during specific times of the year or month.

- **Noise** represents random error or short-term irregular fluctuations in the time series, introducing variability that cannot be explained by trend or seasonality alone.

The mathematical modeling of time series data usually begins with simple models that slowly build complexity as one incorporates more sophisticated ideas. One of the foundational models in time series analysis is the **Autoregressive (AR) model**, which describes a time series based on its previous values. An Autoregressive model of order p, AR(p), is represented as:

$$X_t = c + \sum_{i=1}^{p} \phi_i X_{t-i} + \epsilon_t$$

where X_t is the current value, c is a constant, ϕ_i are the parameters of the model, and ϵ_t is the white noise error term. By averaging past values, the AR model captures temporal dependencies, making it suitable for predicting and analyzing financial time series with momentum.

Another fundamental model is the **Moving Average (MA) model**, which models the time series using past forecast errors. An MA model of order q, MA(q), is expressed as:

$$X_t = \mu + \sum_{i=1}^{q} \theta_i \epsilon_{t-i} + \epsilon_t$$

where μ is the mean of the series, θ_i are parameters of the model, and ϵ_t is the white noise error term. The MA model is often used to smooth out short-term fluctuations and highlight longer-term trends and cycles.

The combination of the AR and MA models leads to the **Autoregressive Moving Average (ARMA) model**, commonly utilized for stationary time series data. The ARMA(p, q) model combines the autoregressive approach and the moving average approach into a single framework:

$$X_t = c + \sum_{i=1}^{p} \phi_i X_{t-i} + \sum_{j=1}^{q} \theta_j \epsilon_{t-j} + \epsilon_t$$

In practice, financial time series often exhibit non-stationary behavior, where statistical properties like mean and variance are not constant over time. To handle such data, the **Autoregressive Integrated Moving Average (ARIMA) model** is employed, which includes a differencing step to transform the non-stationary series into a stationary one. ARIMA(p, d, q), where d denotes the degree of differencing, is expressed as:

- **Differencing:** Apply d levels of differencing to achieve stationarity.

- **ARMA modeling:** Fit an ARMA model to the differenced data.

89

The ARIMA family is extraordinarily flexible and can model a wide array of series, making it a popular tool for economic forecasting.

While traditional ARIMA models address univariate time series, financial markets often require the modeling of multivariate data. This is where **Vector Autoregression (VAR) and Vector Autoregressive Moving Average (VARMA)** models come into play, capturing the linear interdependencies among multiple time series.

A **Vector Autoregressive (VAR) model** of order p, VAR(p), models each variable in a system as a linear function of past values of itself and the past values of all other variables:

$$Y_t = c + \sum_{i=1}^{p} A_i Y_{t-i} + \epsilon_t$$

where Y_t is a vector of time series variables, A_i are matrices of coefficients, c is a vector of constants, and ϵ_t is a vector of error terms.

For markets driven by exogenous factors, a popular model is the **Structural Vector Autoregression (SVAR)** and the **Cointegrated VAR (CVAR or VECM)** which consider underlying relationships and co-movements over the long run, respectively.

Another key aspect of time series analysis in finance is **volatility modeling**. As financial returns often exhibit clustered volatility, models like the **Generalized Autoregressive Conditional Heteroskedasticity (GARCH)** model, introduced by Bollerslev, are extensively used. A typical GARCH(p, q) model includes the following equations:

Variance equation:

$$\sigma_t^2 = \alpha_0 + \sum_{i=1}^{p} \alpha_i \epsilon_{t-i}^2 + \sum_{j=1}^{q} \beta_j \sigma_{t-j}^2$$

where σ_t^2 is the forecasted variance, α_i and β_j are coefficients, and ϵ_t are past forecast errors.

By adopting GARCH models, analysts can predict volatility and adjust investment strategies based on changing risk.

Awareness of seasonality patterns can drive better decision-making, especially for businesses exposed at different times of the fiscal year. Techniques such as **Seasonal Decomposition of Time Series (STL)** and **Exponential Smoothing State Space Model (ETS)** allow the separation of seasonal components to further empower forecasting capabilities.

To validate the efficacy of the models, testing for **stationarity** using the **Augmented Dickey-Fuller (ADF) test**, analyzing the **Autocorrelation Function (ACF)**, and **Partial Autocorrelation Function (PACF)** are important diagnostic methods. Furthermore, model selection is best accompanied by information criterion minimization, such as **Akaike Information Criterion (AIC)** or **Bayesian Information Criterion (BIC)**.

The limitations inherent in traditional time series are being addressed with more contemporary approaches such as machine learning methods, including **Long Short-Term Memory (LSTM) networks** and **Recurrent Neural Networks (RNNs)**, which have shown promising results in capturing complex temporal structures in high-frequency trading and dynamic market prediction.

In real-world applications, time series models are vital for risk management and algorithmic trading strategies. They enable market participants to anticipate future asset performance, optimize portfolios, and gain competitive advantages. Through continuous improvement of computational algorithms and data acquisition capabilities, time series analysis evolves into an increasingly sophisticated means of decoding the past to enhance financial acumen and strategic foresight in an ever-volatile marketplace.

4.4   Mathematical Models of Market Making

Market making stands as a pivotal mechanism underlying the liquidity and functioning of financial markets. Market makers are entities, often financial institutions or individuals, who provide liquidity by offering to buy and sell securities, thereby facilitating trading for investors. The core of market making lies in the ability to manage inventory and hedge risks while profiting from the spread between bid and ask prices. Mathematical models play a crucial role in guiding these market making activities, helping direct decisions under uncertainty, optimizing inventory levels, and managing the risks inherent in their operations.

The essence of market making can be captured through various mathematical models, each devised to address different layers of complexity present in financial markets. Among the most recognized frameworks are those emphasizing inventory management and order placement, each contributing to a comprehensive understanding of strategic mar-

CHAPTER 4.   MATHEMATICS FOR MARKET MAKING STRATEGIES

ket making.

One fundamental model is the **Inventory-Based Model** of market making, where the market maker's primary aim is to maintain a balanced inventory that minimizes risk exposure while maximizing profit from the spread. The concept hinges on the notion that a market maker should avoid holding excessive stock (which risks value loss) or running short (which risks failing to honor purchase commitments).

Mathematically, the inventory-based approach involves setting bid and ask prices dynamically to regulate the inventory level. Consider the inventory level, q, of a market maker:

$$q = q_0 + \Sigma(N_{\text{buy}} - N_{\text{sell}})$$

where q_0 represents the initial inventory level, and N_{buy} and N_{sell} are the number of units bought and sold, respectively. The optimization problem can then be expressed as setting bid (b) and ask (a) prices to achieve a targeted inventory level, by adjusting the spread:

$$\pi = (a - c_{\text{ask}})(N_{\text{sell}}) + (c_{\text{bid}} - b)(N_{\text{buy}}) - \lambda \cdot |q - q_{\text{target}}|$$

where π is the profit, c_{ask} and c_{bid} are external factors (e.g., production cost or the market midpoint), and λ is a penalty reflecting deviation from the target inventory level, q_{target}.

Another sophisticated model is the **Queue-Based Model**, which addresses the sequential nature of trades and the dynamics of orders resting in the order book. Here, a market maker's strategy involves ordering tactics that consider the current queue position, recent trade activity, and anticipated market trends.

In a queue-based model, the market maker adjusts orders based on the expected arrival rates of limit orders (λ_b for bid and λ_a for ask) and the cancellation/transaction rates (μ_b and μ_a):

$$U_t = \max_{b,a} \mathbb{E}\left[\Sigma(\pi_t - c(q_t))\Delta t\right] - \gamma \cdot \text{Var}[\pi_t]$$

where U_t is the expected utility, γ is the risk aversion coefficient, π_t is the net profit over time interval Δt, and $c(q_t)$ is the inventory cost associated with holding a position q_t.

Moving to stochastic modeling, one common framework is the **Stochastic Control Model**, which employs stochastic calculus to derive insights into the optimal strategy for market makers. These models allow the formulation of dynamic programming equations, characterizing the behavior and decisions of market makers. An example is the classical

Avellaneda-Stoikov Model, which provides a probabilistic description of optimal bid and ask quotes, adjusting for transaction costs, risks, and profits.

The Avellaneda-Stoikov model uses the Hamilton–Jacobi–Bellman (HJB) equations to derive the value function $V(x, t)$ representing the maximum expected utility of terminal wealth:

$$V(x,t) = \max_{a,b} \left[-\exp(-\gamma(x + \pi)) \right]$$

where γ is the risk aversion coefficient, x is wealth, and π is the cumulative profit. The optimal bid and ask prices are influenced by inventory risk and volatility, providing a quantifiable equilibrium between supply and demand.

In market environments characterized by high-frequency trading, transactional strategies benefit from **agent-based models** and **reinforcement learning**, which adaptively modify strategies based on real-time data and historical behaviors. These methods incorporate complex algorithms to observe market actions continually, analyze bid-ask spreads, and optimize order execution.

For instance, reinforcement learning models employ the Markov Decision Process (MDP) where a market maker evaluates states defined by current market conditions, chooses actions like price adjustments, and receives rewards linked to trading success or penalties attributed to risk exposure. Through temporal difference learning and deep Q-learning approaches, these systems refine strategies dynamically, tuning responses to shifting market conditions.

Furthermore, **game-theoretic models** are applied to simulate competitive market environments, where multiple market makers operate and interact strategically. The analysis of Nash equilibria provides insights into cooperative versus competitive behaviors, guiding optimal decision-making concerning price setting and inventory distribution.

An ideal market making strategy involves balancing several elements: maintaining liquidity provision, optimizing spread-based profit, managing inventory risk, and adapting to market volatility—all with an eye towards regulatory constraints and prevailing market ethics. Mathematical models facilitate this balance by blending theoretical rigor with empirical insights, directing the development of efficient strategies that ascertain sustainability and profitability in rapid-paced market conditions.

Thus, the interplay of mathematical models in market making underscores a crucial synthesis between quantitative analysis, computational algorithms, and strategic foresight that collectively arm market makers with the requisite tools to thrive in an evolving financial ecosystem. These models serve as both a compass and a guidebook for navigating the intricate landscape of modern market architecture, turning complex quantitative theory into actionable trading acumen.

4.5   Game Theory and Strategic Interaction

Game theory, an area of mathematics devoted to studying strategic interactions among rational decision-makers, plays a critical role in analyzing behaviors and outcomes in financial markets. With its foundation laid by figures such as John von Neumann and John Nash, game theory offers a structured framework to dissect and comprehend competitive and cooperative strategies employed by market participants, including investors, traders, and market makers.

In the context of market making, the application of game theory involves assessing how market participants interact, compete, and form strategies that ultimately influence market dynamics. One of the foundational concepts in game theory is that of a "game," which consists of players, strategies, and payoffs. Each player strives to maximize their payoff by selecting strategies while anticipating the moves of others.

A fundamental concept within game theory is the Nash equilibrium, a state in which no player can benefit from unilaterally changing their strategy, given the strategies of all other players. Identifying Nash equilibria helps market participants predict the outcomes of strategic interactions, guiding decisions on pricing, risk management, and competitive positioning.

Consider a simplified example of two competing market makers, A and B, engaged in setting bid and ask prices. The strategic interaction can be represented in a payoff matrix, with each cell indicating the payoff each market maker receives based on their choice of strategy:

	A's Strategy: High Spread	A's Strategy: Low Spread
B's Strategy: High Spread	(3, 3)	(2, 4)
B's Strategy: Low Spread	(4, 2)	(1, 1)

Table 4.1: Payoff matrix for market makers A and B

In this matrix, the numbers represent payoffs for market makers A and B, respectively. The Nash equilibrium occurs when both choose a low spread, resulting in a payoff of (1, 1), as neither can increase their payoff by unilaterally switching strategies.

Game theory not only analyzes the competitive actions but also delves into cooperative behaviors. Cooperative games, where participants form coalitions to enhance their collective payoff, showcase how market makers might align interests to improve liquidity or stabilize prices during periods of market stress.

A salient aspect of game theory is its application to auction mechanisms and trading protocols. In financial markets, auctions are a common method to facilitate the buying and selling of securities. Game theoretic principles are used to design auction formats that incentivize truthful bidding and efficient price discovery. The Revenue Equivalence Theorem, for instance, helps auction designers understand how various auction rules affect revenue outcomes under certain bidder valuations.

In examining continuous double auctions, where buyers and sellers submit bids and offers continually, game theory aids understanding the conditions for competitive equilibria and efficiency. The strategic interactions in such auctions are complex, often involving rapid decisions and the management of limited information—areas where classical game theory and its computational advancements intersect.

Advanced applications of game theory explore incomplete information scenarios, using Bayesian games where players have beliefs about the strategic types of other players based on probability distributions. In the context of financial markets, this translates to traders making decisions with partial knowledge of other participants' intentions or capabilities, modeling situations like insider trading, asymmetric information, and speculative attacks in currency markets.

The concept of repeated games is also pertinent to financial markets, highlighting the strategic interactions that occur over time rather than in isolated settings. Repeated interaction fosters reputation building and cooperation, which can mitigate the potential for opportunistic behavior.

In the modern era of algorithmic trading, game theory intersects with machine learning and artificial intelligence, providing tools for developing algorithms that adapt and respond to the strategies of others autonomously. Through evolutionary game theory and agent-based modeling, financial markets become a laboratory for testing strategic interactions among a multitude of algorithmic traders.

One paradigmatic example is the Prisoner's Dilemma, frequently used to illustrate how rational strategies lead to suboptimal outcomes, despite cooperative gains being possible. In trading scenarios, it manifests in a situation where competing firms might undercut prices or reduce spreads excessively to capture market share, thereby reducing profitability for all involved.

Game theorists also draw insights from psychological and behavioral data to refine strategies, incorporating elements like bounded rationality, prospect theory, and the psychology of risk into models. Behavioral game theory unveils how irrational factors might drive decision-making, with implications for understanding phenomena like herd behavior, market bubbles, and investor sentiment shifts.

Another extension is the study of signaling games, where participants send costly signals to convey information otherwise obscured by strategic uncertainty. Market participants, such as corporations disseminating earnings forecasts or central banks adjusting interest rates, engage in signaling mechanisms where game-theoretic principles help decode intentions and forecast subsequent actions.

In terms of policy implications, game theory informs regulatory bodies on market structure and anti-competitive practices, ensuring fair competition and protecting investors' interests. By analyzing strategic interactions through game lenses, regulators can design robust frameworks that minimize systemic risk and enhance market integrity.

To synthesize, game theory provides invaluable insights into the strategic realm of financial markets, offering a lens through which the complex network of interactions can be untangled and understood. By analyzing the incentives and strategies inherent in market behavior, game theory not only illuminates the underlying mechanics driving market equilibria but also equips participants with strategic foresight to navigate the intricate chessboard of global finance adeptly. Whether in auction mechanisms, algorithmic trading, or market signaling, the enduring utility of game theory underscores its centrality in the continual endeavor to optimize and regulate the financial marketplace.

4.6 Optimization Techniques for Strategy Development

Optimization techniques form a vital aspect of strategy development within financial markets, providing the mathematically grounded methodologies to enhance decision-making processes. In the context of market making and trading, optimization encompasses the application of mathematical rigor to identify the best strategies under given constraints, improving profitability, reducing risk, and ensuring efficient capital allocation.

Optimization in financial strategy development addresses a variety of goals: maximizing returns, minimizing risks, balancing portfolios, optimizing trading execution, and fine-tuning algorithmic strategies. Given the complexity and dynamism of financial markets, the methodologies extend from classical linear programming to sophisticated, AI-driven stochastic and adaptive approaches.

The cornerstone of quantitative optimization is **Linear Programming (LP)**, a method used to achieve the best outcome in a mathematical model whose requirements are represented by linear relationships. LP is widely used to solve problems where the objective is to maximize or minimize a linear function subject to linear constraints. A simple representation is:

$$\max_{x} c^T x \quad \text{subject to} \quad Ax \leq b \quad \text{and} \quad x \geq 0$$

where x is a vector of decision variables, c is a vector of coefficients, A is a matrix representing constraints, and b is a vector of constraints.

In portfolio management, LP can be used to maximize portfolio return subject to a risk constraint or to minimize risk for a given level of expected return, a formulation conceptually captured in the Markowitz mean-variance model. In this model:

$$\min \frac{1}{2}x^T Q x - r^T x \quad \text{subject to} \quad e^T x = 1,\, x \geq 0$$

where Q is the covariance matrix of returns, r is the vector of expected returns, and e is a vector of ones ensuring full capital allocation.

Despite its utility, real-world financial problems often exhibit non-linearities, necessitating more advanced methods such as **Quadratic Programming (QP)**, which extends LP by considering quadratic objectives. These forms are pivotal in optimizing portfolios with higher-order moments of the return distribution considered, embedding risk metrics such as variance, as seen in multifactorial risk-adjusted return optimization.

In trading strategy development, optimizing execution is another significant area where **Stochastic Optimization** comes into play. In a context where orders must be executed over time in the presence of uncertain and random market conditions, stochastic models are used to probabilistically model asset price paths and insights. Methods such as **Monte Carlo Simulations** facilitate this, enabling traders to simulate various market scenarios and assess the statistical efficiency of proposed strategies over extensive arrays of simulated environments.

Parallelly, **Genetic Algorithms (GAs)** and **Evolutionary Strategies** have gained popularity due to their adaptability and robustness in navigating complex, multi-modal landscapes. These algorithms mimic evolutionary processes and natural selection, iteratively evolving candidate solutions toward optimality via mutation, recombination, and selection. They're particularly well-suited to non-convex optimization tasks, often encountered in developing trading strategies where the search space is vast and fraught with local optima.

Reactive market adaptation—a critical facet in continuously evolving financial environments—benefits from **Machine Learning Optimization** frameworks. Techniques such as **Reinforcement Learning (RL)** directly optimize action strategies by learning from the feedback provided by interaction with the market environment, adjusting actions based on reward signals. Clusters of APIs and trading systems increasingly integrate RL-based agents that fine-tune trade execution, adapt to variable liquidity conditions, and adjust to optimally mimic human-like learning processes.

Another potent approach is **Constrained Optimization**, where constraints represent financial realities such as leverage ratios, capital adequacy, or risk exposure limits. Non-linear constraints often necessitate the application of **Sequential Quadratic Programming (SQP)** methods—an iterative process for solving constrained non-linear optimization problems with a quadratic programming subproblem solved at each iteration.

In algorithmic trading, the **Optimal Execution** problem involves the design of order strategies that minimize market impact and transaction costs over discrete trading intervals. The **Almgren-Chriss Model** offers a structured approach through which the tradeoff between market impact costs and price risk is quantified, seeking an optimal trade trajectory that equilibrates urgency against execution efficiency.

For multi-period financial strategy optimization, **Dynamic Programming (DP)** plays a critical role, particularly through the establishment of Bellman Equations. DP handles time-based decisions where the temporal sequence and variability affect the outcome, essential for managing dynamic portfolios and guiding decision parameters through uncertain forecasting horizons.

Moreover, **Robust Optimization** techniques are gaining prominence due to their inherent ability to manage uncertainty explicitly. In a robust fashion, strategies are developed that remain effective under worst-case scenario misspecifications—accounting for parameter sensitivity and model misspecification risks by safeguarding against the impact of unforeseen market shifts.

Addressing high-dimensional data and variability, **Deep Learning Techniques** complement optimization processes, embedding deep neural networks for complex patterns and correlations detection. Deep learning is increasingly employed to refine predictive models that feed into subsequent optimization modules, enhancing the synergy between prediction accuracies and optimal strategy selection.

The strategic and computational interplay underscores the multifaceted nature of optimization. By weaving together distinct fields of mathematical, statistical, and AI-driven models, the comprehensive optimization landscape offers quantitative traders and market makers a robust toolkit for constructing effective and innovative financial strategies. With financial markets fast evolving, the perpetual refinement of optimization techniques ensures adaptability, resilience, and competitiveness in navigating the intricate choreography of capital markets.

4.7 Risk Measurement and Statistical Models

In the intricate and often volatile environment of financial markets, risk measurement stands as a foundational pillar for informed decision-making and prudent investment management. Understanding and quantifying risk are imperative for market participants, as risks directly affect the stability and performance of investment portfolios. To this end, a wide array of statistical models and methods have been developed to effectively measure and manage risk, providing insights that enable investors to anticipate potential losses and optimize their strategic approaches.

At the core of risk management lies the quantification of different types of risks, including market risk, credit risk, and operational risk. Market risk, primarily driven by fluctuations in market prices, can be assessed through various statistical models that attempt to capture the inherent uncertainties and volatilities.

One of the foremost measures in risk assessment is **Value at Risk (VaR)**, a widely used statistical technique that estimates the potential loss in the value of a portfolio over a defined period for a specified confidence interval. VaR is formally expressed as:

$$\Pr(L > \text{VaR}) = 1 - \alpha$$

where L denotes the loss, and α is the confidence level, typically set at 95% or 99%. VaR provides a threshold value such that the probability of loss exceeding this value is $(1-\alpha)$. It can be calculated using several approaches, including:

- **Historical Simulation**: This non-parametric method leverages past market data to simulate the distribution of possible future returns, directly deriving VaR from historical losses.

- **Variance-Covariance Method**: A parametric technique assuming normal distribution of returns, uses mean and standard deviation to compute VaR based on the portfolio's historical volatility and correlations among asset classes.

- **Monte Carlo Simulation**: An advanced methodology that uses random sampling and statistical modeling to estimate the probability distribution of portfolio returns across numerous scenarios, capturing both linear and non-linear relationships among assets.

Despite its popularity, VaR has limitations—chief among them being its failure to account for extreme events, often dubbed "black swan" events. To address this, the **Conditional Value at Risk (CVaR)** or Expected Shortfall emerges as a more comprehensive risk metric. CVaR focuses on the tail end of the distribution, measuring the expected losses exceeding VaR threshold:

$$\text{CVaR}_\alpha = \mathbb{E}[L|L > \text{VaR}_\alpha]$$

CVaR offers a deeper insight into the risk profile by considering the scale of potential tail losses, thus proving valuable for portfolios with significant exposure to extreme events or instruments with path-dependent risks.

Beyond market risk, addressing **credit risk** becomes especially pertinent in contexts such as derivatives, loans, and bonds. **Credit VaR** and the **CreditMetrics** framework offer methodologies for predicting the likelihood of default and evaluating the impact of changes in credit rating on the return of debt instruments.

Furthermore, multifactor risk models like the **Capital Asset Pricing Model (CAPM)** and **Arbitrage Pricing Theory (APT)** play essential roles in measuring systematic risk and isolating factor-specific contributions to a portfolio's total risk. CAPM encapsulates the relationship between expected return and market risk, expressing it as:

$$E(R_i) = R_f + \beta_i(E(R_m) - R_f)$$

where $E(R_i)$ is the expected return on asset i, R_f is the risk-free rate, β_i represents the sensitivity to market return ($E(R_m)$) changes, and $(E(R_m) - R_f)$ reflects the market risk premium.

APT, in contrast, extends CAPM by allowing multiple risk factors, providing a multilinear equation:

$$E(R_i) = R_f + \sum_{j=1}^{k} \beta_{ij} F_j$$

where β_{ij} reflects the sensitivity of asset returns to factor j, and F_j denotes the set of risk factors.

Volatility measurement is another critical component of risk evaluation. Techniques such as the **Generalized Autoregressive Conditional Heteroskedasticity (GARCH)** model aid in understanding time-varying volatility patterns:

$$\sigma_t^2 = \omega + \sum_{i=1}^{p} \alpha_i \epsilon_{t-i}^2 + \sum_{j=1}^{q} \beta_j \sigma_{t-j}^2$$

where ω, α_i, and β_j are model parameters capturing past shocks and variance persistence. GARCH models are instrumental in deriving correlated volatility clusters—marked periods of high volatility followed by relative calm—and offer predictive capabilities essential for forecasting future risks.

Moreover, **stress testing** and **scenario analysis** provide robust frameworks for risk measurement by assessing how portfolios respond to significant market disruptions or simulated catastrophic events, determining capital adequacy, and ensuring resilience against worst-case outcomes.

Complementing these traditional statistical techniques, advancements in **Machine Learning** and **Artificial Intelligence** are transforming risk management landscapes. Machine learning algorithms, such as **Random Forests** and **Support Vector Machines (SVMs)**, are adept at pattern recognition, enhancing risk assessment accuracy by incorporating large, multidimensional datasets often impervious to conventional methods. Neural networks facilitate dynamic modeling, revealing hidden structures in data and improving stress-testing procedures.

As quantitative finance evolves by integrating computational capacities, **quantum computing** holds the potential to revolutionize statistical risk modeling through unparalleled processing speeds and complex problem-solving capabilities, enabling the exploration of massive risk horizons with unprecedented precision.

Risk measurement, therefore, manifests as an intricate synergy between statistical paradigms and technological innovations. By leveraging an array of quantitative tools, financial professionals can architect strategies resilient to the multidimensional risks characterizing the financial realm. As models evolve and datasets expand, the art of risk measurement continues to assert itself as a cornerstone for strategic prowess, fiscal prudence, and sustainable advantage within global markets.

Chapter 5

Risk Management in Market Making

In this chapter, the focus is on identifying and managing the types of risks specific to market making, including liquidity, market, credit, and operational risks. Techniques for risk assessment such as Value at Risk (VaR) and stress testing are explored to quantify and control exposures. Capital allocation strategies and risk limits are discussed to ensure financial robustness and compliance. The chapter covers hedging strategies and portfolio diversification as key risk mitigation practices. Adaptive risk management approaches are highlighted to address the challenges of dynamic market environments, emphasizing the integration of real-time data and technology.

5.1   Identifying Risks in Market Making

Navigating the landscape of market making requires a thorough understanding of the diverse risks inherent to the process. Market makers, by their very function, are exposed to numerous types of risk, which, if not identified early and managed effectively, can lead to significant financial setbacks. This section aims to elucidate these risks in detail, providing both a foundational understanding and deeper insights suitable for readers at all levels of experience.

Market making involves facilitating liquidity in financial markets by being ready to buy and sell securities at publicly quoted prices. While this essential function helps ensure smoother and more efficient markets, it simultaneously exposes market makers to various risks, including liquidity risk, market risk, credit risk, and operational risk. Understanding these risks in their full breadth and depth is crucial for developing robust risk management strategies.

- **Liquidity risk** encompasses the challenge faced by market makers in transacting at or near current market prices during times of financial stress. This form of risk emerges when there are insufficient buy orders to meet sell orders or vice versa, potentially leading to price impacts or forced sales that erode profit margins. A vivid illustration of liquidity risk can be drawn from the global financial crisis of 2007-2008, where many market makers found themselves with illiquid positions that could be liquidated only at substantial losses. To mitigate liquidity risk, market makers often diversify their order flow sources and maintain relationships with a wide network of trading partners.

- **Market risk**, perhaps the most well-recognized form of financial risk, involves the possibility of losses due to adverse movements in market prices. For market makers, who are constantly buying and selling securities, this risk is ever-present. Market risk can be systemic, such as broad-based price declines across asset classes, or idiosyncratic, affecting only specific assets. For example, a sudden interest rate hike could sharply affect the equities, fixed income, and derivatives in which a market maker holds positions. Understanding the sensitivity of portfolios to different market variables, known as the Greek letters in options trading (Delta, Gamma, Vega, Theta, and Rho), helps market makers manage this risk.

- **Credit risk** in market making refers to the danger that a counterparty might default, failing to fulfill contractual obligations. This risk is particularly relevant when trading over-the-counter (OTC) derivatives or in less-regulated segments of the market. Examples include a scenario where a counterparty cannot deliver the securities as promised, or lacks the funds to complete a purchase. The collapse of Lehman Brothers illustrated the domino effect of credit risk, where other market participants were left with large exposures to a defaulted counterparty. To mitigate credit risk, market makers employ techniques such as collateral management, credit default swaps, and rigorous due diligence processes.

- **Operational risk** entails the potential for losses resulting from inadequate or failed internal processes, systems, human errors, or external events. Given the high-frequency nature of market making activities, even a brief systems outage or a trading error can lead to substantial financial consequences. For instance, in August 2012, a programming error by Knight Capital led to a $440 million loss within 30 minutes, highlighting the catastrophic impact of operational mishaps. Market makers often invest heavily in their technology infrastructure and training to minimize operational risks, with comprehensive backup systems and robust protocols in place to deal with potential disruptions.

While these four risks are the core challenges faced by market makers, it is important to recognize that these risks are often interconnected, potentially amplifying one another under certain conditions. For example, a liquidity crunch could elevate market risk if market makers are forced to trade at disadvantageous prices, while simultaneous operational failures could exacerbate the situation.

Moreover, regulatory and compliance risks also play a vital role in the risk landscape for market makers. With regulatory bodies continually evolving their standards and requirements, market makers must remain vigilant to ensure that their operations adhere to current laws, including the Dodd-Frank Act and the European Market Infrastructure Regulation (EMIR). Regulatory breaches can incur hefty fines and damage reputations, further emphasizing the importance of compliance in managing overall business risks.

The advent of digital platforms and automated trading has further nuanced the nature of risks in market making. Algorithmic trading, though enhancing speed and efficiency, introduces complexities such as algorithmic risk. This is the risk that trading algorithms may behave undesirably due to coding errors, unintended market impacts, or incorrect parameter settings. Hence, rigorous pre-deployment testing and continuous monitoring of algorithms are necessary to mitigate these risks.

Additionally, the increase in cyber threats poses an ever-evolving risk for market makers. Cybersecurity risks are omnipresent in the digital age, with data breaches having the potential to jeopardize client information, trading algorithms, and overall market stability. Implementing robust cybersecurity measures and ensuring vigilance at all organiza-

105

tional levels thus becomes indispensable components of effective risk management.

Understanding and identifying these risks mark the first step toward formulating effective management strategies. Market makers, therefore, stand at the forefront of financial stability within the markets, their ability to identify and mitigate risks directly correlating with the broader health of the financial ecosystem. By proactively addressing these risk factors, market makers not only protect their interests but also uphold the integrity of the markets they serve.

5.2   Risk Assessment and Measurement

Effective risk management in market making hinges on the thorough assessment and measurement of potential risks. This process is fundamental in not only identifying risks but also in quantifying their potential impact, thus enabling market makers to adopt appropriate strategies for mitigation. In this section, we delve deeply into the methodologies and tools that underpin risk assessment and measurement, providing expert insights that benefit both novice and seasoned professionals in the domain.

Risk assessment serves as the foundation of a risk management framework. It involves a systematic process of understanding and analyzing the characteristic risks relevant to market making, which include market risk, credit risk, liquidity risk, and operational risk. The primary goal of assessment is to provide a quantitative basis for decision-making by evaluating both the likelihood of risks occurring and their potential impact on the market maker's financial health.

One of the central tools for risk measurement is Value at Risk (VaR), a statistical technique used to estimate the potential loss a portfolio might face within a given time frame at a certain confidence level. VaR is a cornerstone in risk management, widely used due to its ability to condense diverse sources of risk into a single figure, thereby simplifying the complexity for ease of interpretation and communication. For instance, a daily VaR of $1 million at a 95% confidence level implies that there is only a 5% probability that losses will exceed $1 million on any given day.

The calculation of VaR can be approached through different methods: historical simulation, variance-covariance (also known as parametric VaR), and the Monte Carlo simulation. Historical simulation involves using historical data to model and simulate potential losses, relying on the assumption that past market behaviors, to a certain extent, predict future risks. The variance-covariance method, on the other hand, assumes that returns are normally distributed, which allows for a straightforward quantitative calculation using statistical parameters like mean and standard deviation. Monte Carlo simulation, a more complex and computational technique, involves generating a vast number of random price paths to model the potential outcomes for a portfolio under numerous hypothetical scenarios. Each approach has its strengths and weaknesses, and the choice often depends on the specific context and resources available to the market maker.

Beyond VaR, Conditional Value at Risk (CVaR), also known as Expected Shortfall, offers an extension by not only measuring the VaR threshold but also evaluating the average loss that occurs beyond this threshold. This makes CVaR particularly useful in capturing tail risk — extreme losses that may occur with low probability but have significant consequences. CVaR provides a more comprehensive picture of potential losses in volatile market conditions, offering insight that is particularly valuable during market crises.

Stress testing is another fundamental tool in the risk assessment and measurement arsenal. Unlike VaR and CVaR, stress testing does not rely on normal market conditions but rather evaluates a portfolio's resilience to extraordinary, though plausible, adverse events. This could include scenarios like a sudden economic crisis, major geopolitical event, or an unexpected surge in market volatility. Stress testing helps market makers ascertain how extreme shocks would affect their risk exposure, thus enabling them to bolster their defensive strategies against such disruptions.

To complement these quantitative metrics, scenario analysis is used to evaluate specific predetermined future events, such as interest rate changes or equity market shifts, and their possible impacts. Scenario analysis often supplements other measures by offering a more qualitative approach that takes into account market dynamics not reflected in historical data or statistical assumptions.

Additionally, liquidity risk assessment tools have become increasingly important. These tools assess the potential difficulties in closing large positions without impacting market prices significantly, especially during periods of financial turmoil. Utilizing liquidity-adjusted VaR (LVaR) allows market makers to incorporate both price risk and liquidity considerations into their risk management frameworks, providing a more holistic view of potential exposures during times of market stress.

Another critical aspect of comprehensive risk assessment is leveraging technology and data analytics. With the rise of big data, machine learning, and artificial intelligence, quantitative models have become more sophisticated, offering real-time risk assessments that are both dynamic and adaptive to changing market conditions. These technologies enable market makers to process vast amounts of data to identify patterns, correlations, and anomalies that could signal emerging risks, providing a proactive rather than reactive approach to risk management.

Effective risk measurement also relies heavily on robust internal controls and governance frameworks. Regular risk audits and the establishment of risk committees ensure that risk measurement processes remain aligned with industry standards and organizational objectives. Such practices drive consistency, transparency, and accountability in risk management activities, ultimately enhancing the market maker's capacity to anticipate and adapt to potential risks.

Lastly, it is important to highlight the emerging role of regulatory frameworks in shaping risk measurement practices. With increased regulatory scrutiny, market makers are required to not only measure risks accurately but also demonstrate that they can withstand specific stress scenarios through regulatory stress tests, such as those mandated by Basel III or the Comprehensive Capital Analysis and Review (CCAR) conducted by the Federal Reserve. Compliance with these regulations not only assists in maintaining financial stability but also endows market makers with credibility and resilience in the eyes of investors and regulators alike.

In sum, the assessment and measurement of risk represent essential components of effective risk management within market making operations. By utilizing a combination of quantitative tools, technological advancements, and rigorous governance frameworks, market makers can gain invaluable insights into their risk landscape, thus positioning themselves to navigate market uncertainties with an informed, decisive approach.

5.3   Capital Allocation and Risk Limits

In the intricate world of market making, the strategic allocation of capital plays a pivotal role in driving profitability while simultaneously managing risk. This section delves into the principles and practices of capital allocation and the establishment of risk limits, exploring how these elements form the backbone of a resilient financial strategy that safeguards against volatility and regulatory pressures.

Capital allocation refers to the process of distributing financial resources among various trading activities and risk elements in a way that maximizes return while adhering to acceptable risk levels. The primary aim of capital allocation for market makers is to optimize the use of capital to support liquidity provision, facilitate market stability, and achieve sustainable profitability. Effective capital allocation is intricately tied to the risk exposure that each trading activity represents, and this dynamic interplay necessitates a keen understanding of both the markets and regulatory expectations.

The allocation process begins with a comprehensive risk assessment that evaluates the risk-return profile of different asset classes, trading strategies, and market conditions. This assessment enables market makers to determine where and how to deploy financial resources most effectively. Risk-adjusted return measures such as the Sharpe Ratio, Treynor Ratio, and Sortino Ratio are often employed to gauge the expected returns relative to the assumed risks, providing insights that guide capital distribution decisions.

A key aspect of capital allocation involves setting aside sufficient capital buffers to absorb potential losses, particularly in turbulent markets. Regulatory standards, such as those outlined in the Basel III framework, prescribe minimum capital requirements that financial institutions must meet to mitigate systemic risk. These requirements ensure that market makers maintain enough capital to remain solvent even under adverse market conditions. For instance, the Basel III Accord mandates that banks hold a Tier 1 capital ratio of at least 6%, ensuring that core capital is available to cover losses without disrupting operations.

Strategic capital allocation also takes into account the concept of economic capital, which represents the amount of capital a firm needs to cover its risk profile as comfortably as possible. Unlike regulatory capital dictated by external requirements, economic capital is determined internally, reflecting the firm's unique risk appetite and business model. By aligning economic capital with the firm's strategic goals, market makers ensure that resources are utilized efficiently and in a manner that supports long-term growth and resilience.

In tandem with capital allocation, setting risk limits is a critical mechanism for managing exposure and preventing excessive risk-taking.

Risk limits are predefined thresholds that outline the maximum permissible level of risk for different activities, positions, or market scenarios. They act as guardrails, ensuring that the firm's risk exposure remains within acceptable bounds and that operations align with strategic objectives and regulatory standards.

Risk limits can be established at multiple levels within a market-making operation, including enterprise-wide, business unit, and individual trader levels. Enterprise-wide limits provide a macro-level view of total risk exposure, ensuring that cumulative risks do not exceed the firm's overall risk appetite. Business unit limits focus on the specific risks associated with individual trading desks or strategies, allowing for targeted risk management that reflects the unique characteristics and goals of each unit. At the individual level, trader-specific limits ensure that no single position or trade exceeds acceptable risk levels, thereby preventing outsized losses from impacting the broader operation.

The process of setting risk limits involves a combination of quantitative methods, expert judgment, and ongoing monitoring. Quantitative approaches leverage statistical models and historical data to estimate potential losses under various scenarios, while expert judgment incorporates qualitative insights to address factors that may not be fully captured by quantitative models. Continuous monitoring ensures that risk limits remain relevant in the face of changing market dynamics and evolving business strategies.

Dynamic risk limits allow market makers to adapt flexibly to shifts in market conditions, adjusting exposure levels as necessary to capitalize on opportunities or mitigate threats. For example, during periods of heightened volatility, a market maker may choose to tighten risk limits to protect the firm from unexpected market swings. Conversely, in more stable conditions, the firm might loosen these limits slightly to take advantage of potentially lucrative opportunities.

The integration of technological advancements, such as real-time data analytics and automated trading systems, has further enhanced the effectiveness of capital allocation and risk limits. These technologies provide market makers with unparalleled insights into market dynamics, enabling them to make informed decisions about capital deployment and risk management. Automated systems, in particular, facilitate the seamless execution of strategies that adhere to pre-set risk parameters, reducing the likelihood of human errors and enhancing operational efficiency.

In addition to internal strategies, adherence to external frameworks and guidelines is crucial for ensuring compliance with regulatory standards. Regulatory bodies such as the Securities and Exchange Commission (SEC) and the European Securities and Markets Authority (ESMA) provide guidance on the implementation of sound capital and risk management practices, emphasizing the need for transparency, accountability, and prudent risk-taking. By aligning with these guidelines, market makers not only fulfill their regulatory obligations but also enhance their reputation among investors and stakeholders.

The strategic allocation of capital and the establishment of robust risk limits are indispensable components of successful market-making operations. These practices enable firms to strike a delicate balance between pursuing profitable opportunities and maintaining financial stability, ultimately supporting resilient performance in a dynamic and often unpredictable market environment. By continuously refining capital allocation strategies and fine-tuning risk limits, market makers can confidently navigate the complexities of modern financial markets, delivering consistent value to both their clients and their organizations.

5.4   Hedging Strategies for Risk Mitigation

In the multifaceted world of market making, hedging stands out as a cornerstone strategy for managing and mitigating financial risk. As market makers constantly engage in buying and selling, they encounter an array of risks, including market fluctuations, currency variations, interest rate changes, and price movements. Hedging offers a systematic approach to buffering these exposures, thus enabling firms to safeguard against adverse market conditions while continuing to provide liquidity and stabilize markets.

Hedging, at its core, involves taking an offsetting position in a related security or financial instrument to mitigate potential losses from fluctuations in price or market movements. The idea is to create a financial result that offsets the losses in one area of the portfolio with gains in another. This section delves into various hedging strategies used by market makers, enriched with detailed explanations and examples to illustrate their practical applications and effectiveness.

One of the primary tools for hedging is the use of derivatives, financial instruments whose value is derived from the performance of an underlying asset. Derivatives such as options, futures, forwards, and swaps provide market makers with flexibility and precision in tailoring

111

their hedging strategies to specific risk profiles.

Options, for instance, give buyers the right, but not the obligation, to buy or sell an asset at a predetermined price before a specified expiration date. They can be used in multiple hedging strategies, such as protective puts, where a market maker holds a long position in a stock and buys a put option to protect against a drop in the stock's price. Conversely, a covered call strategy involves holding a long position in an asset while writing a call option on the same asset to generate additional income, thus hedging against minor price declines while leveraging additional earnings from the option premium.

Futures contracts, another form of derivative, obligate the buyer and seller to transact a set amount of an asset at a predetermined price on a future date. Market makers use futures to lock in prices and hedge against adverse price movements in underlying assets. Consider a scenario where a market maker expects the price of crude oil to rise. By purchasing futures contracts, the market maker can lock in today's price, thereby protecting against potential price increases that could erode profitability when fulfilling client demands for crude oil transactions in the future.

Swaps, which include various types such as interest rate swaps, currency swaps, and commodity swaps, allow for the exchange of cash flows or financial instruments based on different conditions or indices. An interest rate swap, for example, can convert a variable interest rate obligation into a fixed rate, thus hedging against the risk of interest rate increases. This is particularly valuable for market makers who may have received funding based on variable rates but prefer to manage a fixed cost structure to mitigate cash flow variability.

Beyond derivatives, market makers also employ natural hedges, a technique that involves structuring operations to naturally offset exposures without using financial instruments. For instance, a firm conducting transactions in multiple countries might match its cash outflow in one currency with inflows in the same currency from a different business line or geographic region, thereby reducing exposure to currency fluctuations.

The use of diversification as a hedging strategy cannot be overstated. By spreading investments across a wide array of asset classes, industries, or geographic areas, market makers can reduce unsystematic risk — risks associated with specific companies or industries. A diversified portfolio is less likely to be significantly affected by fluctuations in any one asset, hence providing a form of passive risk mitigation. For example, if a particular sector or region experiences disruption, diversified holdings in other more stable or booming sectors can cushion the blow.

Additionally, market makers often utilize beta hedging to manage exposure to broad market movements. By calculating the beta of a portfolio, which measures its sensitivity compared to the overall market, a hedging strategy can be implemented by taking offsetting positions in market indices or corresponding securities to neutralize the portfolio's market-related volatility.

The strategic utilization of stop-loss orders is another important hedging tool. A stop-loss order is an instruction to sell a security once it reaches a certain price level, limiting potential losses. This acts as an automated risk control mechanism, helping market makers minimize losses without constant manual intervention. For example, in high-frequency trading environments where rapid execution and protection against abrupt price movements are crucial, stop-loss orders become invaluable in executing a disciplined approach to risk management.

However, while hedging is effective, it is not without costs and limitations. Implementing hedges typically incurs transaction costs and may limit potential profits. By locking in prices or creating offsetting positions, market makers might also forgo potential gains that could have been achieved through unhedged positions. Therefore, it is crucial for market makers to conduct a thorough cost-benefit analysis to determine the viability of specific hedging strategies for their unique risk profiles and market conditions.

The effectiveness of hedging also depends on accurate risk assessment and timely execution. Market makers must identify and quantify their exposures precisely, leveraging sophisticated risk management systems and real-time market data to inform their hedging decisions. Additionally, maintaining flexibility to adjust hedging strategies in response to evolving market dynamics is key to sustaining effective risk management and ensuring alignment with the firm's overarching financial objectives.

Moreover, with the growing complexity of financial markets, technology has become a pivotal enabler in enhancing the precision and responsiveness of hedging strategies. Algorithmic trading platforms, empowered with machine learning capabilities, can execute hedging decisions rapidly and adaptively by analyzing vast datasets and identifying market trends and correlations that might elude traditional analytics.

Ultimately, effective hedging strategies offer market makers a powerful means to navigate the turbulent waters of financial markets, protecting against downside risks while capitalizing on opportunities. By judiciously balancing risk and reward through a repertoire of hedging instruments and techniques, market makers can continue to fulfill their critical economic function of providing liquidity and enabling price discovery, all while safeguarding their financial solidity and competitive edge.

5.5   Portfolio Diversification

Portfolio diversification stands as a fundamental principle of risk management within market making and trading, serving as a vital strategy to distribute risk exposure across various asset classes, sectors, or geographical regions. By spreading investments, market makers and investors alike aim to mitigate unsystematic risk—also known as specific risk—while potentially enhancing returns. This section delves into the intricacies of portfolio diversification, its theoretical underpinnings, practical applications, and its intricacies in a market-making context, enriched with illustrative examples and insightful analyses.

Diversification is rooted in the classic financial theory introduced by Harry Markowitz in the 1950s, known as Modern Portfolio Theory (MPT). The essence of MPT lies in optimizing the balance between risk and return through carefully curated portfolios. Markowitz's theory posits that holding a mixture of non-correlated or negatively correlated assets can lead to a portfolio with lower risk than the sum of the individual risks. This is because the performance volatility of various securities may offset each other, reducing overall portfolio variance and increasing the potential for more stable returns.

For market makers, who continually switch between buying and selling securities, diversification helps to shield against adverse price movements in specific securities or markets. It offers the robustness required to withstand market shocks by reducing the exposure to any single asset or event. Consider the scenario of a market maker involved in both equity and bond markets. If equities face a downturn due to an economic slump, a portfolio also holding government bonds—which often behave inversely to equities—can buffer against market losses, as bonds tend to perform better when interest rates are cut to stimulate the economy.

It's important to note, however, that diversification does not eliminate all risks. Systematic risk—also known as market risk—stems from broader economic, political, or social changes that affect all assets and cannot be mitigated through diversification alone. This distinction reaffirms the importance of strategic asset allocation and consistent portfolio reviews to ensure alignment with evolving market conditions.

In the context of geographical diversification, market makers can leverage the diversity of global markets to their advantage. By holding assets in different countries, they can mitigate the risk associated with local economic downturns or regulatory changes. For instance, if European markets are underperforming due to recessionary pressures, a globally diversified portfolio can still benefit from robust performance in emerging Asian markets or stable growth in North American economies. This approach also allows market makers to capitalize on time zone differences, trading across different markets as they open, thus optimizing capital use around the clock.

Sectoral diversification is another vital component, involving the distribution of investments across various industries or sectors such as technology, healthcare, consumer goods, and energy. This approach helps mitigate sector-specific risks—such as regulatory changes impacting pharmaceuticals or technological shifts affecting traditional manufacturing industries. By spanning multiple sectors, market makers can ensure that a downturn in one sector is potentially offset by stability or growth in another. For example, while the energy sector might suffer from fluctuating oil prices, technology stocks might thrive due to innovation drivers, thus balancing the portfolio's performance.

Moreover, diversification strategies can integrate different investment styles and vehicles. Market makers can include a mixture of value and growth stocks, large-cap and small-cap companies, or developed and emerging market equities in their portfolios. Each investment style or vehicle responds differently to market changes, providing an additional layer of risk management. Value stocks may offer stability in times of heightened volatility, whereas growth stocks might outperform during economic expansions.

Diversification can also be achieved through the inclusion of alternative investments in a portfolio. Investments such as real estate, commodities, and private equity often have low correlation with traditional asset classes, offering further risk reduction. For instance, investing in gold, which is often viewed as a safe haven during times of economic uncertainty, can hedge against inflationary pressures and currency fluctuations. Similarly, real estate investments provide protection against inflation while generating rental income and potential capital appreciation.

On the practical side, achieving optimal diversification requires careful consideration of transaction costs, liquidity, and the potential for over-diversification—a situation where excessive diversification leads to diminished returns without proportional risk reduction. The balance between diversification and concentration is crucial. While a well-diversified portfolio can provide stability, excessive diversification might lead to an average performance with limited upside potential, as notable gains from strong performers may be offset by weaker assets.

Moreover, in a market-making environment, the dynamic nature of markets necessitates ongoing portfolio rebalancing to maintain optimal diversification levels. As market conditions change, certain asset classes or sectors may become more favorable than others, prompting a review and adjustment of the portfolio's weightings. Market makers must thus constantly monitor the market environment and adjust their diversification strategies accordingly to capitalize on opportunities and manage risks effectively.

Technological advancements have further enhanced the ability of market makers to diversify their portfolios efficiently. Advanced analytics, algorithmic trading, and machine learning tools enable the analysis of vast datasets to identify diversification opportunities and correlations that may not be immediately obvious. These technologies facilitate quicker decision-making, allowing market makers to initiate or adjust diversification strategies with precision and speed in response to rapidly changing market conditions.

Furthermore, the rise of exchange-traded funds (ETFs) and mutual funds has made diversification more accessible, enabling market makers to achieve diversified exposure through a single investment vehicle. ETFs, for instance, offer broad exposure to specific indices, sectors, or asset classes, often with lower expense ratios and greater liquidity than individual securities. This ease of access and simplicity of execution make them an attractive option for market makers seeking diversified exposure while managing transaction costs.

Finally, in summary, postulating without repetition, while diversification is a powerful tool for managing risk, it is not a one-size-fits-all solution. The effectiveness of diversification hinges on a comprehensive understanding of the underlying assets and their interactions within a portfolio. By employing diversification thoughtfully and aligning it with broader strategic goals, market makers can enhance their operations' resilience, ensuring stability and success in the face of an ever-evolving market landscape.

5.6 Adaptive Risk Management Strategies

The fast-paced and ever-evolving nature of financial markets requires market makers to adopt adaptive risk management strategies to effectively navigate uncertainty and volatility. Unlike traditional approaches that may rely on static risk models, adaptive strategies leverage real-time data analysis, technological advancements, and flexibility to respond dynamically to changing market conditions. This section provides an in-depth exploration of adaptive risk management strategies, emphasizing the critical role they play in enhancing the resilience and competitiveness of market-making operations.

Adaptive risk management begins with the acknowledgment that markets are inherently dynamic, characterized by rapid shifts in sentiment, economic indicators, regulatory environments, and macroeconomic events. As a result, market makers must refine their risk management frameworks to incorporate adaptability as a core principle. Rather than applying a one-size-fits-all approach, adaptive strategies adjust risk exposure in response to market signals, enabling market makers to mitigate risks effectively while capitalizing on emerging opportunities.

At the heart of adaptive risk management lies the ability to harness real-time data. Advanced analytics and big data technologies provide market makers with access to vast, diverse datasets that offer insights into market trends, investor behavior, and economic indicators. By integrating these data streams into their risk management processes, market makers can identify potential risks and opportunities at their inception. For instance, analyzing social media sentiment, news feeds, and economic reports in real time helps market makers anticipate market movements, adjust positions, and protect portfolios from unforeseen developments.

Machine learning and artificial intelligence (AI) are pivotal in facilitating adaptive risk management. These technologies enable market makers to build predictive models that learn and evolve over time, recognizing patterns and anomalies that may act as precursors to market events. By doing so, AI-driven models enhance the accuracy and speed of risk assessments, empowering market makers to make informed decisions with greater confidence. For example, AI algorithms can detect subtle shifts in market volatility or liquidity, prompting timely adjustments to hedging strategies or capital allocation to mitigate potential losses.

Scenario analysis and stress testing equipped with adaptive capabilities further enhance risk management frameworks. Unlike conventional stress tests based on historical data, adaptive stress testing incorporates hypothetical scenarios that reflect potential future market conditions. By exploring a range of extreme but plausible scenarios, market makers can assess the resilience of their portfolios and strategies, identifying potential vulnerabilities and guiding proactive measures. Adaptive scenario analysis helps market makers prepare for a variety of contingencies, such as sudden geopolitical tensions, unexpected regulatory shifts, or drastic changes in consumer behavior.

Real-time monitoring systems play a vital role in adaptive risk management strategies. Implementing continuous surveillance mechanisms allows market makers to track risk metrics, key performance indicators (KPIs), and market developments as they unfold. These systems facilitate the quick identification of deviations from established risk thresholds, enabling prompt corrective actions to maintain risk exposure within acceptable limits. For instance, if a sudden spike in counterparty credit risk is detected, market makers can swiftly reduce exposure or seek alternative trading partners to safeguard their positions.

In addition to leveraging technology, adaptive risk management requires a cultural shift within market-making organizations. Building a culture of adaptability involves fostering collaboration across departments, encouraging innovation, and promoting continuous learning. Risk management teams must work closely with trading desks, technology experts, and data analysts to develop integrated strategies that align with the firm's objectives. Regular risk management reviews and cross-functional communication ensure that adaptive strategies remain agile and effective, even in the face of evolving market landscapes.

Flexibility in decision-making also characterizes adaptive risk management. By recognizing that market conditions can change rapidly, market makers must be prepared to modify their strategies and approaches as needed. This might involve adjusting risk limits, reallocating capital, or revising trading strategies in response to unexpected market developments. For example, during periods of heightened global uncertainty, a market maker may opt to increase diversification across asset classes or regions, reduce leverage, or enhance liquidity buffers to withstand potential shocks.

Furthermore, adaptive strategies encourage market makers to explore alternative risk mitigation techniques. This might include employing contingent strategies, such as dynamic hedging, wherein market makers adjust hedging positions as market conditions evolve, rather than relying on static hedges. Seizing opportunities to employ options, futures, or other derivative contracts in a flexible manner enables market makers to mitigate downside risks while capturing potential upside gains.

Regulatory compliance is another crucial facet of adaptive risk management. As regulatory frameworks evolve, market makers must ensure that their risk management processes remain aligned with applicable laws and guidelines. This requires staying informed about regulatory changes, conducting regular compliance audits, and integrating adaptive mechanisms to accommodate evolving rules. Adopting adaptive compliance strategies not only prevents legal and reputational risks but also enhances the firm's credibility and trustworthiness within the industry.

Technology modernization, including cloud computing and infrastructure upgrades, supports adaptive risk management efforts by enabling seamless access to data and computing power. The cloud provides market makers with flexible, scalable solutions for processing large volumes of data and executing complex simulations, reducing reliance on legacy systems and enhancing operational agility. By investing in technology capabilities, market makers can facilitate real-time analysis, model updates, and scenario testing, thereby staying ahead in rapidly changing markets.

Lastly, adaptive risk management involves evaluating and improving risk models continuously. Regular model validation ensures that predictive models remain accurate, relevant, and aligned with current market dynamics. This includes scrutinizing model assumptions, recalibrating parameters, and incorporating emerging data sources to enhance forecast precision. By continuously refining risk models, market makers can maintain a competitive edge and execute strategies effectively in a dynamic trading environment.

Adaptive risk management strategies are indispensable for market makers seeking to thrive in today's fast-paced and unpredictable markets. By embracing technology, fostering agility, and integrating real-time insights into decision-making, market makers can navigate risks prudently while seizing opportunities for growth. Through ongoing adaptability and innovation, they can maintain their pivotal role in providing liquidity and stability to financial markets, ensuring long-term success and resiliency in the face of uncertainty.

5.7   Regulatory Compliance and Reporting

In market making, regulatory compliance and reporting form critical components of operational integrity and credibility. Financial markets are subject to comprehensive regulations that aim to maintain market stability, protect investors, and promote transparency. For market makers, adhering to these regulations is not only a legal obligation but also a strategic imperative that enhances trust and mitigates legal and reputational risks. This section provides an exhaustive exploration of regulatory compliance and reporting requirements for market makers, enriched with detailed insights into key regulatory frameworks and best practices for implementation.

Regulatory compliance encompasses a wide array of rules and standards set forth by regulatory bodies at both national and international levels. These regulations are designed to manage systemic risk, enhance market transparency, and protect participants from market abuse. For market makers, who are crucial intermediaries providing liquidity and facilitating price discovery, compliance with these regulations ensures that their operations align with broader market objectives and contribute positively to the financial ecosystem.

One of the fundamental tenets of regulatory compliance is ensuring the integrity and fairness of trading practices. Market makers must adhere to stringent conduct rules to prevent manipulative practices such as front-running, insider trading, or market manipulation. To maintain compliance, market makers establish robust internal controls and compliance programs that monitor trading activities, enforce conduct standards, and ensure alignment with regulatory requirements. These programs often include surveillance systems that detect unusual or suspicious trading patterns, reinforcing adherence to ethical standards.

Regulatory frameworks such as the Markets in Financial Instruments Directive II (MiFID II) in Europe and the U.S. Securities and Exchange Commission (SEC) guidelines lay out comprehensive requirements for market transparency, trade reporting, and investor protection. For example, MiFID II mandates pre-trade and post-trade transparency for equity and non-equity markets, requiring market makers to disclose key information such as order book depth, transaction execution times, and trade prices. This transparency enhances market efficiency and allows investors to make informed decisions.

In conjunction with these frameworks, the European Market Infrastructure Regulation (EMIR) and the Dodd-Frank Act in the U.S. impose stringent reporting obligations on derivatives trading and over-the-counter (OTC) markets to mitigate counterparty risk. Market makers involved in derivatives transactions must report trade details to trade repositories, ensuring that regulators have comprehensive oversight of market activities. This helps manage systemic risk by providing regulators with data needed to assess market exposure and identify potential threats to financial stability.

Compliance with anti-money laundering (AML) and "know your customer" (KYC) regulations is paramount for market makers to prevent financial crime and ensure the integrity of financial markets. AML and KYC procedures involve verifying client identities, monitoring transactions for suspicious activities, and performing ongoing due diligence to detect potential money laundering or terrorist financing. Effective compliance programs often leverage technology solutions such as automated identity verification and real-time transaction monitoring to enhance the efficiency and accuracy of these processes.

Regulatory compliance further necessitates strict adherence to capital adequacy requirements, which are designed to ensure that market makers maintain sufficient financial resources to withstand market volatility. Frameworks such as Basel III enforce guidelines on capital reserves, leverage ratios, and liquidity coverage ratios. By holding adequate capital buffers, market makers can sustain operations during adverse conditions, thus safeguarding their solvency and protecting the wider financial system against systemic shocks.

Data protection and cybersecurity regulations, such as the EU's General Data Protection Regulation (GDPR) and the California Consumer Privacy Act (CCPA), impose obligations on market makers to protect client data and maintain robust cybersecurity defenses. Compliance with these regulations involves implementing data encryption, access controls, and incident response plans to protect sensitive information from unauthorized access and cyber threats. Market makers must also ensure that data collection, processing, and retention practices align with legal requirements, enhancing client trust and reducing the risk of penalties.

Reporting requirements are integral to regulatory compliance, demanding accuracy, timeliness, and transparency in documenting market ac-

121

tivities. Market makers must submit regular reports to regulatory authorities detailing transaction data, risk exposures, financial statements, and compliance activities. These reports provide regulators with insights into market trends, risks, and the overall health of the financial ecosystem. Automated reporting systems aid market makers in meeting these obligations by streamlining data collection, validation, and submission processes.

Effective compliance and reporting frameworks require a strategic approach that combines technological solutions with a strong compliance culture. Market makers invest in advanced compliance technologies, such as real-time monitoring systems, data analytics platforms, and machine learning algorithms, to enhance their ability to detect, prevent, and respond to compliance breaches. These technologies enable the proactive identification of potential risks, facilitate swift remediation measures, and ensure that compliance programs remain agile and responsive to evolving regulatory landscapes.

Building a culture of compliance involves fostering ethical behavior, continuous education, and accountability across the organization. Market makers emphasize the importance of regulatory compliance through regular training programs, workshops, and communication channels that reinforce compliance objectives and raise awareness of emerging regulatory changes.   Compliance personnel play a critical role in guiding the organization through complex regulatory requirements, acting as advisors and enforcers to ensure that compliance remains a top priority.

Furthermore, maintaining open and transparent communication with regulatory authorities is essential for successful compliance. Engaging in constructive dialogue with regulators enables market makers to gain clarity on regulatory expectations, seek guidance on ambiguous requirements, and provide feedback on industry challenges. Collaborative interactions contribute to a more cooperative regulatory environment and facilitate the development of tailored compliance strategies that align with both regulatory and operational objectives.

Adapting to regulatory changes requires vigilance and agility. Regulators continually update frameworks to address new market developments, technological advancements, and emerging risks. Market makers must stay informed about regulatory changes through industry associations, legal advisories, and compliance networks. Proactive adaptation to regulatory shifts involves revising policies, updating procedures, and reallocating resources to ensure ongoing compliance and operational efficiency.

Regulatory compliance and reporting are cornerstones of responsible market-making operations, encompassing a wide spectrum of obligations that ensure market integrity, protect investors, and promote stability. By integrating robust compliance programs, leveraging advanced technologies, and fostering a culture of ethical behavior, market makers can navigate the complex regulatory landscape with confidence, contributing to the long-term resilience and sustainability of financial markets. Through continuous adherence to regulatory requirements and proactive engagement with regulators, market makers uphold their commitment to transparent and fair markets, safeguarding the interests of all stakeholders involved.

Chapter 6

Statistical Arbitrage and Mean Reversion

This chapter examines statistical arbitrage based on exploiting market inefficiencies and anomalies using quantitative techniques. Mean reversion is explored as a pivotal concept guiding many arbitrage strategies, with a focus on pairs trading and the selection of correlated assets. Various quantitative models are analyzed to identify arbitrage opportunities, complemented by discussions on the risk-reward dynamics and challenges faced during implementation. The chapter concludes with methods for evaluating and optimizing the performance of statistical arbitrage strategies, aiming for enhanced profitability while mitigating risks.

6.1   Concept of Statistical Arbitrage

In the intricate landscape of financial markets, the concept of statistical arbitrage stands as a beacon for those seeking to exploit inefficiencies through data-driven strategies. At its core, statistical arbitrage hinges on the recognition of market anomalies and the subsequent application of quantitative models to capitalize on these discrepancies. The foundational ideas of statistical arbitrage can be traced back to the notion of efficient markets, which posits that asset prices fully reflect all available information. However, empirical evidence has illustrated that markets are not always efficient, presenting traders and investors with potential opportunities for profit.

The essence of statistical arbitrage lies in identifying and exploiting temporary mispricings in securities by leveraging mathematical models. These opportunities typically manifest in the form of price deviations from an expected equilibrium level, often reverting to the mean over time. This reversion provides a compelling rationale for employing statistical indicators to predict future price movements. Unlike traditional arbitrage, which seeks riskless profit through price differences across markets or instruments, statistical arbitrage accepts that these anomalies might not resolve immediately or guaranteedly, hence carrying inherent risk.

One of the key aspects of statistical arbitrage is the use of high-frequency trading (HFT). With the advent of advanced computing technology and sophisticated algorithms, traders can efficiently analyze vast datasets at unprecedented speeds. This allows them to detect patterns and price actions that human traders would likely overlook. The algorithmic execution of trades ensures that positions are opened and closed at optimal times, maximizing the probability of a successful outcome. Despite its potential, incorporating HFT into a statistical arbitrage framework requires rigorous testing and calibration to mitigate the risks associated with market volatility and liquidity shortages.

The mathematical underpinning of statistical arbitrage is grounded in statistical concepts such as mean reversion, co-integration, and principal component analysis. Mean reversion is based on the assumption that prices will revert to a historical average over time, allowing traders to identify overbought or oversold conditions. Co-integration examines the long-term equilibrium relationship between asset prices, suggesting that while prices may diverge in the short term, they will converge over a more extended period. Principal component analysis, on the other hand, helps in understanding the underlying factors driving price movements, enabling traders to isolate specific elements that may contribute to mispricing.

A practical example of statistical arbitrage can be seen in the context of a pairs trading strategy. In pairs trading, a trader identifies two assets with historically correlated price movements. Suppose an unusual divergence occurs between these assets. In that case, the statistical arbitrageur anticipates a convergence back to the mean and consequently takes long and short positions in the respective assets, aiming to benefit from this reversion. The success of such a strategy depends on careful pair selection, precise timing, and effective risk management to account for model uncertainty and the potential continuation of divergence.

The pursuit of statistical arbitrage requires not only quantitative acumen but also a profound understanding of market behavior and economic fundamentals. Profitable opportunities often elude those who overlook broader economic indicators, geopolitical events, or sector-specific developments. Hence, integrating macroeconomic analysis with quantitative models enriches the robustness of statistical arbitrage strategies, lending them resilience in the face of fluctuating market conditions.

Furthermore, in constructing a successful statistical arbitrage strategy, data quality and selection play a pivotal role. Inaccurate or outdated data can skew modeling results, leading to erroneous trading signals and unintended financial consequences. Thus, a comprehensive data sourcing and cleansing process is indispensable to ensure that modeling inputs accurately reflect current market realities. Furthermore, incorporating real-time data feeds enhances decision-making agility, providing a competitive edge in rapidly evolving markets.

Open-source data analytics platforms like Python's Pandas, SciKit-Learn, and MATLAB have democratized access to powerful analytical tools, leveling the playing field for independent traders and small firms. The use of machine learning algorithms further augments statistical arbitrage by enabling the discovery of hidden patterns and predictive features within complex datasets. These technologies facilitate the continual refinement of models based on real-time feedback and performance metrics, allowing traders to adapt dynamically to market shifts.

The risk management aspect of statistical arbitrage cannot be understated. Given the reliance on quantitative models, traders must be vigilant about model risk and parameter instability. Periodic backtesting, stress testing, and scenario analysis become indispensable to evaluate a strategy's robustness across different market conditions. Moreover, diversification across different trading horizons, asset classes, and geographies can help mitigate systemic risks, offering a buffer against adverse market movements.

In financial ecosystems marked by growing complexities and interdependencies, regulatory considerations also play a crucial part in strategy implementation. Compliance with market regulations, including trading limits, reporting standards, and anti-manipulation laws, is essential. Adhering to these frameworks ensures not only operational legality but also preserves the ethical integrity of trading practices, enhancing institutional reputation.

Statistical arbitrage, while replete with lucrative opportunities, is not devoid of challenges. The fierce competition among market participants often results in a rapid erosion of arbitrage opportunities, necessitating continuous innovation in strategy design. The cyclical nature of financial markets also dictates that the performance of statistical arbitrage may ebb and flow, influencing returns unpredictably. As such, astute arbitrageurs maintain the flexibility to pivot strategies and methodologies in response to evolving market paradigms.

The ongoing digital transformation within the financial sector promises to redefine the scope of statistical arbitrage further. Emerging trends in financial technology, such as blockchain, decentralized finance, and artificial intelligence, are poised to introduce new dimensions of data sources, analytical methodologies, and execution channels. Embracing these advancements is integral for traders looking to remain at the vanguard of statistical arbitrage, ensuring sustainability and long-term success.

Ultimately, the concept of statistical arbitrage epitomizes the synthesis of mathematical ingenuity, technological prowess, and market acuity. It challenges market participants to transcend traditional boundaries of trading, advocating for a holistic appreciation of quantitative insights and strategic foresight. As the quest for alpha continues, statistical arbitrage remains an enduring testament to the evolving art and science of trading.

6.2   Mean Reversion Theory

Mean reversion theory is a cornerstone of financial economics, asserting that asset prices and returns tend to move towards their historical mean over time. This idea contrasts with the concept of an efficient market hypothesis, which assumes that prices follow a random walk and incorporate all available information instantly. The tenet of mean reversion holds particular significance in the realm of trading and investing, offering a foundation for numerous strategies aimed at capturing returns from fluctuations around an intrinsic value.

At the heart of mean reversion is the statistical property that data points cluster around the mean in a time series, which can be applied to stock prices, interest rates, and even macroeconomic indicators. When an asset's price deviates substantially from its historical mean, mean reversion theory suggests that there is a high probability for a correction or reversal back toward the average. Traders leveraging this insight often rely on historical data analysis to identify reversion patterns, deploying strategies that anticipate and exploit these predicted moves.

To formalize the concept, consider the mathematical expression of mean reversion in a stochastic process. A common model used is the Ornstein-Uhlenbeck process, defined by the equation:

$$dX_t = \theta(\mu - X_t)dt + \sigma dW_t$$

Here, X_t represents the price at time t, μ is the long-term mean level, θ is the speed of reversion to the mean, σ is the volatility, and dW_t is a Wiener process. This formula encapsulates how the expected change in price is proportional to the deviation from the mean, with added volatility dynamics. The quantification of such parameters is critical in constructing trading signals and managing risk in a mean-reverting strategy.

The practical application of mean reversion is evident across different financial contexts. Consider statistical arbitrage strategies like pairs trading, where traders seek out two historically correlated securities. If these securities diverge beyond a statistically defined threshold, traders might short the overvalued security while simultaneously going long on the undervalued counterpart, anticipating a reversion to their established mean correlation.

Another compelling example of mean reversion is found in the behavior of interest rates. Over decades, interest rates exhibit mean-reverting characteristics, returning to a normal range despite short-term fluctuations driven by economic cycles and central bank policies. Fixed income traders and economists often model this tendency when devising investment strategies or forecasting economic conditions, utilizing the evidence of reversion to gauge future pricing of bonds or interest rate swaps.

In equities, mean reversion can be particularly powerful in identifying overextended movements in stock prices. Consider the investment strategy of value investing, popularized by gurus like Benjamin Graham and Warren Buffett. Although not overtly framed as a mean-reversion strategy, the underlying principle is similar: identifying stocks trading significantly below their intrinsic value suggests a likely reversion to mean historical valuations over time, thus providing an appealing investment opportunity.

Technical analysis also furnishes tools built upon the concept of mean reversion.   Moving averages, Bollinger Bands, and the Relative Strength Index (RSI) are quintessential instruments that capture mean-reverting signals.   For instance, when using moving averages, traders compare the short-term moving average with a long-term average to detect potential buy or sell signals based on deviations. Bollinger Bands expand this notion by adjusting the bands to encapsulate price volatility, encouraging trades when prices hit extreme highs or lows relative to these bands, suggesting overbought or oversold conditions.

In practice, implementing a mean reversion strategy requires careful consideration of several factors.   First is the selection of assets with demonstrated mean-reverting properties, often through backtesting historical price data.   Second is the determination of appropriate time-frames for analysis.   Short-term traders might benefit from observing minute-by-minute or hourly data, while long-term investors may rely on daily, weekly, or even monthly trends.

Understanding and managing risk is paramount to successful mean-reversion strategies. Volatility can obscure mean-reverting behaviors, leading to prolonged deviations from the mean and potential losses. Incorporating stop-loss mechanisms or hedging techniques, and adjusting portfolio allocations dynamically, can mitigate some of these risks. Furthermore, systematic risk factors, driven by broader economic changes or geopolitical events, may alter an asset's perceived long-term mean, necessitating a flexible approach.

The appeal of mean reversion theory also extends into behavioral finance, where it attempts to rationalize why trading opportunities persist. Behavioral finance suggests that mean reversion may arise due to investors' cognitive biases, such as overreaction to news events or herd behavior, leading to initial overshooting of prices beyond fundamental values. As market participants adjust their positions, prices revert, thereby creating profit opportunities for those astutely anticipating these corrections.

Despite its strengths, mean reversion theory is not without limitations. It presupposes a consistent historical mean, which might be disrupted by structural market changes or regime shifts. These shifts could result from technological innovations, regulatory changes, or global events that fundamentally alter market dynamics, such as the COVID-19 pandemic. Practitioners must remain vigilant to these evolving conditions, continuously adapting their strategies to align with real-world developments.

In an era characterized by incessant data generation and analysis, mean reversion finds new relevance through machine learning and artificial intelligence. Advanced algorithms can identify mean-reverting signals in large, multidimensional datasets, offering insights that are often inaccessible through traditional methods. As technology continues to evolve, so too will the models and strategies underpinning mean reversion, enriching its applicability in increasingly complex market environments.

In summary, mean reversion theory serves as a vital principle in understanding and navigating financial markets. Its application across diverse assets and strategies underscores the multifaceted nature of trading and investing. By discerning temporal mispricings and remaining attuned to market conditions, practitioners can harness mean reversion to generate returns, manage risk, and achieve their financial objectives.

6.3 Pairs Trading Strategies

Pairs trading is a market-neutral strategy that plays a vital role in the repertoire of statistical arbitrageurs, exploiting temporary price divergences between two correlated instruments. This strategy's central premise rests on constructing a pair of securities with a historical correlation, taking advantage of its deviation and convergence dynamics. By trading one asset long while simultaneously shorting the other, traders hedge market risk—particularly systemic risk—while capitalizing on relative value discrepancies.

The inception of pairs trading can be attributed to quantitative research desks in major financial institutions, particularly during the onset of algorithmic trading in the 1980s. As computational finance blossomed, so did the systematic approaches that allowed pairs trading to thrive. The allure lies in its apparent simplicity and its robustness against market-wide fluctuations, appealing to both institutional traders and individual investors eager for a market-neutral stance.

To construct a pairs trading strategy, a thorough understanding of correlation and co-integration is imperative. Correlation measures how two asset prices move in relation to one another but does not imply a stable, long-term equilibrium relationship. Co-integration, however, extends this notion by asserting that while individual asset prices may wander over time, their linear combination remains stationary, enhancing predictive reliability in pairs trading.

The selection of asset pairs is a meticulous process, often performed through rigorous statistical testing. Potential pairs might include equities within the same industry, ADRs paired with their domestic counterparts, or even derivatives like options or futures based on a singular underlying asset. The historical relationship is typically scrutinized using statistical measures such as the Pearson correlation coefficient and the Engle-Granger co-integration test.

Once a pair is selected, the next phase in executing a pairs trading strategy involves establishing trading signals based on deviations from the mean of the price spread between the two assets. This spread, defined as the price difference or ratio between the two instruments, oscillates around a statistical mean. When the spread widens significantly from this mean, rendering it statistically unlikely (usually beyond a predefined threshold of standard deviations), the strategy dictates entry into a long position on the undervalued asset and a short position on the overvalued one.

Monitoring the spread is crucial, and traders often employ tools such as moving averages and z-scores to gauge entry and exit points. The z-score quantifies the spread's distance from the mean in terms of standard deviation units, offering a normalized measure to compare across different pairs. If $S(t)$ denotes the spread at time t, μ_S the mean of the spread, and σ_S its standard deviation, the z-score is defined as:

$$Z(t) = \frac{S(t) - \mu_S}{\sigma_S}$$

A z-score exceeding a positive threshold would signal overextension, prompting a convergence trade. Similarly, a z-score below a negative threshold indicates the reverse.

Undoubtedly, pairs trading is not without its challenges. Parameter estimation, dynamic model tuning, and timely execution can significantly impact the trade's profitability. The assumption of mean reversion may fail during turbulent economic environments or structural breaks, where historical relationships are rendered obsolete. This risk illustrates the necessity for continuous strategy evaluation and risk management practices.

The effectiveness of pairs trading is largely contingent on transaction costs, especially in high-frequency trading environments. Employing high-frequency data and automated order execution systems enhances precision, but it requires careful calibration to ensure costs do not erode potential returns. Thus, pairs trading is often coupled with robust back-testing frameworks, enabling the fine-tuning of parameters such as thresholds, holding periods, and stop-loss levels.

Beyond traditional equities, pairs trading finds applicability across various asset classes. In commodities, spreads between different grades or delivery months of the same product offer fertile ground for pairs logic. Foreign exchange markets also present intriguing pairs trading opportunities, with traders examining interest rate differentials, geopolitical stability, and economic indicators to predict relative movements.

Consider a pairs trading example involving two major tech giants with historically stable correlations: Company A and Company B. Assume that through co-integration tests, a trader discerns that their stock prices co-move closely. If macroeconomic news disproportionately impacts Company A, causing its price to surge, the trader might evaluate whether this divergence is justified. Assuming it is not, they would short Company A and go long Company B, betting that the prices will eventually converge as earlier patterns suggest.

The psychological disciplines underpinning pairs trading cannot be overlooked in a behavioral finance context. Market participants frequently exhibit cognitive biases, such as overreaction or anchoring, which contribute to temporary inefficiencies. Understanding these behaviors enriches the pairs trading strategy, providing empirical context to the reversion phenomenon.

Moreover, machine learning is increasingly integrated with pairs trading strategies, elevating their adaptability and performance. Advanced techniques like support vector machines and neural networks learn from non-linear historical data patterns to enhance predictive accuracy. These technologies facilitate quicker adaptation to market changes while also exploring deeper options such as dynamic hedging ratios and non-linear pricing surfaces.

In summary, pairs trading strategy marries quantitative rigor with intuitive market insights, enabling traders to pursue profits through relative value plays without succumbing to overall market trends. While its implementation demands careful statistical analysis and prompt execution, the rewards align well with the risks when handled strategically. Pairs trading remains a testament to the nuanced interplay of market forces and statistical acumen, continually evolving as technology and global markets advance.

6.4 Quantitative Models for Arbitrage

Quantitative models for arbitrage represent the fusion of mathematical rigor with financial insight, forming the backbone of contemporary statistical arbitrage strategies. These models are meticulously designed to identify and exploit price discrepancies across financial markets with precision and speed. In an era characterized by exponential data growth and computational advances, quantitative models have evolved into complex frameworks deploying sophisticated algorithms, enriched by the advent of machine learning and artificial intelligence.

The foundation of quantitative arbitrage models resides in statistical theories and econometric techniques, harnessed to unearth actionable trading signals. Among the diverse array of quantitative models, factor models, time series analysis, and machine learning stand out as pivotal methodologies employed to discern and capitalize on market inefficiencies.

Factor models represent a class of financial models that use various economic indicators or factors to explain asset returns. The most compelling aspect of factor models in arbitrage is their ability to decompose returns into systematic risk factors and idiosyncratic components. The Capital Asset Pricing Model (CAPM) is a quintessential example, postulating that expected returns on a security are proportional to its exposure to systematic risk, encapsulated by beta:

$$E(R_i) = R_f + \beta_i(E(R_m) - R_f) \tag{6.1}$$

where $E(R_i)$ is the expected return of the investment, R_f is the risk-free rate, β_i is the beta of the investment, and $E(R_m)$ is the expected return of the market. More advanced multifactor models, such as the Fama-French Three-Factor Model, introduce size and value factors alongside market risk to better explain variations in asset returns. Exploiting these factors, arbitrageurs can construct market-neutral portfolios that hedge against systematic risk, isolating alpha derived from perceived mispricings.

Time series analysis adds another dimension, with autoregressive integrated moving average (ARIMA) models and GARCH models among popular tools for forecasting financial time series. These models are adept at capturing temporal dependencies and volatility clustering characteristic of asset prices. For instance, an ARIMA model captures both autoregressive and moving average components, facilitating the prediction of future price movements based on past values:

$$Y_t = c + \phi_1 Y_{t-1} + \cdots + \phi_p Y_{t-p} + \theta_1 \varepsilon_{t-1} + \cdots + \theta_q \varepsilon_{t-q} + \varepsilon_t \quad (6.2)$$

Trading strategies built on time series forecasts focus on mean-reverting behavior or momentum-based patterns, introducing signals for buying undervalued securities and selling overvalued ones.

Machine learning techniques have redefined the landscape of quantitative models. Algorithms ranging from supervised learning techniques like regression trees and ensemble methods to unsupervised learning like clustering and deep learning models such as neural networks, facilitate data-driven decision-making in arbitrage. With the capacity to detect non-linear relationships and complex patterns in vast datasets, machine learning empowers traders to adapt dynamically to market conditions, enhancing predictive accuracy and trade execution. Techniques such as random forests and gradient boosting excel in providing robust predictions through ensemble methods that combine multiple weak predictors to improve prediction stability and accuracy.

In practical applications, quantitative models encompass a broad spectrum of strategies tailored to diverse financial instruments. Consider merger arbitrage—a strategy hinging on the outcome of pending mergers or acquisitions. Quantitative models in this domain evaluate probability distributions of deal closure, market sentiment, and regulatory impact, subsequently generating positions that hedge against deal failure while profiting from successful closures.

Convertible arbitrage provides another domain enriched by quantitative modeling, leveraging convertible bonds' mixed equity-debt characteristics. It applies pricing models like Black-Scholes to gauge options embedded within convertibles, orchestrating positions that exploit pricing errors in the bond's conversion terms relative to the underlying equities.

Quantitative models thrive on data, and the explosion of financial data sources has both broadened opportunities and heightened the challenge of integrating diverse datasets. High-quality, real-time data feeds are indispensable, ensuring models operate on updated information reflective of current market conditions. Data cleaning and preprocessing are crucial in eradicating outliers and correcting errors that could distort model output.

Backtesting remains a cornerstone of model validation, allowing traders to simulate strategy performance under historical market conditions. It serves to identify strengths, highlight vulnerabilities, and refine parameters before deployment in live trading environments. Collaboration with high-performance computing platforms augments backtesting capabilities, facilitating rapid iteration and optimization of complex quantitative models.

Risk management, intertwined with model deployment, is vital. Quantitative models must be equipped with mechanisms to evaluate exposure to market volatility, liquidity constraints, and operational risks. Scenario analysis and stress testing provide insights into a model's resilience amid adverse conditions, fostering robust tail-risk management.

The successful implementation of quantitative arbitrage models also necessitates compliance with prevailing regulatory frameworks. Navigating complex legislation governing data usage, market transactions, and financial reporting demands vigilance, ensuring adherence to ethical and legal standards. Compliance is not merely an operational requirement but reinforces market integrity and fosters investor confidence.

Emerging trends in financial technology promise to further enhance quantitative modeling capabilities. Blockchain initiatives, alternative data sources such as satellite imagery or social media sentiment, and real-time analytics platforms offer new frontiers for model exploration. Innovations in quantum computing may redefine computational constraints, facilitating unprecedented model complexity and precision.

In summary, quantitative models for arbitrage encapsulate the essence of modern trading—a synthesis of statistical theory, computational sophistication, and strategic foresight. As financial markets continue to evolve, these models embody the cutting-edge tools required to thrive amid competition, anticipating opportunities while meticulously managing risk. The continuous evolution of methodologies and technologies will likely usher in new paradigms of arbitrage, driven by a relentless pursuit of market efficiencies.

6.5   Risk and Reward in Statistical Arbitrage

The intricate balance between risk and reward is a fundamental aspect of statistical arbitrage, shaping the decision-making processes of traders and investors. Within this domain, practitioners meticulously analyze potential returns against inherent risks, seeking strategies that maximize profitability while minimizing exposure to adverse market conditions. Statistical arbitrage, unlike traditional arbitrage, inherently involves a degree of uncertainty, due to its reliance on statistical assumptions, model accuracy, and market dynamics.

At the core of statistical arbitrage is the hypothesis that market prices will eventually revert to a statistical mean, allowing discrepancies to be exploited. However, price movements driven by a confluence of microeconomic, macroeconomic, and psychological factors present risks that can obfuscate mean-reverting patterns. Consequently, understanding the risk and reward matrix in statistical arbitrage necessitates a multi-dimensional approach that accounts for model risk, market risk, and operational risk.

Model risk is paramount in statistical arbitrage and arises from the potential inaccuracies of the quantitative models employed. These models, whether based on machine learning algorithms, time series analyses, or factor models, are only as effective as their underlying assumptions and data inputs. Inaccurate assumptions about mean reversion dynamics or co-integration can lead to erroneous trading signals. To mitigate model risk, traders engage in rigorous backtesting, employing out-of-sample testing and cross-validation to ensure robustness across various market scenarios.

Market risk is another critical element, encompassing the potential for losses due to changes in market prices, volatility, or liquidity. Statistical arbitrage often involves trading in highly liquid markets to facilitate rapid entry and exit from positions, yet liquidity can evaporate unexpectedly, leading to slippage or unexecuted orders. Moreover, abrupt changes in market volatility, driven by economic releases, geopolitical events, or sudden investor sentiment shifts, can amplify risk. Traders employ volatility-adjusted position sizing, stop-loss orders, and diversification across asset classes to manage and spread market risk effectively.

An intriguing facet of statistical arbitrage is the so-called "convergence risk." This risk materializes when asset prices, expected to converge based on historical correlations or spreads, continue to diverge due to structural changes or prolonged market shocks. The 2007-2008 global financial crisis vividly illustrated convergence risk, where correlations between ostensibly related securities broke down, leading to unexpected losses for statistical arbitrageurs.

In the face of these risks, capturing potential rewards in statistical arbitrage relies on the execution of well-calculated trades rooted in quantitative research and timely market insights. One of the appealing aspects is the ability to achieve consistent returns with reduced exposure to broader market swings. By maintaining a market-neutral stance—

balancing long and short positions—practitioners isolate systematic risks and focus on relative performance. The reward structure in statistical arbitrage aligns closely with the alpha it seeks to generate, with efforts concentrated on identifying securities mispriced relative to each other rather than the market as a whole.

Consider, for instance, a pairs trading strategy applied to two technology stocks. If Stock A and Stock B demonstrate a historically stable price correlation, a sudden divergence might present an arbitrage opportunity. Statistical models might predict that Stock A is undervalued relative to Stock B, prompting the trader to go long on Stock A and short on Stock B. The primary reward materializes as the prices revert, realigning with their historical equilibrium. The use of statistical models enhances the precision of such trades, augmenting the potential for reward while necessitating vigilant risk management to navigate potential divergences.

Operational risk, while often less emphasized, plays a significant role in executing statistical arbitrage successfully. This includes the reliability of the trading infrastructure, the accuracy of data feeds, and the competence of personnel managing algorithms and models. Technological failures can lead to costly disruptions, especially in high-frequency trading environments leveraging statistical arbitrage. Redundant systems, regular audits, and continuous staff training are essential practices to mitigate operational risk and ensure seamless strategy implementation.

Regulatory risk is also an integral aspect of the broader risk landscape. Compliance with financial regulations is mandatory, with stringent rules governing algorithmic trading, short selling, and capital adequacy. Regulatory changes can unexpectedly impact statistical arbitrage strategies, necessitating ongoing vigilance and adaptability. Comprehensive understanding of jurisdiction-specific regulations and proactive engagement with compliance frameworks safeguard against potential legal issues and reinforce market transparency.

In an ever-evolving financial environment, quantifying the precise risk-reward trade-off in statistical arbitrage remains challenging. Advanced risk metrics such as the Sharpe Ratio, Value-at-Risk (VaR), and Conditional Value-at-Risk (CVaR) aid practitioners in assessing strategy performance. The Sharpe Ratio, for instance, measures the excess return per unit of standard deviation, offering insights into risk-adjusted returns:

$$\text{Sharpe Ratio} = \frac{E[R_p - R_f]}{\sigma_p}$$

where $E[R_p]$ is the portfolio's expected return, R_f the risk-free rate, and σ_p the standard deviation of portfolio returns. By prioritizing risk-adjusted performance, traders fine-tune strategies to prioritize capital preservation alongside return generation.

Emerging technologies and data sources are reshaping how risk and reward are managed in statistical arbitrage. Machine learning models provide unprecedented predictive capabilities, learning from complex and high-dimensional data patterns to enhance risk assessment and trading decisions. The incorporation of alternative data sources, ranging from satellite imagery to social media sentiment, enriches model inputs, potentially unveiling new opportunities and risks that traditional datasets might overlook.

Ultimately, the pursuit of risk and reward in statistical arbitrage encapsulates the quintessential trading endeavor: maximizing returns while preserving capital. The nuanced interplay between sophisticated quantitative models and pragmatic risk management strategies ensures that statistical arbitrage remains a compelling proposition for adept traders. As financial markets become progressively intricate, the synthesis of technological advancements with empirical trading principles will continue to redefine the risk-reward paradigm, propelling statistical arbitrage toward new frontiers of innovation and ingenuity.

6.6 Implementation Challenges

Implementing statistical arbitrage strategies in real-world trading environments presents a host of challenges that require careful consideration and adept navigation. While the theoretical underpinnings of statistical arbitrage may appear robust, transitioning these concepts from a theoretical framework to an operational trading strategy involves overcoming numerous practical hurdles. These challenges span across data quality, model selection, execution tactics, transaction costs, and scalability, each of which can significantly impact the efficacy and profitability of the strategy.

One of the foremost challenges in implementing statistical arbitrage is ensuring the quality and reliability of data. The accuracy of any quantitative model is only as good as the data inputs on which it re-lies. Thus, obtaining high-quality, clean, and precise data is crucial. Fi-nancial markets generate vast amounts of data, including price quotes, volume, and trade execution details, but this data is often riddled with inaccuracies, missing values, and outliers. Data vendors may provide inconsistent formats, leading to discrepancies that can distort model predictions. Data preprocessing, therefore, becomes an essential step wherein datasets are cleaned, normalized, and transformed to ensure robustness and reliability.

Synchronizing data, particularly at high frequencies, is another signifi-cant challenge. When dealing with multiple data sources or analyzing correlations between different securities, time-stamping discrepancies can result in mismatches that undermine co-integration analyses or spread calculations. Implementing precise timestamp alignment pro-cesses is essential to minimize signal inaccuracies attributed to data lag or misalignment.

Another critical facet of implementation is model selection and valida-tion. Different models vary in their assumptions and parameters, and choosing the optimal model for a particular market condition can be an intricate process. Practitioners must weigh the merits and limitations of various statistical and machine learning models, such as linear re-gression, support vector machines, or neural networks. Model risk is an inherent challenge, arising from overfitting to past data—where the model captures noise rather than fundamental relationships—or from misinterpreting historical trends as future forecasts. Continuous vali-dation through out-of-sample testing, stress testing, and refinement is necessary to sustain model performance amidst evolving market dy-namics.

Execution risk, encompassing the risk of not executing trades at an-ticipated prices or volumes, is also a significant concern. Slippage, the difference between the expected price of a trade and the actual price, can erode potential returns, especially in highly volatile or illiq-uid markets. High-frequency traders encounter execution challenges extensively, necessitating the deployment of sophisticated algorithms to optimize order execution and minimize market impact. These al-gorithms might include limit orders, peg orders, or slicing techniques that disperse large orders into smaller parts to avoid excessive market influence.

Transaction costs, comprising both explicit costs like commissions and implicit costs such as market impact, are another challenge that can significantly affect profit margins. Strategies that involve frequent trading, such as high-frequency statistical arbitrage, are particularly impacted by transaction costs. Reducing these costs involves negotiating competitive commission rates with brokers, optimizing execution strategies to minimize market impact, and leveraging technological solutions that streamline trade processing and settlement.

Scalability presents yet another hurdle. As strategies expand in scale, either in terms of capital deployed or the number of simultaneous trades, operational complexities increase. Larger operations require greater infrastructure for data processing, storage, and computation. Additionally, the risk of execution imbalances and latencies grows, potentially leading to decreased efficiency or increased exposure. Implementing automated systems with load balancing, parallel processing, and failover mechanisms ensures that scalability does not compromise performance or risk controls.

Additionally, risk management frameworks must be adapted to handle the intricacies of large-scale implementations, necessitating advanced measures like portfolio margining, dynamic hedging strategies, and real-time risk monitoring systems.

Regulatory concerns add another layer of complexity to the implementation of statistical arbitrage strategies. The regulatory landscape is ever-evolving, with financial authorities worldwide instituting rules that govern trading activities to maintain market fairness and stability. Traders must comply with various regulations pertaining to short selling, leverage restrictions, and reporting requirements. Additionally, the use of proprietary algorithms and the prevalence of high-frequency trading have drawn increased scrutiny, with regulators focusing on ethical considerations, market manipulation concerns, and systemic risk implications.

Compliance departments thus play an essential role in ensuring that strategies align with legal requirements. Implementing robust compliance protocols, including regular audits, transparent reporting practices, and ethical trading guidelines, mitigates the risk of regulatory breaches and reinforces the legitimacy of trading operations.

Technological infrastructure is yet another critical component, given that statistical arbitrage relies heavily on computational resources. Implementing advanced models requires high-performance computing systems capable of handling intensive data processing and model simulations. Latency, or the delay in data transmission and processing, is a persistent challenge, especially for strategies dependent on real-time data and higher frequencies. Building low-latency trading platforms involves investing in cutting-edge technology, including proximity hosting, co-location services, and custom networking solutions, to ensure that execution speeds meet the demands of competitive trading environments.

Lastly, talent acquisition and retention play a pivotal role in the successful implementation of statistical arbitrage. The integration of cross-disciplinary teams, combining expertise in quantitative finance, computer science, and economics, ensures that strategies are both technically robust and market-aware. As the demand for quantitative talent continues to rise, firms must foster cultures that promote innovation, continuous learning, and collaborative problem-solving to attract and retain top-tier professionals.

While statistical arbitrage offers compelling opportunities for capturing market inefficiencies, its implementation is fraught with challenges that require a multi-faceted approach. Addressing these challenges through meticulous data handling, adept model selection, effective execution, cost management, regulatory compliance, technological investment, and talent cultivation enhances the potential for success in this competitive arena. As markets continue to evolve and technology advances, the capacity to adeptly navigate these challenges will determine the resilience and profitability of statistical arbitrage strategies in the future.

6.7 Performance Evaluation and Optimization

Performance evaluation and optimization are critical components in the lifecycle of statistical arbitrage strategies, ensuring that they remain robust, efficient, and profitable over time. In the fast-paced and highly competitive world of trading, the ability to accurately assess the effectiveness of a strategy and continually refine it in response to market dynamics is paramount.

At the foundation of performance evaluation is a comprehensive set of metrics that encapsulate the strategy's risk-return profile, efficiency, and impact on capital allocation. The primary goal of performance evaluation is to quantify the success of the strategy against predefined objectives, incorporating both absolute and risk-adjusted return measures along with other informative metrics.

One of the most widely used metrics is the Sharpe Ratio, which measures the excess return per unit of volatility:

$$\text{Sharpe Ratio} = \frac{E[R_p - R_f]}{\sigma_p} \tag{6.3}$$

Here, $E[R_p]$ is the expected portfolio return, R_f the risk-free rate, and σ_p the standard deviation of the portfolio's return. A higher Sharpe Ratio indicates a more favorable risk-adjusted performance, providing a clear indicator of the strategy's ability to generate returns above the risk-free rate after accounting for volatility.

Complementing the Sharpe Ratio, the Sortino Ratio refines risk assessment by considering only downside volatility. This distinction emphasizes the differing impacts of negative and positive volatility, addressing the asymmetry that can be particularly relevant in assessing statistical arbitrage strategies:

$$\text{Sortino Ratio} = \frac{E[R_p - R_f]}{\sigma_D} \tag{6.4}$$

where σ_D is the standard deviation of negative returns. This metric is beneficial for strategies that might exhibit skewed return distributions or be particularly sensitive to downside risks.

Alpha, the measure of an investment's performance over and above the market benchmark, is crucial for assessing the inherent value a statistical arbitrage strategy brings through its trades. In a market-neutral strategy like statistical arbitrage, alpha reflects the strategy's skill in capturing inefficiencies independent of market movements, underlining the qualitative aspects of strategic implementation.

Beyond these traditional metrics, more granular performance indicators such as maximum drawdown, recovery time, and the Calmar Ratio enhance the understanding of how strategies perform under stress conditions. The maximum drawdown measures the peak-to-trough decline during a specific period, offering insights into potential vulnerability under adverse market conditions. The Calmar Ratio, which relates the annual return to maximum drawdown, serves as a risk-adjusted return gauge particularly suited to understanding long-term sustainability:

$$\text{Calmar Ratio} = \frac{\text{Annual Return}}{\text{Maximum Drawdown}} \tag{6.5}$$

Performance evaluation transcends statistical metrics, extending into the qualitative assessment of model assumptions, operational efficiency, and compliance adherence. A strategy's operational efficiency, encompassing execution speed, transaction costs, and slippage management, critically influences net returns. Consistent model assumption validation, alongside real-time monitoring systems, ensures that strategies not only meet theoretical expectations but also thrive in actual trading environments.

Optimization in statistical arbitrage involves iterative refinement of models and strategies to enhance performance outcomes. Central to optimization is the continuous process of parameter tuning, where key model attributes like thresholds for entry and exit signals, volatility adjustments, and capital allocations are fine-tuned to align with evolving market conditions. Optimization heavily relies on backtesting frameworks that simulate strategy performance under historical market scenarios, allowing for the identification and mitigation of weaknesses before live deployment.

An effective optimization strategy integrates machine learning techniques, facilitating predictive analytics that adaptively alter model parameters in response to new data. Machine learning models, with their ability to learn complex patterns and relationships, assist in uncovering latent inefficiencies and modeling deviations from mean-reverting equilibriums. Algorithms like reinforcement learning allow for an adaptive approach, engaging in dynamic parameter setting based on historical and incoming data streams.

Stochastic optimization techniques, such as genetic algorithms and particle swarm optimization, offer powerful avenues for exploring high-dimensional parameter spaces, mitigating local optima issues often associated with more traditional methods. These techniques leverage evolutionary computation frameworks to iteratively evolve solution populations, honing in on optimal parameters that enhance robustness and profitability.

Another layer of optimization involves transaction cost analysis, a crucial factor in maintaining edge in high-frequency trading environments. By understanding the nuances of order execution and latency, traders optimize algorithms for efficient execution, minimizing adverse price impacts. Automated trading systems, coupled with real-time data analytics, facilitate proactive adjustment of trade execution strategies, ensuring minimal friction and optimized performance.

Risk management optimization is equally indispensable, encompassing advanced hedging techniques, real-time risk analytics, and stress testing protocols. By employing value-at-risk (VaR) and conditional value-at-risk (CVaR) analyses, traders quantify potential losses and adjust strategies to align with risk tolerances. Dynamic hedging strategies, incorporating derivatives like options and swaps, provide further avenues for tailoring risk exposure without hindering return potential.

In the context of optimization, the human element should not be overlooked. The intuition and creativity of experienced traders provide invaluable insights that often transcend algorithmic outputs. Ensuring a robust dialogue between systematic models and human oversight cultivates an environment where strategic foresight and adaptive learning can thrive harmoniously.

Ultimately, the success of performance evaluation and optimization in statistical arbitrage hinges on a holistic approach. It involves blending quantitative metrics with qualitative insights, engaging sophisticated analytical tools alongside strategic human ingenuity, and fostering an organizational culture committed to continuous improvement and learning. As the landscape of financial markets evolves with technological innovations, the capacity to adapt and optimize statistical arbitrage strategies will remain paramount, influencing the trajectory of performance outcomes and sustaining competitive advantages in the quest for alpha.

Chapter 7

Machine Learning Techniques for Market Prediction

This chapter explores the integration of machine learning into market prediction, underscoring key algorithms and their applications in financial forecasting. It covers data preprocessing and feature engineering as foundational steps for effective model training. Supervised and unsupervised learning techniques are detailed, alongside their roles in market analysis and pattern recognition. Time series forecasting models are highlighted for their significance in predicting market trends. The chapter also addresses model evaluation, focusing on metrics and methods to ensure robust predictive performance, and delves into advanced techniques like deep learning to push the boundaries of market prediction accuracy.

7.1 Overview of Machine Learning in Finance

Machine learning, a subset of artificial intelligence, is reshaping the landscape of financial markets by enhancing prediction accuracy, automating processes, and uncovering deeper insights from vast datasets.   At its core, machine learning enables the discovery of complex patterns and data-driven decisions through model training. In this section, we delve into the critical role machine learning plays in finance, elucidating key concepts, applications, and examples that showcase its transformative impact.

The financial markets are characterized by their complexity and the dynamic interaction of multiple factors. Historically, financial forecasting depended heavily on econometric and statistical models. These traditional models, while effective, often struggled to capture non-linear patterns and adapt to the rapid changes in market conditions. Machine learning offers a more flexible approach that goes beyond conventional models by allowing algorithms to learn and improve from data without being explicitly programmed for specific tasks.

One of the primary applications of machine learning in finance is market prediction.   This involves forecasting asset prices, identifying market trends, and gauging the overall direction of the market. Machine learning models, such as decision trees, support vector machines (SVM), and artificial neural networks (ANN), have shown remarkable potential in improving prediction accuracy. For instance, neural networks, inspired by the human brain's interconnected structure, can model complex hierarchical data patterns, which are prevalent in financial datasets.

Consider a scenario where a machine learning algorithm is used to predict stock prices. The input data could include historical prices, trading volumes, economic indicators, and even sentiment data from news articles and social media. By learning from this diverse input, machine learning models can identify patterns that may not be immediately apparent to human analysts. These predictions, while not foolproof, provide traders with valuable insights that improve decision-making under uncertainty.

Algorithmic trading, another critical domain within finance, extensively employs machine learning to develop automated trading strategies. These strategies leverage algorithms to make split-second trading decisions, capitalizing on market inefficiencies and trends. For example, quantitative analysts, often known as quants, might apply reinforcement learning—a technique where models learn optimal actions through trial and error—to design trading systems that adapt to changing market conditions over time.

Moreover, machine learning algorithms play a pivotal role in risk management, an integral component of any financial strategy. Machine learning models can assess and predict risk by analyzing historical data and recognizing patterns that correlate with risk factors. Techniques such as clustering, anomaly detection, and predictive modeling help financial institutions identify credit risk, detect fraudulent activities, and manage operational risks more effectively. For instance, clustering can group similar credit applicants, aiding lenders in understanding risk profiles and making informed lending decisions.

Beyond prediction, machine learning enhances portfolio management by optimizing asset allocation and enhancing returns. Modern portfolio theory primarily focuses on diversifying assets to achieve an optimal risk-return trade-off. Machine learning augments this by integrating alternative data sources, such as satellite imagery and consumer purchasing trends, to gain an edge in market insights. Techniques like genetic algorithms and portfolio optimization models are increasingly used to construct and rebalance portfolios dynamically.

To illustrate the versatility of machine learning in finance further, consider its application in sentiment analysis. Financial markets are significantly influenced by investor sentiment, which can often lead to irrational behaviors. By using natural language processing (NLP) techniques, machine learning models can analyze text data from news feeds, blogs, and social media platforms. This allows investors to gain insights into market sentiment and potential impacts on asset prices. Sentiment analysis helps traders anticipate market movements driven by collective emotional responses, thus providing a strategic advantage.

Despite its numerous benefits, deploying machine learning in finance is not without challenges. One significant challenge is the quality and availability of data. Financial data is often noisy, incomplete, and subject to biases that can affect model outcomes. Additionally, the dynamic nature of financial markets means that models must continuously adapt to new information. This requires robust data preprocessing techniques, continuous model training, and retraining strategies to maintain accuracy and reliability.

Furthermore, the interpretability of machine learning models remains a critical concern, especially in highly regulated industries like finance. While complex models such as deep learning can provide exceptional accuracy, they often function as "black boxes," making it difficult to understand how decisions are made. This lack of transparency can pose significant risks, particularly in auditing models for compliance and ethical use. Efforts to improve model explainability, through methods such as model agnostic techniques and local interpretable model-agnostic explanations (LIME), are crucial in addressing these challenges.

Machine learning in finance is also profoundly affected by regulatory factors. Regulatory bodies such as the Securities and Exchange Commission (SEC) and the European Securities and Markets Authority (ESMA) have stringent requirements around data usage, model transparency, and risk management. Financial institutions must navigate these regulations while deploying machine learning solutions, balancing innovation with compliance. This necessitates a careful consideration of the ethical implications of machine learning, ensuring that models do not perpetuate biases or lead to discriminatory practices.

The advent of machine learning in finance has opened the door for greater collaboration between human expertise and artificial intelligence. Financial professionals equipped with machine learning skills can work alongside models to enhance analytical capabilities, thus fostering more informed decision-making processes. For instance, while a machine learning model might efficiently analyze large datasets to highlight potential investment opportunities, a human analyst can provide contextual understanding and strategic insight, ensuring that decisions align with broader financial goals.

In practical terms, the integration of machine learning in finance has led to the emergence of FinTech companies, which leverage technology to offer innovative financial services. These companies often use machine learning to provide personalized financial products, automated investment platforms, and real-time risk assessments, challenging traditional banking systems and driving industry-wide innovation.

The future landscape of finance will undoubtedly be shaped by continued advancements in machine learning technologies. As computing power and data availability grow, the potential for more sophisticated algorithms and models will increase. Innovations such as quantum computing and neuromorphic processing might further revolutionize the field, pushing the boundaries of what is currently achievable in market prediction and financial analysis.

The journey of integrating machine learning into finance is ongoing, complex, and fraught with challenges, yet the potential for transforming market prediction and decision-making is immense. As the financial sector continues to embrace these technologies, professionals, stakeholders, and regulatory bodies must work in unison to ensure that this integration is both effective and ethically responsible, ushering in a new era of financial innovation and precision.

7.2 Data Preprocessing and Feature Engineering

In machine learning, particularly within the intricate environment of financial markets, the quality of input data is paramount. "Garbage in, garbage out" is a well-worn adage that holds especially true for data-driven financial models. This section explores the critical processes of data preprocessing and feature engineering as foundational steps for crafting effective machine learning models. These processes transform raw data into a structured and informative format, readying it for the analytical rigor demanded by high-stakes financial predictions.

Data preprocessing is the initial phase, involving the cleansing and preparation of raw data. Financial data is often plagued by inconsistencies such as missing values, outliers, and noise. These irregularities can severely skew model performance if left unaddressed. For instance, missing values in stock price data can arise from non-trading days, such as weekends or holidays. To tackle missing data, techniques like imputation or interpolation are employed, filling the gaps with plausible values based on surrounding data points. Another strategy might be carrying forward recent data points (last observation carried forward) to maintain continuity.

Outliers are another pivotal concern in financial datasets. These unusual data points can distort model training, leading to skewed predictions far removed from reality. Outlier detection methods, such as Z-score analysis or the use of interquartile range (IQR), help mitigate this risk by identifying and handling anomalous data points before they affect the model.

Noise reduction is equally important, as financial data can be volatile. Smoothing techniques, like moving averages or exponential smoothing, can be applied to distill the underlying trends of time series data, thus providing a clearer signal for model analysis. In doing so, data preprocessing not only rectifies imperfections but also enhances the stability and reliability of subsequent analyses.

A crucial aspect of data preprocessing is normalization—scaling the data to a uniform range. This step is vital in financial data because different variables, such as stock prices, trading volumes, and interest rates, exist on disparate scales. By normalizing data using techniques such as min-max scaling or z-score standardization, models are better equipped to process and learn from these inputs without being unduly

151

influenced by their original scale.

Transitioning to feature engineering, this process involves creating new variables or features from the existing dataset to improve model performance. In the financial sector, feature engineering can be particularly challenging yet essential, as it requires both a deep understanding of financial systems and the creativity to derive insightful metrics. For example, instead of solely relying on raw stock prices, engineers might calculate relative returns, which are percentage changes over a given time period, to normalize the data and make comparisons across different securities feasible.

Another powerful feature engineering technique is the derivation of technical indicators—metrics used by traders to analyze historical price and volume data—to forecast future price movements. Common indicators include moving averages, relative strength index (RSI), and Bollinger Bands, each serving to highlight momentum, volatility, or trend direction. Including these indicators as features can substantially enrich the dataset with predictive nuances omitted by raw data alone.

Moreover, sentiment analysis features, derived from textual data, can augment traditional numerical datasets. By analyzing news articles, financial reports, and social media posts, one can extract investor sentiment metrics, such as polarity scores or sentiment averages, which provide insight into market moods and potential price movements. This information is crucial, as it can help models anticipate market reactions based on public sentiment trends.

Feature selection, closely related to feature engineering, involves choosing the most relevant features for model training. In finance, this process can mean sifting through a vast array of potential inputs, such as economic indicators, macroeconomic data, and sector-specific variables. Techniques such as principal component analysis (PCA), recursive feature elimination (RFE), and regularization methods (like LASSO) help refine and reduce the feature set to its most informative components, enhancing model performance and training efficiency.

Dimensionality reduction plays a similar role, compressing data while maintaining its essential characteristics. In financial markets, where datasets can be extensive and convoluted, dimensionality reduction techniques are invaluable. Methods like PCA and t-distributed stochastic neighbor embedding (t-SNE) transform high-dimensional data into more manageable forms, emphasizing important correlations while reducing computational overhead.

Data transformation, a component of feature engineering, further refines data by improving its distribution properties. Logarithmic transformations, for instance, are often applied to financial data to stabilize variance and normalize skewed distributions, making them more amenable to statistical analysis.

Hypothesis generation is a less talked about yet significant facet of feature engineering in finance. Here, domain experts posit hypotheses about market behavior, which are then translated into engineered features. For example, a hypothesis might suggest that certain trading patterns precede market rallies, prompting the creation of features that encapsulate these patterns for model evaluation. It is through this symbiotic relationship between theoretical speculation and empirical validation that truly innovative features emerge.

Despite the immense potential of data preprocessing and feature engineering, challenges remain. One such challenge is the risk of overfitting, where the model becomes too tailored to the training data and loses generalization capability. This is especially pertinent in finance, where overfitting could lead to significant financial losses. Careful cross-validation and testing against out-of-sample data are critical to ensuring that feature-engineered models maintain robustness across various market conditions.

Additionally, feature engineering often involves a delicate balance between complexity and interpretability. While intricate features can capture subtle data patterns, they also risk transforming models into opaque systems, difficult for stakeholders to understand or trust. Striving for a middle ground ensures that models remain both powerful and comprehensible.

Advancements in automation, often referred to as automated feature engineering or feature learning, offer promising solutions by leveraging machine learning algorithms to autonomously discover features. Deep learning, for instance, automatically extracts hierarchical features from raw financial data, alleviating some of the burdens traditionally associated with feature engineering. Nonetheless, the nuanced expertise of seasoned financial professionals remains invaluable in guiding these automated processes.

Ultimately, the role of data preprocessing and feature engineering in finance cannot be overstated. These processes form the bedrock upon which machine learning models are built, serving as the conduits through which raw data is transformed into strategic intelligence. As financial markets continue to evolve, the refinement of these techniques will be key to unlocking deeper insights, driving innovative strategies, and maintaining a competitive edge in a rapidly changing landscape. Through continuous development and adaptation, data preprocessing and feature engineering ensure that machine learning applications in finance remain not only effective but also cutting-edge, paving the way for greater precision and foresight in financial decision-making.

7.3   Supervised Learning Algorithms

Supervised learning stands as a cornerstone of machine learning, characterized by its reliance on labeled datasets to train models. In the financial markets, supervised learning algorithms serve as powerful tools for predictive analytics, enabling the identification of patterns that inform investment decisions. This section delves into several prominent supervised learning techniques, illustrating their applications, advantages, and limitations within the context of finance, all while highlighting the nuances that practitioners must navigate when deploying these methods.

At the heart of supervised learning is the concept of a labeled dataset— a collection of input-output pairs where the output is known. In finance, these labeled datasets can represent historical data where each feature vector might include variables such as stock prices, trading volumes, and economic indicators, paired with an output variable that represents a target prediction, like future price movement or stock classification.

A foundational supervised learning technique is linear regression, which models the relationship between input variables and a continuous output by fitting a linear equation to the observed data. Linear regression is prized for its simplicity and interpretability, making it an excellent starting point for financial modeling. It functions well in cases where the relationship between variables is approximately linear. For example, linear regression can predict returns based on past performances of stock prices, assuming that past trends will continue modestly into the future.

However, the financial world often defies linear simplicity, yielding to complexities better captured by more sophisticated algorithms like decision trees. A decision tree algorithm splits the dataset into subsets based on the value of input features, using a tree-like model of decisions. This method excels at capturing non-linear patterns, offering a versatile fit to financial data. Moreover, decision trees provide intuitive

154

visualizations, aiding in model interpretation and transparency—a crucial aspect when justifying decisions to stakeholders.

Extending the decision tree concept, ensemble methods, such as random forests and gradient boosting machines, combine multiple decision trees to improve predictions. Random forests, for instance, create a "forest" of decision trees using bootstrap aggregating (bagging) to reduce variance and enhance robustness against the overfitting common to single decision trees. These techniques shine in finance by delivering predictive stability and accuracy across diverse datasets. An application might involve predicting bond rating changes based on a variety of market indicators, where ensemble methods mitigate the volatility inherent in market data.

Support Vector Machines (SVM) bring a different approach to supervised learning by finding the hyperplane that best separates data into classes. In finance, SVMs can be particularly useful for classification tasks, such as categorizing stocks as buy, hold, or sell based on performance indicators. SVMs handle high-dimensional data well and can be adapted with kernel functions to solve non-linear classification problems. However, they require careful parameter tuning and computational resources, which can be intensive, especially with large datasets.

Neural networks, inspired by the architecture of the human brain, have gained popularity in finance due to their capacity to model intricate, non-linear relationships. By connecting layers of synthetic neurons, neural networks transform inputs through multiple layers to capture complex patterns. In financial markets, neural networks are adept at tasks ranging from option pricing to high-frequency trading strategy design. Their flexibility and power come with challenges of interpretability and the risk of overfitting, necessitating strategies like dropout and regularization to enhance model robustness.

One application of supervised learning particularly relevant in finance is stock price prediction. Consider the use of historical price data, macroeconomic indicators, and sentiment scores as inputs. Machines trained in supervised learning algorithms can seek patterns suggesting future price movements. For instance, a neural network might identify subtle correlations between certain economic indicators and price upticks, enabling traders to act on nascent trends before they become obvious.

Another significant application is credit scoring, where supervised learning models assess the likelihood that a borrower will default on a loan. By training on historical data encompassing borrower characteristics and loan outcomes, these models—most commonly logistic regression—estimate default probabilities, aiding financial institutions in risk management and decision-making. The models balance simplicity with effectiveness; however, they must carefully consider ethical implications and biases in the data.

Supervised learning also finds its place in algorithmic trading systems, which automate trades based on predefined rules inferred from past data. Algorithms trained with supervised techniques can adapt to changing market dynamics, adjusting trade strategies to optimize returns or minimize risks. These systems use inputs such as price movements, trading volumes, and other financial indicators, applying models like SVMs and neural networks to execute trades that align with evolving market conditions.

The challenges of using supervised learning in finance are multifaceted, beginning with the need for high-quality, representative datasets. Financial markets are subject to multitudes of externalities that can alter the historical relevance of data. Issues of overfitting, where models learn noise rather than signal, are prevalent. Mitigation strategies include extensive cross-validation, the use of regularization techniques to penalize overly complex models, and vigilant feature selection to ensure model generalization.

Moreover, supervised models must be continuously monitored and updated to reflect new market realities. The data drift—where the data distribution changes over time—can undermine model reliability and necessitate retraining with recent data. Ensuring that the models remain current involves a blend of automation and human oversight, where financial expertise guides machine learning practitioners in maintaining model efficacy.

Interpretability remains a core concern, especially in regulated environments where transparency is mandated by governance and compliance standards. While algorithms like linear regression and decision trees offer clearer insight into decision processes, complex models such as neural networks often require supplementary tools like SHapley Additive exPlanations (SHAP) and Local Interpretable Model-agnostic Explanations (LIME) to make their predictions comprehensible. The tension between model complexity and interpretability necessitates careful consideration to maintain the trustworthiness of financial decisions.

To harness the full potential of supervised learning algorithms in finance, practitioners combine them with advanced data sources, including alternative data like social media sentiment and satellite imagery. By incorporating vast and varied data inputs, models can capture a broader swathe of insights, translating nuanced data characteristics into coherent financial strategies.

The trajectory of supervised learning in finance is guided by ongoing advancements in computational techniques and data availability. As these technologies evolve, so too will the sophistication and accuracy of supervised models, offering unprecedented opportunities for innovation. These models help stakeholders navigate the turbulent waters of financial markets with a blend of data-driven precision and visionary acumen, ensuring they are not merely observers of financial trends but active participants shaping market dynamics.

7.4   Unsupervised Learning and Clustering

Unsupervised learning represents a powerful segment of machine learning concerned with discovering hidden patterns in unlabeled data. Unlike supervised learning, where models are trained on known input-output pairs, unsupervised learning deals with datasets that lack explicit labels, making it ideal for exploratory data analysis and pattern recognition. Within the realm of finance, unsupervised learning techniques, particularly clustering, provide invaluable insights into market behavior, customer segmentation, and investment strategies.

Clustering, a predominant unsupervised learning technique, involves grouping data points based on inherent similarities, without predefined categories. In finance, clustering can unveil underlying structures within complex datasets, aiding in tasks such as identifying market segments, customer profiling, and anomaly detection.

One widely used clustering method is K-means clustering. The K-means algorithm partitions data into k clusters by minimizing the variance within each cluster while maximizing the variance between clusters. In the financial sector, K-means can be employed for segmenting investment portfolios, whereby securities are grouped based on characteristics such as volatility, return rates, and market capitalization. Traders can then tailor their strategies according to these clusters, aligning with risk appetites and desired outcomes.

A practical example of K-means clustering in finance involves customer segmentation in banking. By inputting data such as customer demographics, transaction behaviors, and credit histories, banks can classify customers into distinct segments. These segments inform personalized marketing strategies and product offerings, enhancing customer

157

satisfaction and loyalty.   Additionally, K-means clustering assists in fraud detection by grouping transactions and identifying anomalies that deviate from established patterns.

Despite its utility, K-means requires specifying the number of clusters beforehand, which can be challenging in complex financial systems. This challenge is mitigated by methods like the Elbow Method or Silhouette Analysis, which offer empirical techniques to determine the optimal number of clusters, thus enhancing model accuracy and interpretability.

Hierarchical clustering, another essential technique, builds a tree-like structure (dendrogram) comprising nested clusters. This method is especially useful for understanding hierarchical relationships within data. In finance, hierarchical clustering can delineate asset correlations, identifying hierarchical tiers of asset groups based on their correlations. Investors use these insights to diversify portfolios across distinctive asset classes, reducing exposure to systemic risks.

For instance, hierarchical clustering can help visualize relationships among different stock indices, currencies, or commodities.   By constructing a dendrogram, traders discern which stocks or commodities move synchronously, thereby optimizing hedging strategies and risk assessments.

One limitation of hierarchical clustering is its computational intensity, particularly with large datasets. Nonetheless, it provides a comprehensive framework for exploring the relationships within financial data, supporting strategic asset allocation decisions.

An advanced clustering technique is Gaussian Mixture Models (GMM), which assumes that data is generated from a mixture of several Gaussian distributions. In finance, GMMs offer a probabilistic approach to clustering, giving a nuanced understanding of data distributions. For example, GMMs can be applied in risk management to model the distribution of returns, enabling the identification of different market regimes characterized by distinct volatility or return patterns.

GMMs are particularly valuable in environments characterized by overlapping clusters, where traditional methods might struggle. They provide probabilities that a data point belongs to a particular cluster, offering nuanced insights into uncertain market conditions.

Another avenue for unsupervised learning in finance is Dimensionality Reduction, where the focus is on reducing the number of input variables without losing essential information. Techniques like Principal Component Analysis (PCA) and t-distributed stochastic neighbor embedding (t-

SNE) transform high-dimensional data into a lower-dimensional space, highlighting key patterns.

In the context of finance, PCA can analyze the covariance structure of asset returns to identify principal factors driving market movements, simplifying the complexity inherent in multifaceted financial datasets. Traders and analysts use PCA to construct factor models that capture the essence of market behavior, thereby refining their trading strategies and risk management approaches.

For more visual tasks, t-SNE excels in clustering high-dimensional data into a 2D or 3D space, preserving local structure while reducing dimensions. An example use case in finance is visualizing clusters of similar trading days based on market indicators or sentiment scores. These visualizations help traders identify periods of market stability or instability, guiding strategic decision-making processes.

Unsupervised learning also plays a critical role in anomaly detection— a vital facet of fraud prevention, risk assessment, and compliance within financial services. By modeling normal behavior through clustering techniques, systems can flag anomalous activities that warrant further investigation. For instance, transactions far removed from established clusters might indicate fraudulent activities, prompting preventative measures from financial institutions.

A significant challenge in unsupervised learning is the scarcity of ground truth labels, which can complicate the evaluation of model performance. Validation often involves using domain expertise to assess patterns' plausibility or employing semi-supervised learning methods, where limited labeled data aids unsupervised learning.

Furthermore, unsupervised learning demands robust feature engineering to extract meaningful insights. In finance, features must capture relevant aspects of market dynamics or customer behavior to reveal substantive patterns. The process involves iterative refinement and continuous learning to adapt to market changes, ensuring the longevity and reliability of insights extracted.

Incorporating market context is critical; understanding regulatory environments and economic conditions can significantly influence the clustering process and outcomes. Thus, financial professionals must blend technical proficiency with domain knowledge to extract actionable intelligence from unsupervised learning algorithms.

The integration of alternative data further amplifies the capabilities of unsupervised models in finance. By incorporating unconventional datasets, such as social media sentiment or geospatial data, algorithms gain a richer and more diverse view of market phenomena. This expansion allows for the identification of novel patterns that might elude traditional analysis, offering competitive advantages in rapidly evolving markets.

Innovative approaches like Deep Learning-Based Clustering are also emerging, leveraging neural networks to autonomously learn complex data representations. These methods hold promise for managing ever-growing datasets, providing scalable solutions for clustering tasks that benefit from deep learning's capacity to model intricate relationships.

As unsupervised learning continues to advance, its role in finance will undeniably expand. The ability to extract hidden structures and patterns from complex, unstructured datasets will drive more informed and strategic decision-making processes, transforming how financial analysts, traders, and risk managers approach market analysis. Unsupervised learning, especially when integrated with supervised techniques, builds comprehensive models that adapt to the dynamic nature of financial markets, ensuring resilient and innovative strategies for managing uncertainty.

Ultimately, unsupervised learning and clustering are poised to revolutionize the financial industry by advancing data exploration and interpretation practices, equipping financial experts with the tools necessary to navigate an increasingly data-driven world. Through continued research and application, these techniques will increasingly inform financial insights, risk management, and strategic innovation, charting new territories in the financial landscape.

7.5   Time Series Forecasting with ML

Time series forecasting is a pivotal aspect of financial analysis, providing insights into future market conditions based on historical data sequences. In this context, machine learning techniques have emerged as transformative tools, offering sophisticated methods for predicting complex financial time series such as stock prices, interest rates, and economic indicators. This section explores the intricacies of time series forecasting using machine learning, highlighting prominent models, their applications in finance, and the challenges researchers and practitioners face.

Time series data, characterized by observations collected sequentially over time, demands specialized forecasting techniques that account for temporal dependencies and patterns. Traditional statistical models, such as ARIMA (AutoRegressive Integrated Moving Average), have long been employed for time series analysis, leveraging their ability to model linear relationships and temporal lags effectively. ARIMA, with its autoregressive component and moving average mechanism, allows analysts to capture seasonalities and trends by differencing the time series to achieve stationarity.

Despite the efficacy of ARIMA in modeling simpler time series data, financial markets often exhibit complex non-linearities and abrupt shifts that transcend the linear frameworks of traditional models. Machine learning approaches offer a deeper understanding of these patterns, leveraging data-driven insights to forecast future states.

One of the most significant advancements in time series forecasting with machine learning is the introduction of Long Short-Term Memory (LSTM) networks. As a specialized type of recurrent neural network (RNN), LSTMs are designed to overcome the vanishing gradient problem inherent in standard RNNs, thus excelling at capturing long-term dependencies in sequential data. In financial markets, LSTMs are particularly effective due to their capacity to learn intricate temporal patterns and dynamic changes, essential for making accurate predictions in volatile environments.

A systematic application of LSTM in finance might involve predicting daily stock prices based on a comprehensive dataset comprising historical prices, trading volumes, and sentiment indicators. By processing this wealth of information, LSTMs can generate forecasts that account for immediate market trends and longer-term shifts, thereby granting traders and analysts a strategic informational advantage.

Another increasingly prevalent methodology in time series forecasting is the use of convolutional neural networks (CNNs) in tandem with LSTMs. CNNs excel in feature extraction, capturing spatial hierarchies and patterns from complex datasets. In time series analysis, employing CNNs for preliminary feature extraction followed by LSTMs for temporal pattern recognition has yielded promising results. This hybrid architecture is well-suited for applications like high-frequency trading systems, where rapid responses to market movements are critical.

A specific financial application benefiting from this hybrid approach is the prediction of currency exchange rates. Here, CNNs can process multi-dimensional input features, such as technical indicators and macroeconomic data arrays, while LSTMs subsequently learn temporal dependencies among these features, resulting in more nuanced and responsive forecasts.

In addition to deep learning models, tree-based ensemble methods have also demonstrated effectiveness in time series forecasting tasks. Methods like Random Forests and Gradient Boosting Machines (GBM) offer robust alternative approaches, particularly when dealing with datasets marked by missing values and non-linear relationships. While these models are generally designed for traditional supervised tasks, they can be adapted for time series through lagged variable transformations and rolling forecasting origin techniques.

For example, in predicting economic indicators like GDP growth or unemployment rates, ensemble models can accommodate a wide variety of input features, such as past economic data and external market indicators, offering predictions that are resilient to market noise and structural shifts.

One more innovative framework is the use of Gaussian Processes (GPs) for time series forecasting. GPs provide a probabilistic approach to modeling time series data, offering not only predictions but also uncertainty estimates, which are crucial in financial decision-making where confidence intervals can significantly influence risk management.

In practice, GPs have been applied to forecast commodity prices, leveraging their flexible covariance structures to model complex time dependencies and incorporate market volatility. The uncertainty estimates produced by Gaussian Processes provide valuable insights into potential forecasting errors, aiding in the formulation of hedging strategies.

Despite their promise, machine learning models come with challenges that must be carefully addressed in financial time series forecasting. One fundamental challenge is the need for extensive and high-quality datasets that capture the multifaceted factors influencing market movements. Moreover, financial time series data can be non-stationary, featuring evolving statistical properties over time. To tackle these challenges, comprehensive data preprocessing—including trend and seasonality decomposition, normalization, and smoothing techniques—is crucial.

Another pertinent challenge involves model interpretability and transparency, paramount in financial environments where decisions must be justified to stakeholders and regulatory bodies. While traditional models like ARIMA offer clear mechanisms for interpretation, machine learning models often require additional tools, such as SHAP (SHapley Additive exPlanations) or LIME (Local Interpretable Model-agnostic Explanations), to render their decision-making processes transparent.

Furthermore, model validation and testing pose significant considerations in the financial domain. Strategies such as walk-forward validation and train-validation splits are essential to ensure that predictive models maintain generality and robustness across unseen data and shifting market conditions.

The balance between computational complexity and interpretability is another dynamic that practitioners must manage. While complex neural networks offer enhanced precision, their high computational costs and underlying complexity necessitate a measured approach to deployment, ensuring appropriate cost-benefit considerations align with financial goals.

Recent advancements such as Attention Mechanisms have further enriched time series forecasting capabilities. By selectively focusing on significant parts of input sequences, attention-based models improve the accuracy of predictions in scenarios characterized by disparate temporal patterns. This innovation holds significant potential for enhancing time series models' interpretability, showcasing which time periods or events have the most influence on forecasts.

Machine learning's applicability to time series forecasting in finance marks a dynamic convergence of technological and analytical prowess. The exploration of sophisticated models, from LSTMs and CNNs to ensemble techniques and GPs, equips market participants with cutting-edge tools to anticipate future trends in an ever-evolving landscape. As computational resources expand and algorithms advance, the synergy between traditional expertise and machine learning innovation will continue to redefine the boundaries of financial forecasting, catalyzing strategies that navigate the complexities of market dynamics with unprecedented precision and foresight. Through continued research and development, machine learning models promise to elevate time series forecasting to new heights, pioneering unseen possibilities in financial markets analysis.

7.6   Model Evaluation and Validation

In the domain of financial machine learning, the robustness and reliability of models are paramount. Model evaluation and validation serve as critical processes that ensure a machine learning model's predictive power and reliability in real-world applications. This section delves into the key techniques and considerations for evaluating and validating models within financial settings, highlighting methodologies to assess model performance, prevent overfitting, and optimize model selection.

The initial step in model evaluation involves choosing appropriate performance metrics that align with the model's objectives and the specific characteristics of financial data. For classification tasks, common metrics include accuracy, precision, recall, and F1-score, each providing distinct insights into a model's performance. For instance, in credit scoring, precision and recall are crucial, as they indicate the model's ability to correctly identify defaulters while minimizing false positives, directly impacting economic outcomes.

Accuracy, while a straightforward measure, often requires careful consideration in imbalanced datasets. In fraud detection, for example, the sheer number of non-fraudulent transactions can skew accuracy metrics, misleading stakeholders about a model's true effectiveness. In such cases, precision-recall curves and area under the ROC curve (AUC-ROC) offer more informative views of performance, highlighting trade-offs between true positive rates and false positive rates.

For regression-based tasks, common metrics include Mean Absolute Error (MAE), Mean Squared Error (MSE), and Root Mean Squared Error (RMSE). These metrics assess the deviation between predicted and actual values, offering quantitative insights into model accuracy. In financial forecasting, selecting the appropriate error metric is vital, as forecasts with large deviations can lead to significant monetary losses.

Once performance metrics are selected, model validation techniques are employed to assess how well a model will generalize to unseen data. Cross-validation, a robust statistical method, divides the dataset into multiple subsets, training and testing the model iteratively on different partitions. The most prevalent form, k-fold cross-validation, splits data into k groups, using each for testing while training on the remaining folds. In financial contexts, time-series cross-validation methods are essential, as they respect the temporal relationships inherent in financial data, ensuring that future data points are not used to predict the past.

Among these, walk-forward validation is particularly well-suited for time-series data, where the model is trained on a moving window of data and tested on the subsequent periods, simulating a real-world forecasting process. This approach helps in understanding how well the model adapts to new data and changing market conditions.

Beyond cross-validation, preventing overfitting—a common challenge in financial modeling—merits significant attention. Overfitting occurs when a model captures noise rather than underlying patterns, leading to impressive training results while performing poorly on unseen data. Techniques to mitigate overfitting include regularization methods, such as L1 (LASSO) and L2 (Ridge) regularization, which add penalty terms to the model's loss function to discourage overly complex models by shrinking their coefficients.

Dropout is another technique predominantly used in neural networks, randomly omitting units during training to prevent dependencies on particular nodes, thus enhancing model robustness. Ensemble methods like bagging and boosting also combat overfitting by combining predictions from multiple models, each trained on different subsets of the data, and regularizing variance in predictions.

Hyperparameter tuning forms another crucial aspect of model validation, as hyperparameter settings significantly influence a model's performance. Techniques like grid search and random search test combinations of hyperparameters exhaustively and stochastically, respectively. More advanced methods, such as Bayesian optimization, iteratively refine the search process by building a probabilistic model of the objective function, focusing computational resources on promising hyperparameter spaces.

In practice, leveraging tools such as validation curves and learning curves provides a visual understanding of a model's performance under varying hyperparameter settings and dataset sizes. Learning curves, in particular, illustrate how a model's error changes with the amount of training data, offering insights into whether more data is likely to improve model performance.

Model evaluation also extends beyond technical metrics, encompassing considerations of model interpretability, scalability, and deployment feasibility. In finance, where decisions often require justification to stakeholders, models must be interpretable, providing clear insights into decision mechanisms. Tools like SHAP values and LIME play a pivotal role in explaining model predictions, helping stakeholders trust and understand the model's outputs.

Scalability becomes a focal point when deploying models to production, especially in high-frequency trading environments where rapid decision-making is required. Evaluating a model's computational efficiency and latency is crucial in these scenarios, ensuring the model's predictions align with operational constraints and performance expectations.

Furthermore, potential risks, including model drift and data leakage, require vigilance. Model drift, where the model's performance degrades over time due to changes in data distribution, can be addressed through continuous monitoring and periodic retraining using up-to-date data. Data leakage, the inadvertent use of future information during model training, can lead to overly optimistic performance estimates; robust data handling practices and proper validation frameworks are essential to prevent this issue.

In regulatory contexts, ensuring compliance with financial regulations and ethical standards is imperative. Evaluating models for bias and fairness, particularly in sensitive applications like credit scoring, demands careful scrutiny of training datasets and algorithmic processes to prevent discrimination or unintended harm.

Model evaluation and validation constitute foundational pillars in the construction and deployment of financial machine learning models. By employing rigorous validation frameworks, selecting relevant metrics, and addressing data-driven challenges, practitioners ensure that models remain reliable, interpretable, and aligned with strategic objectives. The process is inherently iterative, involving continuous learning and adaptation to evolving market dynamics and technological advancements. Through these practices, financial institutions and analysts equip themselves with models that not only withstand the complexities of financial markets but also enhance their strategic capabilities, fostering innovation and informed decision-making in an increasingly data-centric world.

7.7   Advanced Techniques and Deep Learning

The incorporation of advanced machine learning techniques, particularly deep learning, has revolutionized the landscape of financial analytics and forecasting. These methods, rooted in the complexity and flexibility of neural networks, open new vistas for handling vast datasets and uncovering non-linear patterns that traditional models might overlook. In this section, we explore the myriad ways advanced techniques and deep learning are applied in finance, the challenges they address, and their transformative potential for market prediction and decision-making.

Deep learning, a subset of machine learning grounded in artificial neural networks, is celebrated for its ability to model intricate patterns and relationships within data. The architecture of deep learning models—comprising multiple layers of interconnected neurons—facilitates the hierarchical extraction of features, making them especially adept at capturing complex non-linear relationships. These capabilities are particularly relevant to financial markets, which are inherently multifaceted and influenced by myriad factors.

One of the cornerstones of deep learning in finance is the application of feedforward neural networks. These networks, while conceptually simple, serve as the foundational architecture for more sophisticated deep learning models. They are particularly useful in forecasting tasks where the relationship between input features and target variables can be leveraged to make accurate predictions. For instance, in stock price prediction, feedforward networks can integrate various indicators—including historical prices, trading volumes, and macroeconomic variables—to generate forward-looking price estimations.

Recurrent Neural Networks (RNNs), particularly Long Short-Term Memory (LSTM) networks, are another groundbreaking deep learning innovation, specifically tailored for sequential data modeling. LSTMs address the shortcoming of traditional RNNs by incorporating gated cells that retain information over extended sequences, thus excelling at processing time series data. In finance, LSTMs prove invaluable for tasks like modeling temporal dependencies in stock price data, enabling more nuanced and dynamic forecasting due to their ability to leverage long-term market trends and patterns.

The synergy between CNNs (Convolutional Neural Networks) and LSTMs underscores another advanced technique—hybrid architectures that capitalize on the strength of each network type. CNNs, with their prowess in feature extraction, work in tandem with LSTMs to handle complex sequences in financial data. This collaboration is evident in applications like high-frequency trading, where CNNs first derive relevant features from multi-dimensional input data before LSTMs model the temporal dependencies increasingly characteristic of market movements.

Autoencoders, an unsupervised learning technique also stemming from the deep learning domain, have found their niche in finance for anomaly detection and data compression tasks. By learning a compressed representation of input data, autoencoders can effectively identify patterns that deviate from the norm, facilitating the detection of anomalies such as fraudulent transactions or atypical market conditions. Their capacity for dimensionality reduction also aids in preprocessing large volumes of financial data, distilling essential features while discarding noise— crucial for efficient data processing and model training.

Another burgeoning application in advanced machine learning is Generative Adversarial Networks (GANs). GANs, consisting of a generator and a discriminator network in a competitive setting, have been leveraged in finance for tasks such as scenario generation and synthetic data creation. For instance, GANs can simulate plausible market conditions, enhancing stress testing practices by generating extreme yet realistic scenarios that gauge a portfolio's resilience against unexpected market shifts. This capability supports risk management and strategic planning processes, offering actionable insights into potential vulnerabilities.

Deep reinforcement learning signifies another frontier of advanced techniques in finance, combining the decision-making framework of reinforcement learning with the hierarchical learning capacities of deep neural networks. It empowers agents to learn optimal strategies through interactions with the market environment, adapting autonomously to changes. Financial domains such as automated trading and portfolio management benefit significantly from this approach, as models iteratively refine their strategies to maximize returns or minimize risk, supporting dynamic and responsive investment decisions.

The use of Transformers, originally developed for natural language processing, marks another leap in applying deep learning to finance. Transformer's attention mechanism allows it to focus selectively on relevant parts of the input data, proving invaluable for time series forecasting where not all points carry equal significance. This selective focus has enhanced strategies in trading, credit risk analysis, and even market sentiment evaluation, providing powerful tools for parsing through extensive datasets efficiently and effectively.

Despite their vast potential, deploying advanced deep learning techniques in finance is not without challenges. The field demands high computational resources, posing logistical challenges, particularly for institutions with limited technological infrastructures. Moreover, the data-intensive nature of deep learning requires access to extensive, high-quality datasets—often a limiting factor in financial environments.

Another critical challenge is model interpretability. Deep learning models, often perceived as "black boxes," raise concerns about transparency and accountability—especially in finance, where decision-making implications are profound. Efforts to address these challenges include the development of interpretable model frameworks and post-hoc explanation tools like SHAP and LIME, which provide insights into model decision processes, enhancing stakeholder trust and compliance.

Overfitting remains a notable concern, given the complex architectures intrinsic to deep learning models. Techniques like dropout, early stopping, and regularization are essential to ensure that models generalize beyond training data and maintain robustness in fluctuating market conditions.

Finally, ethical considerations and biases in model training require vigilance. Financial data can reflect historical biases and systemic inequalities, necessitating conscientious efforts to ensure models not only predict accurately but also uphold ethical standards and promote fair financial practices.

The landscape of financial analysis is experiencing an era of profound transformation fueled by advanced machine learning and deep learning techniques. These technologies unlock unprecedented possibilities in market prediction, risk management, and decision-making, equipping financial institutions to navigate complexity with precision and foresight. As research progresses and capabilities enhance, the collaboration between technological innovation and financial acumen promises to drive even greater advancements, perpetually redefining how markets are understood, anticipated, and influenced. Through synergy with emerging data sources, continuous learning, and ethical consideration, deep learning stands poised to chart the future of finance, crafting a narrative of data-driven opportunities and transformative potential.

Chapter 8

Algorithm Design and Backtesting

This chapter delves into the essentials of designing robust trading algorithms, emphasizing principles like modularity and scalability. It outlines the process of data collection and strategy development, underscoring the importance of thorough testing. Backtesting frameworks are explored as critical tools for validating strategies against historical data, accompanied by discussions on effective performance metrics. Optimization techniques are examined to refine algorithm parameters while preventing overfitting. The chapter also highlights the deployment of algorithms in live environments and the continual monitoring required to sustain performance and compliance in dynamic markets.

8.1   Principles of Algorithm Design

Designing algorithms for trading requires a deep understanding of both financial markets and algorithmic processes. The foundational principles of algorithm design are essential for the creation of robust, scalable, and efficient trading systems. Let's explore these principles in detail, emphasizing the crucial aspects of modularity, scalability, and efficiency.

At the core of successful algorithm design is modularity, which refers to structuring the algorithm in discrete, well-defined components. Each module should perform a distinct function, such as data retrieval, signal generation, risk management, or trading execution. By compartmentalizing complex systems into smaller tasks, developers can manage and troubleshoot these tasks more efficiently. Modularity not only facilitates debugging and code maintenance but also allows for easier updates and modifications. When market conditions change or new strategies emerge, modular systems can adapt quickly with minimal disruption. For instance, replacing a module responsible for a specific execution strategy can be achieved with minimal impact on the remaining system components.

Scalability is another cornerstone of algorithmic design, enabling the algorithm to function across various markets and timeframes without significant re-engineering. An algorithm that is scalable can handle increasing amounts of data and transactions, adjust to different trading volumes, and adapt to various trading environments. The key to achieving scalability lies in efficient data handling and processing, as well as optimizing computing resources. Designing algorithms with parallel processing capabilities exemplifies scalable design. For instance, using distributed computing solutions such as Apache Hadoop or leveraging cloud-based infrastructures can significantly enhance an algorithm's ability to process vast amounts of market data efficiently.

Efficiency in algorithm design pertains to both computational and operational efficiency. Computational efficiency ensures that algorithms execute rapidly with minimal latency, an essential aspect for high-frequency trading where milliseconds can determine profitability. This efficiency is achieved through optimized coding practices, such as minimizing loop operations, effectively managing memory allocation, and choosing the right data structures. Implementers must carefully select algorithms that provide a balance between speed and accuracy to avoid unnecessary computational burdens.

Operational efficiency, on the other hand, involves designing algorithms that can execute trades with minimal market impact and transaction costs. Algorithms must be developed to handle real-time data streams, swiftly respond to market changes, and execute buy/sell orders seamlessly. Concepts like order slicing—dividing large orders into smaller ones to reduce market footprint—and employing smart order routing strategies highlight operational efficiency within algorithm execution.

Incorporating robustness into algorithm design safeguards against unexpected market events and data anomalies. Robustness can be achieved by implementing safeguards, such as stop-loss orders, maximum drawdown limits, and circuit breakers, which automatically halt trading activity upon detecting abnormal market conditions. For instance, the infamous "flash crash" of 2010 highlighted the importance of such protective measures, where algorithms need clear limit settings to prevent cascading losses.

Risk management is an integral part of trading algorithm design. Effective algorithms assess risk by calculating potential losses under various scenarios and adjusting strategies accordingly. Techniques such as Value at Risk (VaR), Conditional Value at Risk (CVaR), and stress testing are commonly used to evaluate risk exposure. Implementing a sound risk management framework ensures that algorithms not only aim for profit maximization but also safeguard capital under adverse conditions.

Example-driven algorithm development is critical for grounding the design in real-world applicability. Backtesting with historical data allows developers to iterate on their designs by evaluating performance, identifying weaknesses, and understanding the dynamics of their strategies. Examples include testing a moving average crossover strategy against a decade's worth of market data to assess its robustness and profitability across different market cycles.

Conceptual clarity in design also plays a pivotal role. Clear, well-defined objectives are essential for aligning the algorithm's functionality with the intended trading strategy. Whether it's capturing spreads in a market-neutral setup or exploiting momentum in trending markets, each design choice should reflect these objectives clearly. Clear documentation of the algorithm's logic and assumptions helps maintain fidelity between the developer's intent and the algorithm's actions, reducing the risk of misalignment in execution.

The design process should also incorporate adaptability, ensuring that algorithms remain relevant as markets evolve. Markets are dynamic, influenced by various macroeconomic factors, technological advancements, and regulatory changes. Algorithms that are adaptable can modify their parameters or switch strategies in response to new market conditions, typically incorporating machine learning techniques to augment adaptability. For instance, reinforcement learning algorithms can adaptively learn optimal policies by interacting with the trading environment directly.

Simulating real-world conditions is essential in the algorithm design process to ensure the algorithm's resilience and effectiveness. Simulations allow developers to test algorithms under hypothetical scenarios that mirror potential future market conditions, including high volatility, liquidity shortages, and varied execution slippage levels. Such simulated environments provide opportunities to refine algorithms further before deployment in live trading contexts.

Finally, algorithm design must integrate compliance measures to adhere to the ever-evolving regulatory landscape. Regulations such as the Markets in Financial Instruments Directive (MiFID II) and the Dodd-Frank Act impose stringent requirements on algorithmic trading activities, particularly around transparency and reporting. Therefore, algorithms should be designed with built-in compliance checks to ensure they function within regulatory frameworks, thereby preventing legal repercussions and promoting ethical trading practices.

In designing a trading algorithm, success is embedded in thoughtful planning and the integration of these core principles. By focusing on modularity, scalability, efficiency, robustness, and adaptability, developers create algorithms that are not only effective in optimizing trading strategies but also resilient in navigating the complexities of the financial markets.

8.2   Data Collection and Processing

Data collection and processing form the backbone of any algorithmic trading strategy. The quality and timeliness of the data directly impact the effectiveness and profitability of trading algorithms. This section explores the methodologies involved in collecting and processing data, emphasizing the importance of data quality, storage solutions, and real-time processing capabilities necessary for today's fast-paced trading environments.

The first step in the data collection process is identifying the types of data required for developing trading algorithms. Common data types include market data, such as price, volume, and order book information, as well as financial statements, economic indicators, and alternative data sources like social media sentiment or satellite imagery. Market data can be further classified into historical and real-time data. Historical data is essential for backtesting and creating baseline models, while real-time data feeds are crucial for executing algorithms in live market conditions.

Once the dataset requirements are articulated, the next phase is sourcing the data. Data can be sourced from a variety of providers, ranging from traditional exchanges that provide price and volume data, to data aggregators and specialized firms that offer enriched datasets like tick-by-tick data or sentiment scores. The choice of data provider often depends on the specific requirements of the algorithm and the trading strategy. For high-frequency trading, low-latency data feeds from dedicated financial data services such as Bloomberg or Thomson Reuters might be necessary. In contrast, for algorithms based on fundamental analysis, financial statement data from sources like EDGAR or Bloomberg Terminals can be invaluable.

After sourcing, data ingestion involves systematically collecting and organizing data for storage and processing. Data is often ingested in real-time through APIs that connect to data providers or via batch processing where data is compiled at set intervals. A robust ingestion system must be capable of handling spiky traffic and high volumes of data without loss or delay. Stream processing platforms like Apache Kafka or real-time databases such as InfluxDB and kdb+ offer high throughput options essential for efficient data ingestion and preprocessing.

The quality of data is paramount in trading algorithm performance. Data quality pertains not only to accuracy but also to consistency, completeness, timeliness, and relevancy. Inaccurate or outdated information can lead to erroneous signals and suboptimal trading decisions. Therefore, implementing data validation processes is crucial. Techniques like cross-referencing dataset values against multiple sources or using error detection algorithms to flag anomalies help maintain data integrity.

Data cleaning is another necessary step to ensure the dataset is usable and error-free. Cleaning tasks may include removing duplicate entries, filling missing values, adjusting for corporate actions (such as stock splits or dividends), and aligning timestamps across different datasets. Consistent formatting of data points, including standardizing date formats and decimal placements, further aids in reducing computational errors during analysis.

Once cleaned, data storage becomes a critical consideration. Efficient storage solutions need to balance availability, security, scalability, and cost. For large volumes of historical data, cloud storage solutions such as AWS S3, Google Cloud Storage, or specialized time-series databases enable flexible and scalable data management. These solutions not only provide virtual access across different geographies but also support redundancy and failover capabilities, ensuring data persistence.

Real-time processing capabilities are essential for latency-sensitive trading strategies. Real-time processing involves the continuous input, processing, and output of data within milliseconds. Technologies such as Apache Storm, Flink, or Spark Streaming are designed for real-time data handling, enabling algorithms to respond promptly to rapid market changes. Using these technologies, trading systems can observe data streams, detect patterns, and trigger actions or alerts instantly based on pre-defined rules or evolving conditions.

A critical aspect of real-time data processing is overcoming the inevitable lag and noise that characterizes market data. Latency issues, resulting from network delays, need tackling through the use of high-speed networks, distributed computing, and proximity hosting or colocation services. Reducing noise can involve statistical techniques like smoothing functions or employing machine learning models to discern informative signals from high-volume data streams systematically.

Integration of machine learning in data processing enhances both predictive accuracy and pattern recognition, especially when dealing with vast and unstructured datasets. Methods such as natural language processing (NLP) extract sentiment from news or social media, expanding the breadth of data beyond traditional market feeds. Similarly, anomaly detection algorithms can identify outliers or unusual market movements that might indicate trading opportunities or the need for protective action.

Throughout data collection and processing, ensuring compliance with data privacy laws and regulations such as GDPR or CCPA is imperative. Compliance involves obtaining necessary data usage permissions, anonymizing sensitive data when necessary, and securing datasets against unauthorized access. This step preserves the ethical standing of trading activities while protecting client and proprietary data.

Finally, data processing workflows should incorporate redundancy and backup mechanisms to prevent data loss in case of system failures. Techniques such as data deduplication, replication, and regular backups ensure that data remains available and resilient to disruptions. Automated data reconciliation practices, triggered at regular intervals, help verify transaction lists, while real-time alerts can notify stakeholders of discrepancies or potential system failures.

Conclusively, a comprehensive data collection and processing framework is fundamental to building robust trading algorithms. It ensures a high level of data integrity, availability, and responsiveness, forming the foundation upon which trading decisions are executed. By investing in reliable data infrastructures and methodologies, algorithmic traders position themselves to effectively capture and capitalize on opportunities while mitigating risks inherent in the financial markets.

8.3   Strategy Development and Testing

The development and testing of trading strategies is a critical component in the algorithmic trading lifecycle. This section delves into the methodology of constructing trading strategies, including the formulation of hypotheses, iterative testing, and refinement processes. It further highlights the importance of rigorous testing frameworks and the disciplined approach necessary to ensure the reliability and profitability of trading algorithms.

Central to strategy development is the clear articulation of a trading hypothesis. A hypothesis in trading specifies the expected behavior or condition under which a trading strategy should perform effectively. For example, a hypothesis may state that "stocks experiencing a sudden increase in trading volume, alongside positive earnings announcements, are likely to outperform the market over the following week." The clarity in hypothesis formulation allows for measurable objectives and reduces ambiguity, providing a benchmark for evaluating strategy performance.

The choice of strategy is often guided by the trader's specific objectives, risk tolerance, and market understanding. Strategies can broadly be categorized into mean-reversion, trend-following, arbitrage, and market-making, among others. Mean-reversion strategies, for example, assume that prices will revert to a mean over time, and trend-following strategies aim to capitalize on sustained market movements. Each strategy type requires distinctive logic and execution mechanisms, tailored to capture predicted market dynamics based on historical behavior.

Once the hypothesis and strategy framework are articulated, the next phase is defining precise entry and exit signals or criteria. Entry signals might be based on technical indicators, such as moving averages or momentum oscillators, while exit signals could involve profit targets or stop-loss limits. These signals serve as automated triggers within the algorithm, specifying exactly when to initiate or close trades. Ensuring precise and unambiguous rule definitions is critical to avoid discrepancies and misinterpretations during live trading.

Backtesting forms the cornerstone of strategy testing, enabling traders to objectively evaluate their trading strategy against historical data. This process involves running the strategy in a simulated environment based on the dataset reflecting actual market conditions from the past. A crucial element of backtesting is the maintenance of realistic assumptions, such as accounting for transaction costs, slippage, and potential execution delays. Overlooking these factors can lead to overestimation of strategy performance and subsequent underperformance in real-world conditions.

During backtesting, a variety of metrics are employed to evaluate strategy efficacy. These include the Sharpe ratio, which measures returns relative to risk; maximum drawdown, which assesses the largest peak-to-trough decline; and the profit factor, comparing gross profits to gross losses. Analyzing these metrics helps in gaining insights into the risk and return characteristics of the strategy, allowing for refinements and targeted adjustments.

Nevertheless, the risk of overfitting during backtesting cannot be overstated. Overfitting occurs when a strategy is overly tailored to past data, capturing noise rather than genuine market patterns. This is a common pitfall as traders tend to adjust parameters exhaustively to achieve the desired backtest outcome, sacrificing robustness in the process. One way to mitigate overfitting is by incorporating out-of-sample testing and walk-forward analysis. Out-of-sample testing evaluates the strategy on a separate data set not involved in the backtest, while walk-forward analysis methodically assesses the strategy over successive periods to ensure consistent performance.

Aside from quantitative backtests, scenario analysis and stress testing play vital roles in examining strategy resilience under extreme market conditions. Scenario analysis evaluates the performance impact under predetermined hypothetical scenarios, such as economic shocks or sudden interest rate changes. Stress tests impose extreme, yet plausible, market situations to understand the threshold beyond which strategy breaks down, providing insights into potential vulnerabilities.

Iterative refinement is intrinsic to the development process. As gaps or inefficiencies are identified through testing, iterative adjustments refine strategy rules, logic, and parameters, gradually perfecting predictive capabilities. Incorporating feedback loops, where insights gained from the testing phase further inform revisions, ensures continuous improvement. For example, adjusting a stop-loss threshold based on high-drawdown periods could significantly limit risk exposure.

Implementing machine learning techniques into strategy development introduces adaptability and flexibility, particularly in analyzing large-scale multivariate data. Techniques such as reinforcement learning enable strategies to improve their decision-making by interacting with simulated markets and learning optimal actions through trial and error. Nonetheless, implementing machine-learning strategies requires a deep understanding of the assumptions, limitations, and underlying biases of the deployed models, along with rigorous feature selection and reduction processes to prevent overfitting and ensure interpretability.

A disciplined record-keeping system is indispensable for tracking strategy adjustments, hypothesis changes, and testing outcomes. Maintaining detailed logs offers a comprehensive history of progressions and informs future decisions. This documentation becomes a reference point for validating developments, revisiting assumptions, and ensuring adherence to pre-defined trading guidelines.

Developers need to be aware of the regulatory implications of deploying any developed strategies in live markets. Strategies involving sensitive information or high-frequency trading apparatuses are subject to enhanced scrutiny, demanding traders abide by regulations such as the MiFID II or Rule 15c3-5 in the United States. Ensuring that compliance measures are embedded within strategy logic preempts legal complications and instills confidence in the trading operation.

In sum, the meticulous development and testing of trading strategies within algorithmic frameworks provide a rigorous pathway for transforming market insights into actionable strategies. By synthesizing clear hypotheses, thorough testing protocols, and adaptive refinement cycles, traders position themselves to achieve sustained and reliable performance in the multifaceted landscape of financial markets.

8.4 Backtesting Frameworks

Backtesting frameworks are instrumental in assessing the viability and performance of trading strategies under historical market conditions. By simulating trades against past data, these frameworks allow traders to evaluate how a strategy might have performed, revealing strengths, weaknesses, and areas for optimization. This section delves into the intricacies of backtesting frameworks, exploring their components, methodologies, and the critical considerations necessary to derive meaningful insights.

The core objective of any backtesting framework is to provide a detailed, unbiased analysis of a trading strategy's potential performance. At its essence, backtesting replicates the decision-making process of a strategy, applying specified rules to historical data in a sequential manner. By so doing, it seeks to uncover potential profitability and identify risks associated with the strategy without the uncertainties associated with future markets.

A robust backtesting framework comprises several key components. Primarily, it involves a data loader that accurately fetches historical data required for testing. This data must be comprehensive, including price, volume, and market depth across all relevant time frames. Moreover, data integrity is paramount; errors, outliers, or incomplete datasets can severely skew results, leading traders to false conclusions. Consequently, pre-backtesting data validation steps are essential to ensure accuracy and completeness.

The next component is the execution engine, which faithfully replicates the mechanics of executing trades within historical data. This engine must account for trading costs, including commissions, fees, and slippage, to provide realistic outcomes. It should also consider order delays and partial fills when dealing with large orders or thin markets, as these factors can significantly affect execution prices.

In addition, the backtesting setup needs a performance analysis module. This component evaluates various performance metrics, such as profit and loss (P&L), drawdown, and risk-adjusted returns like the Sharpe and Sortino ratios. Moreover, it may include sensitivity and scenario analyses to understand the behavior of the strategy under different market regimes.

The choice of backtesting methodology significantly influences the insights derived from the framework. Two predominant backtesting approaches are static and dynamic backtesting.

Static backtesting involves running a trading strategy over a fixed historical period without making any adjustments to strategy parameters during the test. This approach provides a straightforward, objective evaluation of performance over numerous market cycles. By using static backtesting, traders gain insights into how a strategy might behave without interference, thereby identifying inherent strengths and weaknesses.

Dynamic backtesting, on the other hand, allows for parameter modifications in response to changing market conditions during the testing period. It reflects a more realistic trading environment where strategies adapt to evolving data. Dynamic backtesting often incorporates machine learning models for pattern recognition and predictive insights, enabling strategies to adjust signals or weightings based on real-time learning.

Both static and dynamic frameworks have their merits and ideal use cases. While static backtesting excels in exposing systemic strategy flaws or overfitting, dynamic backtesting's adaptability is more aligned with day-to-day trading nuances and market shifts. Hence, traders should choose a methodology that best aligns with the strategy's aims and complexity.

Backtesting's credibility hinges on realistic assumptions about the market environment. Critical among these is the assumption of constant market liquidity. However, during certain market conditions, such as financial crises or specific economic events, liquidity can evaporate, leading to higher execution costs and potential losses. Testing frameworks must therefore simulate varying liquidity conditions, especially for strategies targeting less liquid assets or markets.

Another aspect is transaction slippage, the deviation of actual trade execution prices from expected prices due to market movements. Evaluating this requires incorporating slippage models based on factors like order size and market volatility, offering more refined execution approximations.

Advanced frameworks integrate simulation environments that mimic market microstructure, providing traders with granular insight into how strategies interact with market participants. These environments can test market impact and the propagation of trades, highlighting whether the strategy could influence or be influenced by other participants' actions, particularly in high-frequency trading scenarios.

Institutional backtesting environments might provide access to co-location or virtual market simulations, eliminating network latency to replicate realistic high-frequency trading conditions. They simulate exchanges' order book dynamics, testing if strategies can withstand latency arbitrage or other anti-gaming mechanisms.

Comparatively, leveraging machine learning within backtesting frameworks is becoming increasingly prevalent. Methods like reinforcement learning create agents capable of interaction-dependent learning, dynamically adjusting strategies as they "learn" through simulated trades. Here, frameworks facilitate continuous learning environments where models iteratively refine their trading rules based on performance and feedback loops.

Validation techniques such as cross-verification across multiple datasets are vital to avoid overfitting, a common pitfall where strategies perform excellently on past data but fail under unseen market conditions.   Walk-forward analysis, for instance, divides historical data into training and testing segments performed sequentially, enhancing predictive robustness.

Given the breadth of available backtesting platforms, traders have several options depending on their resources and the strategy's requirements. Professional and open-source platforms like QuantConnect, Backtrader, or Zipline offer comprehensive backtesting suites supported by abundant data and customization options. These platforms often include backtesting APIs, allowing traders to script tailored logic suitably aligned with their trading models.

Ultimately, backtesting frameworks are as effective as the diligence and scrutiny applied in their use. They provide critical insights but must be complemented by sound risk management practices, sensitivity to assumptions made, and an awareness of the potential pitfalls of over-optimistic results. Through meticulous evaluation and refinement, these frameworks remain indispensable tools for validating strategies, enhancing confidence before live market deployment, and guarding against impulsive decision-making in the multifaceted world of trading.

8.5   Performance Metrics and Evaluation

The evaluation of a trading algorithm's performance is a multifaceted process that involves the analysis of a wide array of metrics. These metrics provide quantitative insights into the risk, return, and efficiency of a trading strategy, ultimately guiding decision-making processes regarding refinement, deployment, and scaling. This section explores various performance metrics commonly used in the evaluation of trading algorithms, discussing the significance, calculation, and interpretation of each.

Among the most critical performance metrics is the **Net Profit**, which measures the total profit after accounting for all trading-related expenses, such as commissions and slippage. While net profit provides

182

a direct measure of financial success, it does not contextualize performance; hence, it is often complemented by risk-adjusted metrics.

The **Sharpe Ratio**, a cornerstone of performance evaluation, quantifies returns relative to their risk. It is calculated as the average excess return over the risk-free rate divided by the standard deviation of returns. A higher Sharpe Ratio indicates more return per unit of risk, suggesting an efficiently managed strategy. For instance, a Sharpe Ratio of 1 indicates that the strategy has earned one unit of return for every unit of risk—considered a satisfactory benchmark by many investors. When evaluating Sharpe Ratios, it is essential to compare them to those of similar strategies or benchmarks, such as index funds, for a relative understanding of performance.

The **Sortino Ratio** refines the Sharpe Ratio by isolating downside volatility, recognizing that investors are more sensitive to losses than gains. The Sortino Ratio assesses returns against only the downside deviation, providing a more conservative measure of performance. A high Sortino Ratio suggests that volatility is primarily due to positive returns, aligning with investor preferences. For example, strategies leveraging options might register high volatility due to sporadic gains, benefiting from evaluation through the Sortino Ratio rather than the Sharpe Ratio.

Maximum Drawdown reflects the largest peak-to-trough decline in a trading strategy's equity curve, indicating the worst observed loss. This metric is invaluable for risk management as it highlights the potential losses investors could face. A strategy with a maximum drawdown of 20% means that, at one point, the strategy lost 20% from its highest value before recovering. Evaluating maximum drawdown, alongside recovery time—the time taken to recoup the drawdown—provides insights into a strategy's recovery speed and resilience.

Another crucial metric, the **Calmar Ratio**, computes the annualized return over the maximum drawdown, providing a balanced perspective of return versus risk. A Calmar Ratio of 3, for instance, indicates that the strategy earns three times the return of the risk from the worst-case loss. This metric is particularly relevant for funds and high-net-worth individuals, assisting in budget allocations across diverse strategies.

Furthermore, **Alpha and Beta**, originating from the Capital Asset Pricing Model (CAPM), measure risk-adjusted performance relative to the market. Alpha represents the strategy's excess return over a benchmark, attributing performance to the manager's skill rather than broader market movements. In contrast, Beta expresses sensitivity to market moves, with a Beta above 1 indicating greater market exposure. A strategy with positive Alpha, coupled with a Beta around 1, exemplifies adept market navigation with moderate systemic risk.

The **Information Ratio** extends the concept of excess return by contrasting a strategy's returns against those of a benchmark, scaled for tracking error (the standard deviation of the return differences). Fundamental in hedge fund evaluation, the Information Ratio gauges a strategy's consistency in outperforming the benchmark. A ratio above 0.5 typically signifies strong performance, reflecting consistent excess returns after accounting for risk.

For high-frequency trading algorithms, **Profit Factor** is a key metric, defined as the ratio of gross profits to gross losses. A Profit Factor exceeding one indicates profitable execution, while a lower ratio suggests losses dominate. This metric attributes performance to volumes and trade efficiency, essential for strategies involving numerous small trades.

In evaluating performance, trade-level data provides granular insights into execution efficiency and market impact. Trade metrics such as **Win Rate**, **Average Win**, **Average Loss**, and **Expected Payoff** quantify profitability probabilities and risk thresholds. For instance, a 60% win rate with an average win greater than average loss underscores a strategy's favorable risk-reward profile.

Assessing **Market Impact** evaluates the strategy's influence on market prices. For larger funds, market impact directly affects P&L and is quantified by measuring the deviation of actual trade prices from mid-market prices pre-execution. Algorithms should aim to minimize this impact, preserving favorable pricing conditions.

Capacity and Scalability measure a strategy's potential return as assets under management grow. Algorithms that trade liquid assets in high volumes generally scale better compared to those dependent on niche markets or smaller capacities. Evaluating transaction costs as trade size increases helps gauge capacity limits.

Beyond raw performance metrics, qualitative aspects contribute to evaluation. These include liquidity considerations, strategy complexity, regulatory constraints, and alignment with investors' risk appetites. Evaluators should value these aspects alongside quantitative metrics, ensuring comprehensive justification of strategy selection.

Integrating a robust evaluation framework into algorithmic trading processes aids in maintaining operational discipline and sustained performance. By routinely measuring, comparing, and interpreting these metrics, traders and fund managers can navigate potential pitfalls, optimize existing strategies, and develop superior, adaptive trading systems.

8.6 Optimization and Parameter Tuning

Optimization and parameter tuning are pivotal aspects of refining trading algorithms, enhancing their performance while balancing risk and reward. The process involves adjusting algorithmic parameters to achieve the best possible outcomes under various market conditions without succumbing to overfitting, which occurs when an algorithm performs excellently on historical data but fails to adapt to new data. This section provides an in-depth examination of optimization techniques, the importance of robust parameter tuning, and strategies for achieving an optimal balance in algorithmic trading.

Optimizing a trading strategy begins with identifying key parameters that impact performance. These parameters could include technical indicators, like moving average periods or RSI thresholds, risk management rules, such as stop-loss levels and take-profit points, or execution settings that dictate order size and timing. The choice of parameters depends on the strategy's objectives and the underlying market dynamics it aims to exploit.

One fundamental optimization technique is **Grid Search**, which involves systematically evaluating a pre-defined set of parameter combinations. Traders define ranges and incremental values for each parameter, creating a grid of possible combinations. By conducting backtests across this grid, traders can identify the parameter set yielding the highest performance metrics, such as maximum Sharpe Ratio or profit factor. While exhaustive, the grid search provides clear visibility into parameter interactions and their effects on strategy performance.

However, grid search can be computationally intensive, especially when dealing with multiple parameters with wide ranges. **Random Search** offers an alternative by selecting random combinations from the parameter space to evaluate. While not exhaustive, random search often discovers optimal or near-optimal solutions more efficiently by exploring diverse areas of the parameter space, capturing nonlinear interactions between parameters.

Beyond these techniques, more sophisticated methods like **Bayesian Optimization** and **Genetic Algorithms (GA)** incorporate machine learning principles to guide parameter tuning. Bayesian optimization constructs a probabilistic model of the objective function, predicting the promise of unexplored parameter settings based on prior evaluations. As a result, it intelligently assesses promising areas of the parameter landscape, focusing computational resources effectively. Genetic algorithms, inspired by natural evolution, employ methods like selection, crossover, and mutation to iteratively evolve solutions, potentially discovering novel, high-performing parameter sets.

Walk-Forward Optimization (WFO) is a strategic optimization method that divides historical data into successive windows of time. Starting with an optimization window where parameters are adjusted, the strategy is validated on a walk-forward (test) window. This process iterates, walking through the dataset, engendering insights into parameter stability over time. WFO provides a forward-looking perspective, mitigating overfitting by ensuring rotating, independent datasets validate parameter efficacy.

Optimal tuning continually navigates the **bias-variance tradeoff**—the balance between underfitting and overfitting. Underfitting results from an overly simplistic model, failing to capture meaningful patterns, while overfitting stems from excessive complexity, capturing noise instead of genuine signals. Visualizing parameter performance curves, where sharp peaks suggest potential overfitting risks contrasted with smooth curves, fosters decision-making in model complexity adjustments.

To further avoid overfitting, traders implement techniques like leaving data out for **validation** alongside training datasets. This practice drives honest assessments of strategy performance, guarding against parameter sets optimized solely on historical artifacts instead of substantive predictive patterns. Techniques such as k-fold cross-validation enrich robustness by iteratively rotating dataset portions for training and validation, culminating in parameter selections backed by comprehensive evaluations.

Incorporating **robustness checks** is another critical step, ensuring sensitivity to external factors rather than relying solely on optimized parameters. Robust strategies display consistency across different market conditions, such as varying volatility or liquidity environments. One tactic is testing algorithms on "out of sample" data—datapoints not initially included in development phases. Another involves **stress testing** strategies by simulating extreme but plausible scenarios, encompassing market crashes or liquidity crises, to observe parameter resilience under duress.

An effective optimization process also considers transaction costs and slippage. Though algorithms may appear profitable before including these considerations, hefty transaction costs can erode theoretical gains substantially. Incorporating realistic cost estimates and re-evaluating parameter efficacy post-transaction adjustment ensures traders account for practicalities in execution.

To illustrate optimization's efficacy, consider a simple moving average crossover strategy: Traders optimize the short and long moving average periods. Initial grid search could reveal that a 7-day short moving average and a 21-day long moving average balance rapid responsiveness with stability across bear and bull markets. However, if sensitivity analysis reveals erratic changes in optimal parameters with minor dataset modifications, it indicates potential overfitting. Following this discovery, adopting robustness checks with additional datasets, simulating market regimes, and incorporating Bayesian methods might yield refined parameters with greater real-world potential.

As computational capabilities progress, real-time or near-real-time optimization becomes feasible. Techniques leveraging streaming data platforms or parallel computing structures can dynamically recalibrate parameters, maintaining alignment with rapidly shifting markets. Nevertheless, traders must balance adaptive tuning with ensuring algorithm stability, cautiously managing parameter drift risks.

While optimization empowers traders to maximize strategy prowess, the depth and frequency of parameter tuning should align with strategy complexity and market behavior dynamism. Fast-moving strategies, like high-frequency models, may benefit from more frequent updates, whereas long-term investments might derive sufficient robustness from infrequent recalibrations. Ultimately, optimization requires iterative exploration—a blend of rigorous testing, adaptation, and strategy coherence—to cultivate resilient strategies adapting to uncertain, variegated financial landscapes without succumbing to the allure of overly-tailored yet ultimately fragile solutions.

8.7 Deployment and Monitoring

The deployment and monitoring of trading algorithms are crucial phases that transition a strategy from development to live execution. Deployment ensures that the algorithm is correctly integrated into the trading environment, while monitoring addresses performance, compliance, and risk management in real time. This section elaborates on the key considerations, methodologies, and best practices involved in deploying and monitoring trading algorithms, highlighting the importance of robust infrastructure and vigilant oversight.

Deployment begins with selecting the appropriate trading platform or infrastructure that supports the algorithm's requirements. These platforms may vary from retail trading platforms like MetaTrader and Ninja-Trader to sophisticated institutional-level interfaces such as FIX protocol gateways and proprietary systems. The choice depends on factors such as latency needs, access to liquidity, asset class focus, and integration capabilities.

For high-frequency trading, where speed and latency are vital, co-located servers within exchanges' data centers drastically reduce latency by minimizing geographic data transmission. High-frequency traders benefit from milliseconds of speed advantage, critical in markets where price disparities exist momentarily. Investing in direct market access (DMA) and leveraging colocation arrangements facilitates instantaneous order execution, a cornerstone for time-sensitive strategies.

Ensuring compatibility with market conditions involves thorough system integration testing post-deployment. Integration tests validate that trading systems communicate effectively with broker systems, order management interfaces, and market data feeds, ensuring the smooth operation of buy/sell orders without mismatches or bottlenecks. These tests often simulate live conditions in dedicated environment setups, mirroring real market dynamics without exposing the strategy to actual risks.

Furthermore, adopting fault-tolerant systems is instrumental in counteracting potential deployment risks. Redundancies built into the algorithm infrastructure mitigate single points of failure, guaranteeing that operations continue under adverse conditions like server outages or network failures. Techniques such as load balancing distribute computational requests evenly across multiple servers, bolstering system resilience against unexpected load spikes.

Once deployed, the focus shifts to monitoring, an ongoing process ensuring the algorithm operates as intended under live market conditions. Monitoring systems track strategy performance against predefined benchmarks and thresholds, triggering alerts when deviations or anomalies arise.

A critical monitoring aspect is real-time analytics. By tracking key performance indicators (KPIs) such as returns, volatility, trade volumes, and profitability metrics, traders gain insights into strategy health. Sophisticated dashboards designed for visual data representation provide snapshots of real-time KPIs, assisting in rapid assessment and decision-making. For example, if an algorithm consistently underperforms relative to target returns, immediate investigative action prevents potential losses.

Automated alerts and notification systems bolster monitoring efforts. These systems issue alerts via email, SMS, or application notifications when metrics breach specified boundaries or when unexpected behavior is detected, such as order rejections, abnormal slippage, or protracted downtime. Automated alerts minimize response times, prompting traders to intervene, adjust parameters, or suspend trades where necessary, thus avoiding further undesirable outcomes.

Beyond performance, compliance monitoring ensures adherence to regulations, such as MiFID II, which mandates stringent reporting and transparency in trading activities. Compliance checks validate that algorithms operate within legal constraints, for instance, by limiting trade frequencies, maintaining order-to-trade ratios, or managing liquidity consumption. Compliance tests embedded into system logic automatically flag non-conformities, generating reports for further analysis.

Risk management remains integral to continuous monitoring. Algorithms must adhere to specified risk parameters, such as exposure limits, maximum drawdowns, or leverage ratios. Should a strategy deviate—signaling a risk limit breach or excessive volatility—a failsafe mechanism, such as an automatic trade shutdown or reduction in positions, activates to curtail risk exposure. Queries into risk metrics integrate seamlessly into the monitoring process, ensuring consistent oversight.

Market anomalies and unexpected events command particular attention in monitoring protocols. Sudden market shifts, such as geopolitical escalations or economic announcements, may impact strategy performance, necessitating real-time adaptability. Algorithms with adaptive components—capable of recalibrating in response to volatility spikes or systemic market risks—demonstrate significant advantages, remaining robust amid uncertainty.

Enhancing situational awareness through machine learning-driven analytics augments monitoring capabilities. Algorithms employing anomaly detection models recognize unusual trading patterns or environmental changes, signaling potential issues or opportunities impossible to discern manually. Techniques like reinforcement learning allow algorithms to adjust autonomously based on recent data, improving resilience and performance over time.

Handling exceptional conditions also requires toxic flow prevention, preventing algorithms from becoming inadvertently ensnared in manipulative market practices like spoofing or layering. Monitoring systems leverage pattern recognition to identify and avoid interaction with deceptive activities, preserving strategy integrity.

Finally, feedback loops are crucial for sustainable performance improvements. Insights gleaned from monitoring inform iterative strategy refinements and parameter adjustments, fostering a cycle of learning and enhancement. Historical monitoring data supports optimization processes, revealing sustained underperformance or anomalous behavior requiring remediation.

In summary, deploying and monitoring trading algorithms necessitate technical rigor, strategic planning, and unwavering vigilance. By implementing robust deployment infrastructures and sophisticated real-time monitoring systems, traders not only enhance algorithm reliability but also ensure alignment with market dynamics, regulatory obligations, and risk appetites. Ultimately, these processes fortify confidence in strategies, offering a competitive edge in navigating the complex terrain of financial markets.

Chapter 9

Implementing Market Making Algorithms

This chapter provides a comprehensive guide to the implementation of market making algorithms, starting with selecting appropriate tools and platforms. It details the formulation of trading logic and coding best practices to ensure algorithm efficiency and reliability. Key aspects of order execution and management are discussed to enhance trading effectiveness. The chapter explores the infrastructure for handling real-time market data and the importance of robust monitoring systems. Integration with brokerage and clearing systems is examined to streamline trade execution and compliance processes, ensuring a seamless operation of market making strategies.

9.1   Choosing the Right Tools and Platforms

In the expansive landscape of algorithmic trading, the choice of tools and platforms serves as the foundational step towards implementing effective market making strategies. This initial choice can significantly influence not only the execution efficiency but also the scalability and adaptability of your trading algorithms. When evaluating tools and platforms, consider a comprehensive array of factors that ensure alignment with the specific demands of your market making strategy.

The selection begins with understanding the requirements unique to market making, where rapid order execution, high-frequency data handling, and intricate algorithmic logic are paramount. These requirements lay the groundwork for several critical considerations, including ease of use, scalability, integration capability, cost-effectiveness, and support for multiple asset classes.

Ease of use is a primary factor, particularly if the team lacks deep technical expertise. Platforms that offer intuitive interfaces and extensive documentation reduce the learning curve and enable faster prototyping of market making algorithms. Some platforms provide a code-free environment for strategy development, which can be attractive for traders whose strengths lie outside programming.

Scalability is another vital characteristic, especially for firms anticipating growth in trading volume or asset classes. A platform must efficiently handle increased data throughput and execute larger order quantities without compromising execution speed or accuracy. With the proliferation of cloud computing, many platforms now offer scalable infrastructure that allows on-demand resource allocation, effectively addressing scalability concerns.

Integration capability refers to a platform's ability to seamlessly connect with various data providers, execution venues, and in-house systems. A robust API framework facilitates such integrations, enabling access to diverse markets, streaming real-time data, and executing trades efficiently. Platforms that are agnostic in their data and execution provider integrations often provide the flexibility needed to respond to shifting market conditions and opportunities.

The platform's cost structure is also a crucial consideration, encompassing not only the upfront investment but also ongoing expenses related to data fees, transaction costs, and system maintenance. Budget constraints may influence the choice between commercial platforms and open-source alternatives. While commercial solutions often provide comprehensive support and regular updates, open-source platforms offer customization opportunities, free from licensing costs, but may require more technical expertise to maintain.

A critical advantage in choosing the right tools is the support for multiple asset classes. Market makers frequently operate across different asset classes, needing platforms that accommodate equities, options, futures, forex, and other financial instruments within a single ecosystem. This not only enhances the ability to diversify strategies but also simplifies the operational workflow.

Several platforms stand out in the realm of market making due to their robust features and adaptability. For instance, MetaTrader, known for forex and CFD trading, provides a flexible environment with extensive scripting capabilities via its MQL language. Similarly, MultiCharts offers powerful backtesting and optimization features, making it suitable for developing sophisticated algorithmic strategies.

QuantConnect and Quantopian (though now defunct) represent another category, emphasizing community-driven development and offering cloud-based services that remove the burden of infrastructure management. These platforms allow users to focus on strategy development and testing in a collaborative environment, often accompanied by rich datasets and shared insights from other users.

In evaluating trading platforms, consider the level of support and community engagement. Platforms with active user communities, regular updates, and responsive support can significantly enhance the user experience and provide troubleshooting assistance. For example, platforms offering direct access to developers through forums or customer support lines allow for faster resolution of issues and better implementation of user feedback in platform improvements.

Beyond the platform itself, the selection of the programming environment is equally crucial. Languages such as Python, R, and C++ dominate the algorithmic trading space. Python, with its extensive libraries like NumPy, Pandas, and PyAlgoTrade, is heralded for its simplicity and ease of use in financial calculations and strategy backtesting. C++ is renowned for its execution speed, which is indispensable in high-frequency trading settings, albeit at the cost of longer development time.

Moreover, modern trading systems often require integration with machine learning tools to enhance predictive capabilities. Python again shines in this aspect with libraries like scikit-learn, TensorFlow, and PyTorch, which facilitate the development of models that can adapt and respond to complex market signals, thus augmenting traditional market making algorithms with AI-driven insights.

Security and compliance are also critical concerns, particularly given the sensitive nature of trading data and the regulatory scrutiny surrounding trading activities. A platform must have robust security measures, including data encryption, access controls, and rigorous testing protocols, to safeguard information and comply with financial regulations. Platforms often provide compliance tools that ensure algorithmic strategies adhere to market regulations, thus reducing the risk of penalties.

As we move towards implementing market making algorithms, the consideration of these factors becomes increasingly vital. An effective platform not only enhances the capability of executing strategies efficiently but also empowers traders to innovate and adapt to the dynamic nature of financial markets. The right tools enable seamless adaptation to market changes and create a resilient framework where strategies can be iteratively tested, refined, and deployed with confidence.

In the ever-evolving domain of trading technology, staying informed about emerging platforms and their capabilities can provide a competitive edge. Whether through improved execution speed, lower costs, or advanced analytical tools, staying abreast of technological advancements ensures that your market making strategies remain cutting-edge and adaptable to future market trends. This strategic foresight ultimately defines success in the intricate world of market making.

9.2   Designing Algorithmic Trading Logic

Crafting effective algorithmic trading logic is the heart and soul of any successful market making strategy. It involves not only setting the rules and mechanisms by which trades are executed but also ensuring that these rules can adapt fluidly to the dynamic ebb and flow of the financial markets. In this section, we delve into the essential components, from formulating decision rules to implementing sophisticated order placement logic, all aimed at enhancing the efficiency and profitability of your trading strategy.

At the core of algorithmic trading logic is the concept of decision-making, which in this context refers to the series of rules or conditions that dictate when trades are made. The first step in designing an algorithm is defining the market conditions or signals under which the algorithm will operate. These signals might include price movements, volume patterns, volatility levels, or specific technical indicators. A thorough market analysis is necessary to identify these signals, which serve as the primary inputs into your algorithm.

In developing trading logic, it is essential to incorporate both predictive and reactive components. Predictive logic involves using historical data to forecast future price movements, while reactive components focus on responding to real-time data and market signals. A blend of both can increase the robustness of the trading algorithm. For instance, predictive elements might signal that an asset is likely to rise in value based on historical trends, while reactive elements could trigger a sell if an unexpected market event causes prices to drop rapidly.

Machine learning has increasingly become an integral part of developing predictive models in algorithmic trading. By leveraging algorithms such as regression models, random forests, or neural networks, traders can extract insights from historical data, which help anticipate future price movements or market trends. However, it's important to balance statistical rigor with interpretability and ensure that the models are not overfit to historical data, thus remaining effective in live market conditions.

Order placement logic is another critical aspect of algorithmic trading. Deciding how and when to place orders in the market can significantly affect the execution price and overall strategy performance. Limit orders, market orders, and stop orders are some of the common types utilized within algorithms. Limit orders are often preferred in market making strategies as they allow the trader to specify a price and avoid slippage, but they might not always be executed if the market moves beyond the specified price.

The timing of order placement also influences trading results. A key consideration here is latency, or the delay between market signal detection and order execution. Minimizing latency is crucial, especially in high-frequency trading (HFT), where opportunities can disappear in milliseconds. To achieve low latency, algorithms must be optimized at the code level, and infrastructure should be strategically located close to exchange servers to benefit from colocation services.

Risk management forms the backbone of any trading logic, acting as a safeguard against excessive losses. Effective risk management includes setting stop-loss and take-profit levels, employing position sizing strategies, and ensuring diversified exposure to mitigate risks associated with single trades or assets. Statistical measures, such as Value at Risk (VaR) and conditional VaR, are employed to quantify and manage risk levels within the trading logic.

Furthermore, the deployment of a trading algorithm must consider liquidity management. Market makers thrive on providing liquidity, and hence must continuously assess the depth of the order book and adjust their pricing spreads to maintain profitability while minimizing the risk of holding unsold inventory. The algorithm must dynamically adapt to changes in market liquidity conditions and rebalance positions as required.

Ensuring compliance with market regulations is paramount when designing trading algorithms. Regulatory bodies such as the SEC or FCA have stringent guidelines on market conduct, and algorithms must be coded to adhere to these standards to avoid penalties. This involves embedding compliance checks into the algorithmic logic, such as monitoring for trade consistency and ensuring transparency in execution.

For example, in a market making strategy aimed at stock trading, a trader might develop an algorithm that continuously monitors the spread between the bid and ask prices. If the spread widens beyond a pre-defined threshold, the algorithm might automatically place a buy order at the bid price and a sell order at the ask price, capturing the spread as profit. Such logic must also incorporate risk parameters, halting trading activity in case the total stock position exceeds risk limits or market volatility reaches critical levels.

Stress testing is an often overlooked but critical part of validating algorithmic trading logic. Before live deployment, algorithms should undergo rigorous backtesting against historical data sets to verify their robustness and performance under different market conditions. Moreover, paper trading in simulated environments can provide valuable insights into how the algorithm behaves in real-time, helping to identify potential issues that were not apparent during backtesting.

The iterative process of refining algorithmic logic is continuous. Markets evolve, influenced by macroeconomic factors, technological advancements, and behavioral shifts among market participants. As such, algorithms must be periodically reviewed and updated to account for these changes. This ongoing development requires a feedback loop where performance metrics are analyzed, adjustments are made, and the updated logic is tested again.

Ultimately, designing algorithmic trading logic is as much an art as it is a science. It requires a deep understanding of market dynamics, a strategic application of quantitative and qualitative insights, and meticulous attention to detail in risk and compliance management. When adeptly crafted, this logic not only guides successful trade execution but also provides the agility to navigate and capitalize on the complex landscapes of modern financial markets.

9.3 Coding and Implementation Practices

The journey from conceptualizing a market-making algorithm to its successful implementation is paved with meticulous coding practices and strategic deployment techniques. The efficiency, reliability, and maintainability of the code are pivotal factors that distinguish successful trading algorithms in this highly competitive domain. This section delves into best practices for coding and implementing market-making algorithms, aiming to provide a robust framework that ensures performance and scalability.

At the foundation of effective coding practices lies the principle of clarity and simplicity. Complex and tangled code not only obscures understanding but also introduces errors and maintenance challenges. Writing clean, readable code using descriptive variable names, straightforward logic structures, and appropriate documentation is paramount. Adherence to coding standards and best practices, such as those outlined by PEP 8 in Python, aids in maintaining consistency and readability.

Choosing the right programming language is crucial and should be aligned with the specific needs of the market-making strategy. C++ is favored for its speed, making it ideal for high-frequency trading scenarios where every microsecond counts. Python, with its wealth of libraries and ease of use, is popular for developing and backtesting algorithms due to its extensive support for numerical computation and machine learning. The choice between these languages often hinges on the trade-off between execution speed and development time.

Implementing robust error handling and logging mechanisms is another fundamental practice. Financial markets are dynamic, with unpredictable events that can lead to unforeseen errors. By incorporating comprehensive error handling into the code, algorithms can gracefully manage exceptions without interrupting the trading process. Logging, on the other hand, provides a trail of executed actions, enabling developers to audit performance, diagnose issues, and refine strategies.

Scalability and performance optimization are critical in handling large volumes of data and executing transactions at high speeds. Algorithms should be designed to scale horizontally, meaning they can handle increased loads by distributing tasks across multiple machines or processors. Techniques such as parallel processing and vectorization using libraries like NumPy in Python can significantly enhance computational efficiency.

197

Incorporating unit testing and continuous integration (CI) into the development pipeline ensures that changes to the codebase do not introduce new bugs. Unit tests validate that individual components of the algorithm function correctly. By automating these tests using CI tools, any defects or failures can be quickly identified and resolved, fostering an environment of continuous improvement and reliability.

Version control systems, such as Git, are indispensable in the management and deployment of code. They facilitate collaboration among developers, track changes to the codebase over time, and allow for rollback to previous versions if necessary. Utilizing branches effectively in Git enables experimentation and development of new features without affecting the stability of the main algorithm.

In the deployment stage, selecting the appropriate infrastructure and ensuring robust security measures are paramount. Cloud-based platforms like AWS or Google Cloud offer scalable resources that can be customized to optimize trading performance. These platforms provide advanced security features including data encryption and network isolation, which help protect the integrity and confidentiality of sensitive trading information.

Latency optimization is a critical concern, particularly for market-making strategies that rely on speed. Minimizing the time from data receipt to order execution necessitates optimizing both the software and the underlying hardware. Techniques include utilizing lightweight data structures, streamlining computational processes, and placing services in close proximity to exchange servers via colocation.

Adopting a modular and reusable code architecture enhances maintainability and simplifies future development efforts. By designing the algorithm with distinct modules for tasks such as data ingestion, signal generation, order execution, and risk management, each component can be independently tested, modified, or replaced. This modular approach not only accelerates the development of new strategies but also facilitates the integration of improvements or extensions.

Security practices must be ingrained into every phase of development and deployment. This includes securing data at rest and in transit with encryption protocols like TLS, implementing stringent access controls, and continuously monitoring for vulnerabilities. Given the high stakes involved in trading, ensuring that the algorithm complies with industry regulations and standards mitigates legal and financial risks.

For example, consider an algorithm written in Python which constantly adjusts bids and offers based on real-time trades in the stock market. Performance bottlenecks might initially arise during data parsing or when managing large volumes of historical trading data for backtesting. Solutions could involve optimizing data storage formats, such as using HDF5 files for efficient data access, or leveraging database systems like PostgreSQL for complex data queries.

Implementing advanced data processing techniques is also crucial. Employing in-memory databases or utilizing data streams can drastically reduce access times, thus improving the algorithm's response time to market changes. Moreover, techniques like event sourcing—an architectural pattern where changes to the application state are stored as a sequence of events—can provide a robust solution to efficiently manage and query historical data.

The success of a market-making algorithm is often measured by its resilience in real-world conditions. Before going live, rigorous backtesting against historical data is non-negotiable. Simulating trades over past periods allows developers to tweak parameters and refine logic without financial risk. It serves as an empirical method for verifying that the algorithm performs as expected under various market scenarios.

Further, stress testing algorithms in adverse conditions—such as market crashes or extreme volatility—provides insights into their robustness. This involves simulating market anomalies or outages to ensure the algorithm can handle unexpected events gracefully. Through such exhaustive testing, developers can identify potential weaknesses and implement safeguards, improving the algorithm's ability to withstand real-world trading pressures.

Continuous education and adaptation are vital in staying ahead of the curve in market-making algorithm development. As technology and markets evolve, keeping abreast of the latest advancements in coding practices, infrastructure solutions, and financial regulations is essential. Participation in forums, attending conferences, and engaging with the broader trading community fosters the exchange of ideas and innovations, driving the development of state-of-the-art trading algorithms.

In summary, the journey from coding to deployment encompasses a blend of technical proficiency and strategic foresight, fostering the creation of market-making algorithms that are fast, reliable, and adaptable. By adhering to these best practices, developers lay a solid foundation for their algorithms to excel in the dynamic and challenging world of financial trading.

9.4   Order Execution and Management

Order execution and management lie at the core of successful market making, bridging the strategic design of trading algorithms and their operational performance in the financial markets. This section expounds on the methodologies and techniques to optimize trade execution and the nuanced management of orders, underpinning a well-rounded approach to achieving consistency and profitability.

Efficient order execution is vital to market making, where the margin for profit is often narrow and relies on capturing bid-ask spreads. The execution quality is determined by how swiftly and accurately trades are conducted, alongside the minimization of costs such as slippage — the discrepancy between the expected price of a trade and the actual price at which it is executed. Reducing slippage involves meticulous attention to order types, execution venues, and trading strategies.

The selection of order types is the first pillar of execution strategy. Market orders, typically used for immediate execution, guarantee order fulfillment but expose traders to slippage in volatile markets. In contrast, limit orders execute trades only at a specified price or better, offering control over execution price but risking partial or no fulfillment if the market does not reach the specified levels. Stop orders and their variants — stop-limit and trailing stop orders — add layers of complexity that automate buy or sell decisions once certain price thresholds are triggered.

Algorithmic traders often leverage a hybrid approach, combining different order types to tailor execution based on the prevailing market conditions. For instance, a strategy might involve using limit orders to enter a position and market orders for swift exit during high momentum, safeguarding against potential adverse price movements.

Execution speed, or latency, is a critical factor, especially for strategies engaged in high-frequency trading (HFT). The interval between signal generation and trade execution must be minimized to capitalize on fleeting arbitrage opportunities. Latency can be diminished through the deployment of algorithms on servers located in close proximity to exchange data centers—a practice known as colocation—thereby reducing geographic latency. Moreover, optimizing code and reducing the number of computational steps in the execution path further curtails delays.

Additionally, the utilization of smart order routing (SOR) systems plays a crucial role in navigating fragmented markets. SOR algorithms intelligently direct orders to different trading venues, maximizing fill rates and improving execution quality by tapping into liquidity pools across multiple exchanges and dark pools. These systems dynamically assess conditions such as liquidity depth, transaction costs, and speed of execution, making real-time decisions to identify the most opportune venue for order placement.

The design of execution algorithms, such as TWAP (Time Weighted Average Price) and VWAP (Volume Weighted Average Price), also contributes to improved order management. These algorithms aim to minimize market impact and acquire or dispose of large order sizes without significantly altering the market price. TWAP spreads orders evenly over a pre-defined time interval, while VWAP aligns execution with market volume, ensuring that trades occur in proportion to the overall trading activity.

Effective order management extends beyond execution; it encompasses the ongoing adjustment of strategy parameters, positions, and risk exposure. This dynamic management ensures alignment with evolving market conditions and safeguards against adverse events. Incorporating adaptive algorithms that tweak parameters in response to volatility shifts or liquidity changes is vital. For example, during times of market stress, widening spreads and increased volatility might prompt the algorithm to adjust its pricing model, thereby preserving market share without unduly increasing exposure to risk.

Risk management practices are integral to order management and execution. Setting precise risk limits — such as maximum position sizes, stop-loss levels, and VAR (Value at Risk) thresholds — ensures that each trade aligns with the broader risk appetite of the trading operation. Real-time monitoring systems must be in place to track these parameters, providing alerts or automatic interventions when limits are breached.

The concept of market impact must also be thoroughly understood and managed. Large orders can significantly affect asset prices, introducing adverse price movements that increase transaction costs. Executing such orders gradually over time, using techniques like iceberg orders — where only a fraction of the total order size is visible to the market — can help mitigate market impact.

Furthermore, regular post-trade analysis is essential for refining execution strategies. This involves evaluating metrics such as execution costs, average slippage, fill rates, and time-to-market. By conducting this analysis, traders can ascertain the effectiveness of their execution techniques and identify areas for improvement, driving iterative optimization of their strategies.

Compliance and regulatory adherence are paramount in order management. Trading algorithms must comply with regulations such as MiFID II in Europe, which mandates transparency and fairer markets through trade and transaction reporting, best execution mandates, and controls to prevent market abuse. Integrating compliance checks within the order management system ensures that trades do not breach regulatory standards, minimizing the risk of sanctions.

Consider a practical example where a market-making algorithm is engaged in trading tech stocks on NASDAQ. The algorithm needs to consistently maintain an inventory of shares on both sides of the book. When the market experiences high volatility due to an earnings announcement, the algorithm adapts by using wider spreads to manage risk. Orders are strategically routed using a smart order routing system to optimize execution across various liquidity venues, minimizing slippage and securing competitive pricing—particularly important given the potential for info-arbitrage surrounding such announcements.

In summary, order execution and management are multifaceted pillars of market making that demand a blend of strategic planning, technological sophistication, and regulatory awareness. By mastering these elements, traders can significantly elevate their effectiveness in the fast-paced environment of financial markets, achieving consistent returns while maintaining rigor in risk management and compliance.

9.5   Monitoring and Surveillance Systems

In the intricate realm of market making, robust monitoring and surveillance systems form the bedrock of a resilient trading framework. These systems not only empower traders to oversee algorithm performance in real-time but also play a crucial role in ensuring adherence to regulatory standards and swiftly identifying potential issues that could jeopardize profitability or legal standing. In this section, we delve into the intricacies of building such systems, covering essential components, best practices, and contemporary challenges.

The primary function of monitoring systems is to provide a comprehensive and continuous overview of trading operations. A well-architected system entails several layers of monitoring, including performance tracking, risk management, anomaly detection, and compliance surveillance. At its core, performance tracking involves the meticulous observation of key metrics, such as order execution times, fill rates, latency, and slippage, which collectively inform the trader about the real-time efficiency of their algorithmic strategies.

Implementing real-time monitoring requires a robust data ingestion framework capable of handling high-frequency data with minimal delay. Such a setup must ingest, process, and display data seamlessly, often leveraging stream processing technologies like Apache Kafka or RabbitMQ for efficient data flow. Real-time dashboards powered by analytics platforms like Grafana or Tableau provide intuitive and dynamic visualization, enabling quick decision-making based on up-to-the-second insights.

Risk management monitoring, an integral component, operates simultaneously to track the exposure of trading positions against predefined risk limits. This includes assessing market risk, credit risk, and operational risk inherent in trading activities. Sophisticated risk engines calculate indicators such as Value at Risk (VaR), potential losses, and liquidity risks, providing algorithms with automatic triggers to adjust or exit positions when risk thresholds are breached.

Anomaly detection systems are indispensable in identifying unexpected or suspicious activity. Machine learning models trained on normal trading patterns can alert traders to anomalies that may indicate system failures, data errors, or fraudulent activity. Techniques such as unsupervised learning, including clustering and dimensionality reduction, aid in capturing deviations from typical behavior, thus preventing unauthorized or erroneous actions before they escalate.

Surveillance systems extend beyond operational oversight to ensure compliance with stringent regulatory frameworks. These systems monitor trade activity to detect patterns indicative of market manipulation or abuse, such as spoofing, layering, or insider trading. By integrating surveillance rules that align with regulations like the Market Abuse Regulation (MAR) in Europe or the Securities Exchange Act in the United States, firms ensure their trading operations adhere to both domestic and international legal requirements.

Automated alerts and reporting functionalities are crucial for effective surveillance, providing immediate notifications of compliance breaches or unusual trading patterns. These systems can generate real-time alerts via configurable parameters, such as threshold breaches or complex trade sequences, helping mitigate potential litigation or penalties.

Additionally, comprehensive logging and record-keeping protocols ensure that all transactions are documented, aiding in audits and regulatory reporting.

As an example, consider a scenario where an automated trading system is aggressively involved in high-frequency trading (HFT) across multiple equity markets. To effectively monitor this system, the trading firm leverages a distributed architecture ensuring low latency. Real-time dashboards display metrics such as bid-ask spreads, order book depth, and execution speed, while machine learning models continuously assess for anomalies like sudden spikes in trade volume or unexpected price movements that deviate from historical patterns. Compliance modules analyze historical records and real-time market interactions, visually and algorithmically searching for schemes that could hint at illicit trading practices.

However, implementing effective monitoring and surveillance systems comes with its own set of challenges. One significant challenge is managing the volume and velocity of data, particularly in HFT environments where transactions occur in milliseconds. The system must be capable of storing vast amounts of data without sacrificing performance or responsiveness. This often necessitates big data solutions capable of handling petabyte-scale storage and retrieval, while maintaining low latency for real-time processing.

Scalability is another concern. As a trading firm broadens its activities over various markets and asset classes, the monitoring system must adapt seamlessly, reflecting the associated growth in data volume and complexity. Architecting the system with modularity in mind, where components such as data feeders, processing engines, and visualizations can be scaled or replaced independently, meets these expanding needs more efficiently.

Security is paramount in the design of these systems. Given the sensitive nature of trading data and the potential impact of its compromise, robust security protocols must be in place. This includes encryption of data both at rest and in transit, stringent access controls ensuring only authorized personnel can modify system functions, and continuous security threat assessment to preempt vulnerabilities.

Finally, human oversight must complement technological solutions. Despite advances in automation and analytics, human judgment remains crucial in interpreting the nuanced outputs of monitoring systems. Skilled operators can leverage their experience and intuition to make informed decisions in cases where automated systems may lack context or adaptability to sudden, unprecedented market events.

Proactively evolving surveillance systems parallel to the regulatory landscape is vital. As financial markets become more globally inter-connected and regulations evolve to combat increasingly sophisticated trading frauds, maintaining a proactive stance on compliance ensures long-term operational viability and trustworthiness.

In essence, a robust monitoring and surveillance system forms the crit-ical middle layer between trade execution and strategic oversight. It ensures that market-making activities not only achieve their targets but do so within the bounds of legal compliance and risk management best practices. By fostering a culture of vigilance, adaptability, and continu-ous improvement, firms can harness these systems to sustain competi-tive advantage and operational integrity in the challenging environment of modern financial markets.

9.6 Handling Market Data in Real-Time

In the arena of market making where decisions must be executed within fractions of a second, the capability to handle market data in real-time is an imperative cornerstone. The speed, accuracy, and reliability with which data is processed directly impact the effectiveness of trading strategies, making it a critical focus for implementing market-making algorithms. This section explores the multifaceted aspects of manag-ing real-time market data, addressing challenges, technologies, and strategies to achieve optimal performance.

Real-time market data comprises two primary types: price data and transactional data. Price data includes bid and ask prices, last trade prices, and quotes, while transactional data encompasses order book changes, volume, and trade executions. A market-making system must ingest, process, and react to both types to maintain profitability and competitive advantage.

One of the foundational challenges in handling market data is latency, the delay before a data point is available for processing. Latency can occur at multiple levels—network latency, processing latency, and de-cision latency. Network latency is the time taken for data to travel from its source to the trader's system. To combat this, financial firms often resort to colocation, setting up servers in proximity to major exchanges to minimize the physical distance over which data must travel. Addition-ally, using high-speed terrestrial or undersea fiber-optic cables helps to circumvent network-induced delays.

Processing latency involves the speed with which data is parsed and analyzed once it is received.   The deployment of low-latency architectures, such as using specialized hardware accelerators like Field Programmable Gate Arrays (FPGAs) or Graphics Processing Units (GPUs), can execute complex calculations within milliseconds. In tandem, utilizing efficient data structures and algorithms—all optimized for fast execution and minimal resource usage—helps manage processing speed effectively.   Decision latency involves the time taken for an algorithm to react to processed data, which can be minimized through advance algorithmic decision trees that pre-empt possible scenarios.

Reducing latency at the software level requires implementing data streaming processing frameworks such as Apache Kafka, which facilitate the real-time ingestion and processing of data.   These systems break data processing into multiple stages, allowing for concurrent execution and enabling traders to handle high-throughput environments without bottlenecks. Custom-built algorithms running as microservices in containerized environments ensure that each component of the data pipeline can scale independently according to demand, thus maintaining consistency in performance.

Handling real-time data also demands high degrees of data integrity and accuracy. Any disparity in data can lead to incorrect decisions and potential financial losses. Ensuring data integrity starts with acquiring data from reliable sources and utilizing redundant systems to cross-verify information.   Additionally, implementing robust error correction and anomaly detection protocols helps identify data inconsistencies promptly.

In the context of data integrity, timestamping data with high precision is crucial, allowing traders to synchronize datasets accurately and utilize them effectively for strategy execution. Network Time Protocol (NTP) is commonly used for system clock synchronization, yet in high-frequency trading scenarios where microsecond accuracy is necessary, more precise time synchronization methods like Precision Time Protocol (PTP) are deployed.

To facilitate swift decision-making, running predictive analytics and machine learning models on streaming data is increasingly common. Such models can detect patterns or trends that indicate future price movements before they fully materialize in the markets.   Integration with machine learning libraries such as TensorFlow or PyTorch, along with frameworks like Apache Spark, provides a potent combination for real-time analytics. These systems perform on-the-fly computations, delivering actionable insights directly to trading algorithms.

Managing real-time data must also account for volume spikes—times when data throughput dramatically increases, typically due to significant market events or announcements. Scalable cloud infrastructure enables seamless adaption to these fluctuations, leveraging load balancing techniques to distribute data processing tasks across multiple servers. Furthermore, latest-generation distributed databases such as Apache Cassandra or InfluxDB are optimized for time-series data, providing the necessary throughput and storage capabilities to handle these spikes efficiently.

Automated failover mechanisms and disaster recovery protocols ensure resiliency within real-time data systems. They provide continuity in the event of system failures, seamlessly switching operations to backup systems without disruption. The implementation of circuit breakers and graceful degradation strategies serves to protect systems from overload by throttling incoming data or temporarily switching to batch processing during critical failure modes.

Another crucial aspect is securing real-time data against unauthorized access and breaches. Employing encryption standards like TLS for data in transit and using hardware security modules (HSM) for key management bolsters data security. Additionally, enforcing stringent access controls and continuous monitoring for anomalies or intrusion attempts helps to maintain the confidentiality and integrity of trading data.

Let's consider an example of a market-making algorithm trading currency pairs on the foreign exchange market. Such an algorithm would utilize real-time data streaming from various sources, including price feeds from different exchanges and macroeconomic indicators that influence currency values. It uses a combination of colocation methods, FPGA acceleration for rapid data processing, and machine learning models predicting currency movements based on historical and real-time data. The system is designed with modular containerized services to ensure scalability and employs multiple redundant feed handlers to guarantee data accuracy even if one source fails. During high volatility periods, such as when central bank decisions are announced, the system dynamically scales its resources to manage the increased data load while dynamically adjusting its trading positions based on the insights generated by its predictive models.

Effectively handling market data in real-time therefore requires an intricate balance of cutting-edge technology, strategic planning, and rigorous execution. As markets continue to evolve, staying at the forefront of data handling capabilities will remain crucial for market makers who seek to maintain an edge over competitors. By achieving low latency, high reliability, and exceptional analytical capability, traders secure their operations against volatility and enhance their capability to capture profitable opportunities in an ever-rapid trading ecosystem.

9.7 Integration with Brokerage and Clearing Systems

The seamless integration of trading algorithms with brokerage and clearing systems is an essential element in executing market-making strategies effectively. This integration underpins the infrastructure necessary for trade execution, settlement, and compliance, ensuring that all transactions proceed smoothly from initiation to final settlement. In this section, we explore the various dimensions of integrating brokerage and clearing systems, highlighting the technologies, challenges, and best practices that contribute to an efficient and compliant trading operation.

Brokerage systems serve as the conduit through which traders gain access to financial markets. These systems enable market participants to place orders, receive confirmations, and manage their stock holdings. For a market-making algorithm, integration with these systems must allow for real-time order placement and modification, as well as the reception of trade confirmations and other pertinent market data that informs immediate trading decisions.

Establishing this integration begins with understanding the communication protocols and APIs provided by brokers. FIX (Financial Information eXchange) is the predominant protocol for real-time electronic communication in trading environments. It offers a standardized format for transmitting order information, confirmations, and market data, fostering reliable and efficient interaction between traders and brokers. More contemporary APIs provided by brokers often include RESTful services, which permit flexible integration with modern development environments and programming languages such as Python, Java, or C++.

Critical to the integration process is ensuring low-latency connectivity, which is essential for market makers who engage in high-frequency trading. This often involves colocating trading servers with those of the brokerage firm, minimizing data transmission delays. Additionally, point-to-point leased lines or virtual private networks (VPNs) may be employed to maintain a secure, yet low-latency, communications channel.

Real-time updating and feedback mechanisms are indispensable in this integration. When trades are executed, the algorithm must instantaneously receive execution reports to update its status. Such feedback loops are vital for maintaining accurate portfolio records, managing risk exposure, and reacting promptly to market movements. This necessitates the employment of event-driven architectures that can process these updates with minimal lag, using tools like Apache Kafka or AWS Kinesis, which facilitate rapid data flow and integration.

Clearing systems, on the other hand, are fundamental to the post-trade lifecycle. They ensure that trades are settled according to contractual obligations, involving the confirmation, clearing, and netting of trades. Integration with a clearing system ensures that trades are not only executed but also settled efficiently, mitigating counterparty risk. The clearing organization acts as an intermediary, guaranteeing the trade, managing margin requirements, and ensuring that financial instruments are exchanged timely.

To integrate effectively with clearing systems, automated settlement instructions must be incorporated into the trading system, highlighting the need for accurate and timely reconciliation. Technologies such as SWIFT (Society for Worldwide Interbank Financial Telecommunication) messages facilitate secure exchange of funds and securities between banks and financial institutions, supporting settlement, payment, and messaging compliance.

Beyond technical connectivity, operational processes need sophisticated alignment between market-making strategies and the risk management frameworks employed by clearinghouses. The risk models defined by clearing entities, often based on metrics like SPAN (Standard Portfolio Analysis of Risk) for futures and options, must be seamlessly integrated to monitor leverage and funding requirements, ensuring that all trading operations adhere to margin constraints.

Security and compliance play pivotal roles in integration, as brokerage and clearing systems handle sensitive financial and personal data. Integration efforts must ensure that all transmitted data is encrypted, with robust authentication mechanisms in place to prevent unauthorized access. Compliance with established industry standards, such

209

as those outlined in MiFID II in Europe or the Dodd-Frank Act in the United States, is critical in maintaining the legality and ethics of trading operations.

The need for redundancy and failover mechanisms cannot be overstated in such integrations. System failures can lead to significant financial and operational disruptions. Ensuring alternative communication channels and backup systems ready to assume operation at short notice helps mitigate this risk. Implementing redundant systems with diverse data paths or horizontally scaled architectures can secure operational continuity even in the face of technical challenges or failures.

Consider a scenario where a trading firm integrates its proprietary algorithmic trading system with multiple brokers and clearinghouses for a diversified asset portfolio. Utilizing FIX protocol and REST APIs, the system establishes real-time connectivity, engaging directly with brokerage platforms for trade execution while simultaneously interfacing with clearing systems via SWIFT for settlement processes. The firm employs real-time processing infrastructure using event-streaming platforms to ensure rapid response to market data and execution confirmations. As market volatility impacts portfolio exposure, adjustments to risk models are automated and aligned with clearing requirements using APIs that dynamically pull in current risk metrics.

Technical integration of such depth necessitates ongoing collaboration with brokerage and clearing partners to adapt to system upgrades, policy changes, and evolving technology standards. Continuous testing and validation of APIs ensure resilience to changes, upgrades, and transaction spikes during volatile periods. Regular reconciliation with clearing accounts helps in identifying discrepancies early, thus maintaining operational accuracy and financial integrity.

Overall, effective integration with brokerage and clearing systems sets the stage for the smooth execution of market-making strategies, from trade execution to settlement. By employing cutting-edge technology, maintaining robust risk management practices, and ensuring regulatory compliance, trading firms create a framework capable of leveraging their strategies effectively while minimizing operational risks. This interplay of technology and process ensures that trades are not only performed efficiently but are also aligned with the broader goals of financial security, compliance, and sustainability in the dynamic world of market making.

Chapter 10

Regulatory Considerations and Ethical Implications

This chapter addresses the critical regulatory frameworks and ethical issues affecting market making. It covers compliance with licensing and market manipulation laws, emphasizing the importance of adhering to anti-fraud and data protection regulations. Ethical trading practices are discussed to ensure fairness and transparency in algorithmic activities. The chapter also examines the impact of regulation on innovation within the industry, as well as efforts towards global regulatory harmonization. These discussions provide a comprehensive overview of the challenges and responsibilities faced by market makers in the digital trading environment.

10.1 Regulatory Frameworks for Market Making

Market making, a critical component of financial markets, involves the provision of liquidity by trading firms, which continuously quote both buy and sell prices for securities, thus facilitating smoother market operations. These activities are subject to a myriad of regulatory frameworks that ensure fairness, transparency, and stability in the financial market landscape. Understanding these frameworks is crucial for any market maker operating across different jurisdictions, as they set the foundation for compliance and ethical trading.

Regulatory frameworks governing market making activities have evolved significantly over the years in response to technological advances, financial crises, and the increasing complexity of global markets. At their core, these regulations aim to protect investors, maintain fair and efficient markets, and mitigate systemic risk. However, the specific laws and guidelines vary greatly from one jurisdiction to another, reflecting the economic and political landscape of each region.

In the United States, the Securities and Exchange Commission (SEC) and the Financial Industry Regulatory Authority (FINRA) are primary regulators of market making activities. The SEC enforces rules under the Securities Exchange Act of 1934, which includes the requirement for market makers to register and file regular reports detailing their trading activities. These reports ensure that market makers operate transparently, without engaging in practices that could manipulate market prices unfairly. FINRA, on the other hand, oversees brokerage firms and exchange markets, ensuring that they comply with the rules and operations set forth by the SEC.

Europe's regulatory landscape is notably shaped by the European Securities and Markets Authority (ESMA), which promotes transparency and protects investors across the EU. The Markets in Financial Instruments Directive II (MiFID II), implemented in 2018, is a cornerstone regulation affecting market makers. MiFID II introduced comprehensive transparency requirements for pre-trade and post-trade reporting, thereby increasing market integrity. It requires market makers to systematically disclose their orders, ensuring that investors have access to detailed information about transaction costs and market liquidity.

In the Asia-Pacific region, regulatory bodies such as the Financial Services Agency (FSA) in Japan and the Securities and Futures Commission (SFC) in Hong Kong play pivotal roles. The FSA focuses on encouraging market stability while fostering innovation through its 'Five-year Regulatory Reform Initiative.' This initiative addresses issues like high-frequency trading, requiring that algorithms used by market makers adhere to strict compliance standards. The SFC's regulations are tailored to ensure robust risk management and accountability for market makers, particularly in derivative markets.

A notable global trend is the move toward harmonization of regulatory standards to accommodate the increasingly interconnected nature of financial markets. Organizations such as the International Organization of Securities Commissions (IOSCO) and the Financial Stability Board (FSB) advocate for coherent, cross-border regulatory frameworks. This harmonization effort reflects the need to prevent regulatory arbitrage — a situation where companies exploit differences between national regulations to gain a competitive advantage. Efforts to create a synchronized environment for market making have led to agreements on minimum capital requirements and other key standards. Nonetheless, the challenge remains in balancing national regulatory autonomy with international coherence.

Despite these extensive regulatory efforts, market making poses numerous compliance challenges. The advent of algorithmic trading, for instance, has necessitated additional scrutiny. Regulators must ensure that automated trading strategies do not lead to market abuse or systemic failures. This has led to the introduction of 'circuit breakers' on major exchanges, preventing extreme market volatility by temporarily halting trading when price movements exceed certain thresholds. Moreover, the implementation of risk controls and real-time surveillance systems helps monitor trading activities to curtail potential malpractices.

An illustrative example of regulatory response is the 2010 Flash Crash in the United States, where major stock indices plummeted rapidly due to a confluence of factors including high-frequency trading algorithms. This event catalyzed significant regulatory revisions, including the development of the Consolidated Audit Trail (CAT) — a system designed to track all trading orders on U.S. exchanges. The CAT aims to enable more efficient regulatory oversight by providing granular insights into market activity.

Given the complexities inherent in different regulatory frameworks, market makers must establish robust compliance strategies. These include conducting regular audits, developing comprehensive internal policies, and training personnel to understand and adhere to current regulations. Adopting advanced technological solutions, such as AI-driven compliance monitoring systems, can enhance a market maker's ability to detect and address potential regulatory breaches proactively.

For smaller firms or new entrants into the market making space, navigating the regulatory environment can be particularly daunting. Engaging with legal experts familiar with cross-jurisdictional regulations and collaborating closely with regulators can provide valuable guidance. Furthermore, participating in forums and industry groups enables market participants to stay informed of evolving regulatory landscapes and best practices.

Understanding regulatory frameworks is not merely about avoiding penalties or operational infringements; it is about recognizing the broader impact of regulation on the market ecosystem. By promoting transparency and accountability, regulations help build trust among investors, which in turn supports market liquidity and stability — essential ingredients for healthy market functioning.

As markets continue to evolve, driven by advancements in financial technologies and shifting economic dynamics, the regulatory landscape will undoubtedly adapt. Market makers must remain vigilant, recognizing that regulatory compliance is an ongoing process requiring agility and foresight. By embedding compliance into their organizational culture, market makers can not only ensure seamless operations but also contribute positively to the broader financial system, upholding its integrity for future participants.

10.2   Licensing and Registration Requirements

The licensing and registration of market makers constitute critical processes within the financial regulatory environment, ensuring that entities engaged in market making activities comply with legal standards and operational criteria set by financial authorities. These requirements are designed to uphold market integrity, protect investors, and ensure that market makers have sufficient financial and operational capability to fulfill their roles in the trading ecosystem.

Market makers, by definition, provide liquidity to financial markets by continuously offering to buy (bid) and sell (ask) securities. This liquidity provision is fundamental for the functioning of efficient and transparent markets, making regulatory oversight of these participants essential. Licensing and registration requirements vary across jurisdictions, reflecting local market architectures and regulatory philosophies. However, the underlying principles share a common focus on ensuring market stability and fairness.

In the United States, the licensing and registration process for market makers is primarily governed by the Securities and Exchange Commission (SEC) and the Financial Industry Regulatory Authority (FINRA). To become a registered market maker, a firm must be a member of FINRA, which involves a comprehensive review process. This includes the submission of a detailed application that outlines the firm's business model, operational procedures, and technological infrastructure. Moreover, market makers must have a minimum net capital, as stipulated by SEC Rule 15c3-1, to ensure they have the financial wherewithal to meet their obligations.

Potential market makers in the U.S. must also demonstrate that they have adequate risk management systems in place, particularly in relation to high-frequency trading strategies. This includes having controls to prevent erroneous trades, detailed compliance manuals to guide operations, and regular audits to evaluate internal protocols. The registration process further seeks to verify the firm's ability to maintain orderly trading during periods of market stress, which is crucial for market stability.

In Europe, the role of market maker licensing and registration falls under the purview of national regulatory bodies within the framework established by the European Union. A key harmonizing regulation is the Markets in Financial Instruments Directive II (MiFID II), which delineates specific requirements and obligations for market makers operating in EU member states. Under MiFID II, market makers are required to register with the relevant authority in each market they operate in, providing a thorough overview of their intended trading activities and the markets they wish to engage with.

A critical component of MiFID II is the emphasis on transparency and disclosure. Market makers must report their activities in significant detail, providing data on trade volumes, pricing, and execution quality. This transparency is intended to offer insights into market dynamics and to protect investors by ensuring that market making practices do not artificially manipulate market prices. Additionally, market makers under MiFID II are subject to capital adequacy requirements and ongoing compliance monitoring to align their trading activities with regulatory expectations.

The intricacies of the licensing and registration processes are also evident in the Asia-Pacific region, where countries like Japan and Australia impose their own regulatory frameworks. In Japan, the Financial Services Agency (FSA) oversees the registration of market makers. The process involves a detailed assessment of the applicant's business continuity planning, data security protocols, and ability to manage financial risks. An interesting aspect of the Japanese regulatory approach is its accommodation of innovation within the fintech space, ensuring that market makers leveraging cutting-edge technologies still adhere to strict compliance standards.

Similarly, the Australian Securities and Investments Commission (ASIC) requires market makers to hold an Australian Financial Services License (AFSL). This license mandates that market makers demonstrate competence in risk management, financial resource adequacy, and responsible management practices. ASIC's framework is particularly focused on safeguarding against conflicts of interest and ensuring fair market conduct.

When exploring the intricacy of the licensing and registration landscape, it is crucial to consider the challenges faced by firms seeking to become market makers. These challenges can range from understanding and interpreting complex regulatory requirements to the operational and financial burdens of maintaining compliance. For instance, firms often need to invest heavily in legal expertise and technological infrastructure to ensure they meet all necessary criteria. The administrative burden associated with ongoing reporting and regulatory engagement can also be substantial.

Despite these challenges, effective licensing and registration bring significant benefits. Aside from avoiding legal penalties and service suspensions, regulatory compliance enhances a firm's reputation among investors and trading partners. It instills confidence in the market maker's ability to operate reliably and ethically, thus opening doors to broader participation in financial markets and increased business opportunities.

Given the increasingly global and interconnected nature of financial markets, firms aiming to operate as market makers in multiple jurisdictions face additional hurdles. These firms must navigate diverse regulatory environments, each with unique rules and expectations. A streamlined approach involves engaging with seasoned compliance experts who understand the nuances of each market, enabling firms to develop integrated compliance strategies that respect regional differences while maintaining operational coherence.

Concurrently, the drive for regulatory harmonization, especially through international bodies like the International Organization of Securities Commissions (IOSCO), seeks to ease the burden of cross-border operations. While differences will remain, the goal of harmonization is to cultivate an environment where consistent regulatory principles apply internationally, leading to reduced complexity and enhanced market stability.

As the financial markets continue to evolve, driven by technological advancements and shifts in regulatory thinking, licensing and registration requirements for market makers will undoubtedly adapt. Market participants must remain vigilant, proactive, and informed to navigate these changes effectively. By prioritizing a culture of compliance and continually engaging with regulatory developments, market makers can position themselves to thrive in an ever-changing financial landscape, ensuring that their operations both align with and contribute positively to the broader market ecosystem.

10.3 Market Manipulation and Anti-Fraud Rules

Market manipulation and fraudulent practices have long been areas of concern in financial markets, as they undermine the integrity and efficiency of trading environments while eroding investor confidence. Market makers, given their crucial role in providing liquidity and ensuring market stability, must adhere to stringent anti-manipulation and anti-fraud regulations designed to deter and penalize unethical conduct.

Market manipulation broadly refers to actions deliberately undertaken to interfere with the natural behavior of financial markets, thereby creating artificial, false, or misleading appearances of security prices, market activity, or conditions. These practices can range from classic forms like "pump and dump" schemes to sophisticated techniques involving algorithmic trading strategies. Fraud, on the other hand, generally involves deception or misrepresentation intended to result in financial or personal gain at the expense of others, including insider trading, fraudulent disclosures, and Ponzi schemes.

In the United States, the Securities and Exchange Commission (SEC) takes the lead in the regulation of market manipulation and fraud. Under the Securities Exchange Act of 1934, several key rules and sections delineate prohibited behaviors. Rule 10b-5, for instance, addresses fraudulent and manipulative schemes, prohibiting any act or omission resulting in fraud or deceit in connection with the purchase or sale of any security. Cases of insider trading, where individuals trade on material non-public information, are prosecuted under this rule, underscoring the need for transparency and fairness in trading activities.

The SEC, together with the Commodity Futures Trading Commission (CFTC), has also been active in pursuing cases of market manipulation involving derivatives and commodity futures. For example, "spoofing" — a strategy where traders place large orders with the intention to cancel before execution, thus misleading the market about supply or demand — has been a notable area of enforcement. Regulators employ a range of detection tools and analytical methods, including examining trading patterns and employing sophisticated algorithms to identify suspicious activities indicative of market manipulation.

Europe's regulatory approach to market manipulation and fraud is encapsulated in the Market Abuse Regulation (MAR), which seeks to enhance market integrity and protect investors across the European Union. MAR encompasses directives that prohibit insider dealing, unlawful disclosure of inside information, and market manipulation. Under MAR, entities are required to implement procedures for detecting and preventing market abuse, including detailed reporting obligations on suspicious transactions and the disclosure of any market manipulation detected.

A key highlight of MAR is its emphasis on preemptive compliance measures, where institutions develop systems and controls to identify and mitigate risks associated with market abuse proactively. This includes maintaining comprehensive records of communications and transactions, conducting regular training for staff on anti-manipulation practices, and fostering a culture of transparency and accountability within the organization.

In the Asia-Pacific region, financial regulators similarly uphold rigorous standards against market manipulation and fraud. In Japan, the Financial Services Agency (FSA) enforces the Financial Instruments and Exchange Act, which provides the legal framework for preventing market abuse, ensuring that entities maintain fair trading practices. The Securities and Futures Commission (SFC) in Hong Kong focuses on rigorous surveillance and swift enforcement actions against market manipulation cases, including those involving cross-border transactions, reflecting Hong Kong's role as a key international financial center.

Regulators in these regions often collaborate with their international counterparts to tackle cross-border market manipulation and fraud, given the global nature of financial markets. This coordination is facilitated by organizations such as the International Organization of Securities Commissions (IOSCO), which encourages cooperation and sharing of intelligence among regulators worldwide. Collaborative efforts are particularly crucial in navigating the complexities introduced by digital trading platforms and the increasing sophistication of manipulation tactics.

The role of technology in detecting and preventing market manipulation is increasingly pronounced. Advanced analytics, machine learning, and artificial intelligence are employed to develop surveillance systems capable of monitoring vast amounts of trading data in real-time. These technologies help identify patterns and anomalies that human analysts might miss, providing robust defenses against market abuse. For instance, machine learning algorithms can be trained to recognize specific behavior patterns associated with past manipulation cases, enabling early detection and intervention.

Despite the technological advances and regulatory frameworks in place, challenges remain. One of the key issues is the rapidly evolving nature of trading practices, particularly in the domain of algorithmic and high-frequency trading. These methods, while beneficial for liquidity and price discovery, also provide avenues for subtle manipulation techniques that can be difficult to isolate and prove. As a result, regulators continuously refine their understanding and methodologies to stay ahead of emerging threats.

In addition to legislative and technological measures, the role of market participants themselves cannot be underestimated in fostering an environment that discourages manipulation and fraud. Market makers and other traders have an ethical obligation to conduct their activities with integrity, ensuring their practices align with both the letter and the spirit of the law. Establishing robust internal compliance programs, instilling a strong ethical culture, and encouraging whistleblowing where necessary are vital components of an effective defense against market manipulation.

Education and awareness are also fundamental in strengthening the financial landscape against fraudulent activities. Training programs and industry workshops that highlight emerging trends in market manipulation and the latest regulatory changes equip market participants with the knowledge necessary to navigate a complex trading environment responsibly. Awareness campaigns spearheaded by financial regulators also play a crucial role in alerting investors to potential frauds and schemes, thereby safeguarding the investor community.

Looking ahead, the battle against market manipulation and fraud will require continued vigilance, innovation, and cooperation. As financial markets become more interconnected and technologically advanced, the imperative to maintain high standards of integrity and transparency becomes even more pertinent. Regulators, financial institutions, and market participants must work collaboratively, leveraging international partnerships, technological innovations, and strong ethical standards to uphold the credibility and stability of global markets for generations to come.

10.4 Data Privacy and Security Considerations

As financial markets evolve in an increasingly digitized world, the importance of data privacy and security has become paramount. Market makers, positioned at the nexus of trading activities, handle a vast volume of sensitive information, ranging from proprietary trading algorithms to client-specific trading data. This section delves into the critical considerations surrounding data privacy and security, exploring regulations, best practices, and the technological safeguards necessary to protect sensitive financial information in today's complex trading environment.

In recent years, data breaches and cyber threats have emerged as significant risks for market participants, prompting regulators worldwide to enforce stringent data protection laws. These regulations are designed not only to safeguard data but also to enhance trust in the financial system. One of the most comprehensive frameworks is the General Data Protection Regulation (GDPR), applicable to entities operating within the European Union. GDPR mandates strict guidelines on data collection, storage, and processing, ensuring that market makers handle personal data responsibly and transparently.

GDPR's relevance to market makers extends beyond European boundaries, as its extraterritorial scope affects any firm dealing with EU citizens. Key provisions include the requirement for explicit consent before data processing, the right to data access and rectification by data subjects, and the timely notification of data breaches to regulatory bodies. Non-compliance with GDPR can lead to significant penalties, highlighting the need for robust data governance practices.

In the United States, firms are subject to a combination of federal and state regulations concerning data privacy, including the Gramm-Leach-Bliley Act (GLBA) and the California Consumer Privacy Act (CCPA). While the GLBA focuses primarily on protecting consumer financial information held by financial institutions, the CCPA grants individuals more control over their personal data, including the right to know, access, and delete information collected by businesses. Market makers operating in the U.S. must ensure compliance with these regulations, implementing policies that protect client data from unauthorized access and misuse.

Across the Asia-Pacific region, jurisdictions such as Singapore, Hong Kong, and Australia enforce their own data protection laws, including the Personal Data Protection Act (PDPA) in Singapore and the Privacy Act in Australia. These regulations similarly emphasize the need for informed consent, transparency in data usage, and comprehensive security measures to prevent data breaches.

In addition to meeting regulatory requirements, market makers must proactively implement security technologies and protocols to safeguard data. This involves employing encryption and other cryptographic techniques to protect data at rest and in transit, ensuring that unauthorized parties cannot access sensitive information. Multi-factor authentication (MFA) adds an additional layer of security, requiring users to verify their identity through multiple channels before accessing critical systems.

Intrusion detection systems (IDS) and firewalls play crucial roles in monitoring network traffic and identifying potential threats in real-time. When a suspicious pattern or anomaly is detected, these systems can alert security teams to potential breaches, allowing for rapid intervention and mitigation. Implementing a robust incident response plan is also vital, preparing organizations to react efficiently to security incidents, minimizing damage, and restoring operations swiftly.

Another essential consideration for market makers is data anonymization and pseudonymization. These techniques involve altering data in such a way that it cannot be traced back to individual clients, thereby protecting personal information while allowing data to be analyzed and utilized. Anonymized data can be instrumental in backtesting trading algorithms and conducting market research without infringing on privacy rights.

While technological measures are critical, cultivating a culture of security within the organization is equally important. Regular training programs can equip employees with the knowledge and awareness needed to recognize potential cyber threats and adhere to security best practices. This includes phishing awareness, secure password management, and understanding the implications of regulatory requirements on daily operations.

Market makers must also consider the security of third-party service providers, especially those involved in cloud computing and data analytics. Conducting thorough due diligence before engaging third parties and ensuring they comply with relevant data protection standards is indispensable. Service-level agreements (SLAs) should clearly outline the responsibilities of each party in maintaining data security and privacy.

Despite the comprehensive measures that can be taken, the reality of cyber threats is that they are continually evolving. From ransomware attacks to sophisticated phishing campaigns, the tactics employed by cybercriminals grow more advanced, necessitating continuous innovation and investment in security technologies. Market makers must stay informed about emerging threats and be willing to adapt their security strategies accordingly.

One recent development in cybersecurity is the application of artificial intelligence (AI) and machine learning in detecting and responding to threats. AI systems can analyze vast datasets to identify abnormal behavior patterns that may indicate a security breach. These systems can also adapt and learn from past incidents, improving their accuracy and efficacy over time.

Blockchain technology is another area gaining traction for its potential to enhance data integrity and security. By providing a decentralized and tamper-proof ledger, blockchain can offer secure mechanisms for recording and verifying transactions, thereby reducing the risk of data tampering and fraud.

Ultimately, the landscape of data privacy and security is complex and multifaceted, requiring market makers to employ a balanced approach that considers technological, regulatory, and human factors. By prioritizing data protection and committing to ongoing improvement, market makers can not only shield themselves from regulatory penalties and operational disruptions but also build trust with clients and stakeholders, positioning themselves as responsible and reliable participants in the financial market ecosystem. The path forward will require ongoing collaboration between regulators, industry leaders, and technology innovators to address the challenges and opportunities presented by the digital age.

10.5 Ethical Trading Practices

In financial markets, where market makers play a pivotal role in ensuring liquidity and stability, ethical trading practices have emerged as a vital component of sustainable and responsible market operation. The emphasis on ethics is not merely about adherence to regulatory mandates; it represents a commitment to upholding trust and integrity within the trading ecosystem. As market participants increasingly turn to algorithmic and high-frequency trading (HFT), the potential for ethical dilemmas and conflicts highlights the importance of grounding trading activities in a strong ethical framework.

At its core, ethical trading involves conducting business in a manner that is fair, transparent, and aligned with the broader interests of stakeholders, including investors, regulators, and society at large. This encompasses a range of considerations, from preventing unfair trading practices and maintaining transparency to promoting sustainable financial practices and safeguarding against conflicts of interest.

One key aspect of ethical trading practices is the commitment to transparency. Transparency in trading operations helps ensure that all market participants have access to the information necessary to make informed decisions. This transparency extends beyond pre-trade and post-trade reporting; it also involves clear communication about trading strategies and the rationale behind trading decisions. Ensuring transparency requires diligent disclosure policies and robust information systems that provide real-time and accurate data to all participants.

Fairness is another crucial element of ethical trading. Market makers have the responsibility to treat all counterparties equitably, ensuring that their actions do not unduly disadvantage any particular group. This includes offering fair prices that reflect true market conditions, avoiding practices that manipulate prices or trading volumes, and providing equal access to trading platforms and services. Fair trading practices build confidence in the markets, encouraging participation and fostering liquidity.

The rise of algorithmic trading and HFT poses unique ethical challenges, as these strategies are capable of executing a large volume of transactions at high speeds, potentially impacting market behavior. Ensuring that such algorithms do not engage in manipulative tactics, such as spoofing or layering, is critical. Spoofing involves placing large orders with no intention of executing them, only to cancel them as soon as they influence the market. Layering is a similar strategy where multiple orders are placed to create the illusion of demand or supply, only to be canceled rapidly once the market reacts. Both practices distort market reality and are considered unethical and illegal.

In response to these challenges, many market makers are investing in algorithmic accountability, developing mechanisms to ensure that their trading algorithms adhere to ethical standards. This involves rigorous pre-deployment testing, continuous monitoring, and regular auditing of algorithms to ensure their behavior remains within ethical and legal bounds. The integration of artificial intelligence and machine learning in trading systems further necessitates the establishment of ethical guidelines for their use, ensuring that these technologies are applied in ways that enhance market integrity rather than undermine it.

Moreover, ethical trading extends to the treatment of confidential information. Market makers often have access to sensitive information that, if misused, could provide an unfair advantage. Upholding the confidentiality of client data and trading activity is paramount, aligning with broader principles of data privacy and security. Entities must ensure that robust controls are in place to prevent unauthorized access or misuse of information, thereby maintaining trust and integrity in their operations.

The financial crises of the past have underscored the importance of ethical conduct in preventing systemic failures. Ethical trading practices are integral to risk management strategies that aim to prevent excessive risk-taking and promote responsible decision-making. By embedding ethical principles within their risk management frameworks, market makers can better anticipate and mitigate potential risks that could undermine market stability.

Furthermore, ethical trading practices are closely intertwined with corporate social responsibility (CSR) initiatives, as firms recognize the value of aligning their operations with societal values and contributing positively to the community. Many market makers are adopting sustainability measures and socially responsible investing (SRI) strategies to pursue financial returns while also generating social and environmental benefits. These efforts reflect a broader understanding that business success and social prosperity are inextricably linked.

Conflicts of interest present another significant ethical challenge, particularly in trading environments where financial incentives can misalign with the duty to act in the best interest of clients. Market makers must implement clear policies and procedures to identify, disclose, and manage potential conflicts of interest, ensuring that decisions are made impartially and transparently. This includes separation of duties and erecting Chinese walls within organizations to prevent the undue influence of proprietary interests.

Education and advocacy also play a vital role in promoting ethical trading practices. By fostering a culture of ethics through training programs, workshops, and industry engagements, market makers can enhance awareness and understanding of ethical issues among employees and stakeholders. Engaging with regulators, industry bodies, and peer organizations facilitates the sharing of best practices and the development of industry-wide ethical standards.

Beyond internal measures, the establishment of ethical trading practices requires active dialogue with regulators and other market participants to continually refine and enhance ethical standards. Collaboration across the industry can lead to greater consistency and effectiveness in ethical governance, ultimately supporting a healthy and resilient financial ecosystem.

The commitment to ethical trading practices is both a moral obligation and a strategic imperative for market makers. By aligning their operations with ethical principles, market makers not only safeguard their reputation and contribute to the stability of financial markets, but they also create a sustainable foundation for long-term success in the global marketplace. As financial markets continue to evolve and face new challenges, ethical considerations will remain at the forefront, guiding market participants in building trust and achieving excellence in their trading activities.

10.6   Impact of Regulation on Innovation

The relationship between regulation and innovation in the financial markets is a complex and multifaceted one, where the balancing act between regulatory oversight and technological advancement is critical. Market makers, as pivotal players in the financial ecosystem, operate at the intersection of these dynamics, navigating a landscape shaped by evolving regulatory frameworks while continuously seeking innovative strategies to enhance their trading operations and competitive edge. Understanding the impact of regulation on innovation provides a comprehensive view of how market makers can adapt to and capitalize on the changing regulatory and technological environment.

Regulation in financial markets aims to ensure stability, fairness, and transparency, protecting investors and preserving market integrity. However, these regulatory measures can also pose challenges to innovation by imposing constraints on how market makers develop and implement new strategies and technologies. The key challenge is to strike a balance that supports innovation without compromising regulatory objectives.

One of the primary impacts of regulation on innovation is the imposition of compliance requirements that can limit the pace and scope of technological advancements. Regulatory compliance often necessitates significant time and resources, as market makers must ensure their innovations align with legal standards. This includes thorough testing, documentation, and adaptation to meet the requirements of regulatory bodies such as the Securities and Exchange Commission (SEC) in the United States and the European Securities and Markets Authority (ESMA) in Europe. These processes can slow down the development and deployment of new technologies, as firms navigate the complexities of demonstrating compliance.

Furthermore, strict regulatory frameworks may inadvertently stifle innovation by creating a risk-averse culture. Market makers, wary of potential regulatory breaches and associated penalties, might be reluctant to pursue bold and disruptive innovations. This risk aversion can manifest in a preference for incremental improvements over radical changes, limiting the transformative potential of new technologies. As a result, the pace of technological progress in areas like algorithmic trading, machine learning, and blockchain may be tempered by the need to carefully navigate regulatory landscapes.

However, regulation can also serve as a catalyst for innovation by establishing clear guidelines that encourage the development of technologies designed to enhance compliance and risk management. The introduction of regulations such as the General Data Protection Regulation (GDPR) and the Markets in Financial Instruments Directive II (MiFID II) has spurred market makers to innovate in data management, privacy, and transparency. Technologies like artificial intelligence and data analytics have been applied to develop sophisticated compliance tools capable of automating and optimizing regulatory reporting, monitoring, and auditing processes.

In addition, regulatory frameworks can promote innovation by increasing competition and market participation. For instance, the adoption of MiFID II in Europe has encouraged the emergence of new trading venues and services by dismantling barriers to entry and fostering a more competitive market environment. This increased competition can incentivize market makers to innovate in order to differentiate themselves and capture market share, leading to greater technological advancements and enhanced market efficiency.

Regulatory sandboxes are another example of how regulation can positively impact innovation. These controlled testing environments allow market participants to trial new products and services with temporary regulatory relief, offering a space to experiment without the immediate risk of non-compliance. Regulatory sandboxes foster collaboration between regulators and innovators, providing valuable insights into evolving market dynamics and informing the development of adaptive regulatory policies. This approach has been embraced by regulators like the UK's Financial Conduct Authority (FCA) and Singapore's Monetary Authority of Singapore (MAS), which have established frameworks to support fintech innovation within secure bounds.

A notable example of regulation driving innovation is the rise of RegTech — regulatory technology designed to streamline regulatory compliance and monitoring. The demand for effective RegTech solutions has surged as market makers seek efficient ways to manage regulatory complexities and reduce compliance costs. Innovations in RegTech, such as real-time risk assessment platforms and automated reporting systems, have enabled market participants to comply more easily with regulations while enhancing operational efficiency and accuracy.

In the broader context, the interplay between regulation and innovation is influenced by international efforts to harmonize regulatory standards. As financial markets become increasingly globalized, regulatory harmonization can facilitate innovation by reducing the complexity and variability of compliance requirements across jurisdictions. Harmonized standards can enable market makers to implement innovative strategies and technologies on a larger, cross-border scale, fostering a more integrated and efficient global market environment.

However, pursuing regulatory harmonization poses its own challenges, as individual jurisdictions balance the desire for consistency with the need to address local market conditions and policy priorities. Successful harmonization requires collaboration and dialogue among international regulatory bodies, market participants, and other stakeholders to ensure that regulatory frameworks are conducive to both innovation and market stability.

Ultimately, the impact of regulation on innovation is not a unilateral constraint but a dynamic interaction that shapes the evolution of financial markets. By navigating regulatory challenges and leveraging opportunities for compliance-driven innovation, market makers can develop resilient and adaptable strategies that align with both regulatory requirements and market demands.

To thrive in this evolving landscape, market makers should embrace a proactive approach to regulation, engaging with policymakers and industry bodies to advocate for regulatory frameworks that support innovation while safeguarding market integrity. Regular engagement with regulators can foster a collaborative environment where market participants can share insights, raise concerns, and contribute to the formation of balanced policies that drive both innovation and stability.

Moreover, investing in research and development, fostering a culture of innovation within organizations, and building strategic partnerships with technology firms and academic institutions can enhance market makers' capacity to innovate responsibly and effectively. By integrating ethical considerations and sustainability objectives into their innovation strategies, market makers can position themselves as leaders in a rapidly changing financial ecosystem, ensuring long-term success in the face of regulatory and technological advancements.

10.7   Global Harmonization of Regulations

In the intricate world of financial markets, characterized by globalization and technological advancements, the call for global harmonization of regulations has grown increasingly urgent. Market makers operate within this expansive and interconnected landscape, where cross-border transactions and international trading are the norms. Ensuring consistent regulatory frameworks across diverse jurisdictions is crucial not only for fostering market stability and integrity but also for enabling market makers to innovate and compete effectively on a global scale.

Global harmonization of regulations refers to the process of aligning financial regulatory standards and practices across different countries and regions to minimize inconsistencies, facilitate international trade, and reduce the risks associated with regulatory arbitrage. Regulatory arbitrage occurs when firms exploit the differences in rules between jurisdictions to gain competitive advantages, potentially undermining risk management practices and market stability.

One of the primary motivations behind the push for regulatory harmonization is to address the challenges posed by the globalization of financial markets. Global financial crises, such as the 2008 financial turmoil, have highlighted the interconnectedness of markets and the systemic risks that can arise when regulatory gaps or conflicts exist. A harmonized approach can help strengthen the resilience of the global financial system by providing clearer guidelines and reducing the chances of regulatory oversights that could lead to crises.

International organizations play a crucial role in the harmonization process, facilitating dialogue and cooperation between national regulators. Bodies such as the International Organization of Securities Commissions (IOSCO), the Financial Stability Board (FSB), and the Basel Committee on Banking Supervision provide platforms for developing and promoting consistent regulatory standards. These organizations help coordinate efforts to address emerging global risks, improve transparency, and promote best practices in financial regulation.

One of the most notable examples of harmonization efforts is the Basel III framework, developed by the Basel Committee on Banking Supervision. Basel III establishes comprehensive guidelines for banking regulation to improve the resilience of banks by setting higher capital requirements, introducing new regulatory metrics like the leverage ratio, and strengthening liquidity supervision. This framework is adopted by member countries worldwide, significantly enhancing the global banking sector's ability to withstand economic shocks and financial stress.

Similarly, the European Union's adoption of the Markets in Financial Instruments Directive II (MiFID II) offers insights into regional harmonization. MiFID II harmonizes trading practices within the EU by imposing comprehensive transparency and reporting requirements, promoting competition, and ensuring robust investor protection. While targeted primarily at the EU, MiFID II's influence extends globally, encouraging non-EU entities that engage with European markets to voluntarily adopt or align their practices with its standards.

The harmonization of regulations also profoundly affects innovation and competition. By reducing the uncertainty and costs associated with operating in multiple jurisdictions, harmonized standards encourage firms to expand internationally and invest in new markets and technologies. For instance, a market maker adhering to consistent regulatory requirements across regions can deploy innovative trading strategies and technological solutions on a broader scale, unlocking growth opportunities and fostering cross-border competition.

However, the path to harmonization is fraught with challenges. Differences in legal systems, market structures, and regulatory philosophies between countries can complicate efforts to achieve complete alignment. Each jurisdiction has its unique priorities and economic conditions, which may necessitate tailoring regulations to address local concerns, even if they deviate from global standards.

Moreover, the process of reaching consensus on harmonized standards can be slow and complex, involving negotiations and compromises among a multitude of stakeholders. Balancing the need for comprehensive, global standards with the flexibility to accommodate regional variations is an ongoing challenge that requires diplomatic skills, collaboration, and patience.

Innovation in financial technology (fintech) is another area where global harmonization can have significant implications. As fintech firms increasingly offer innovative solutions across borders, consistent regulatory frameworks can lower entry barriers, streamline approval processes, and facilitate quicker market access. At the same time, harmonized standards can help protect consumers by ensuring that fintech products and services meet universal safety, transparency, and reliability criteria.

In data privacy and security, harmonization efforts strive to establish global norms that address the cross-border nature of data flows in financial transactions. Aligning regulations such as the General Data Protection Regulation (GDPR) in the EU with data privacy laws in other regions can help manage data risks and reinforce consumer trust in global digital financial services.

Despite the numerous advantages of harmonization, it is crucial that such efforts do not lead to a "race to the bottom," where the pressure to align with the lowest common denominator weakens regulatory robustness. Instead, the objective should be to achieve high-quality standards that reinforce market stability and drive innovation, without imposing unnecessary burdens on market participants.

Successful harmonization hinges on open communication and collaboration between regulators, industry participants, and international organizations. Regular dialogue and sharing of experiences can facilitate mutual understanding and trust-building, laying the groundwork for effective alignment. Engaging with industry voices, including market makers and technology providers, is also vital to ensure that harmonized regulations are practical, forward-looking, and conducive to innovation.

Education and capacity-building initiatives are necessary to support harmonization efforts, equipping regulators and market participants with the knowledge and skills needed to implement and comply with global standards. Continuous research and adaptation to evolving market dynamics will further inform ongoing harmonization strategies, allowing them to remain relevant and effective in an ever-changing financial landscape.

Ultimately, the global harmonization of regulations presents both opportunities and challenges for market makers. By embracing harmonization as a strategic priority, market participants can leverage its benefits to enhance their operational resilience, capitalize on new market opportunities, and contribute to a more stable and integrated global financial system. As financial markets continue to evolve, global regulatory coordination will be essential in fostering a sustainable and inclusive trading environment that benefits all stakeholders.

Chapter 11

Performance Evaluation and Optimization

This chapter focuses on evaluating and optimizing the performance of market making strategies. It outlines key performance metrics such as profitability and Sharpe ratio, essential for assessing trading outcomes. Detailed methodologies for analyzing trading performance are presented, alongside strategies for benchmarking against industry standards. The chapter explores techniques for identifying areas of improvement and implementing optimization through parameter tuning and scenario simulations. Emphasis is placed on risk-adjusted performance evaluations to balance returns with acceptable risk levels, fostering continuous improvement and adaptation in ever-evolving financial markets.

11.1   Defining Performance Metrics

In trading and investing, particularly within market-making strategies, performance metrics form the cornerstone of evaluating success. These metrics provide traders, algorithm developers, and portfolio managers with the tools to assess efficiency, profitability, and risk-adjusted returns. By understanding these metrics, it becomes possible to make informed decisions that align with both strategic goals and risk management practices. This section delves into key performance metrics, explaining their significance and application within market-making strategies.

The metric of **profitability** is often the most straightforward yet critical measurement for any trading strategy. Profitability indicates the absolute return generated from trades over a specific time horizon. However, for market makers, profitability encompasses subtle nuances, such as the ability to continuously capture the bid-ask spread while minimizing slippage and adverse selection risks. Consider a market-making algorithm that facilitates thousands of trades in a day—the sheer volume necessitates a robust mechanism to evaluate cumulative profits while factoring in transaction costs.

One example is using the formula for *net profit*, computed as:

$$\text{Net Profit} = \sum_{i=1}^{N}(P_i \times Q_i - C_i) \tag{11.1}$$

where P_i is the price at which the i-th trade is executed, Q_i is the quantity traded, and C_i represents the transaction costs associated with that trade. This formulation provides a clear quantitative measure of a strategy's effectiveness over time.

Another key metric is the **win/loss ratio**, which offers insights into the consistency and reliability of a strategy. This ratio is defined by the number of winning trades divided by the number of losing trades. A higher win/loss ratio suggests a strategy's success in making more profitable trades rather than merely maximizing the size of winning trades, which aligns with the market-making philosophy of frequent, small gains.

However, relying solely on raw winning trades can be misleading. Consider two algorithms: one with a win/loss ratio of 2:1 and another with 1:1. If the latter generates significantly larger profits in its winning trades compared to the losses endured during negative trades, it might outperform the former. Thus, the interplay between profit per trade and the win/loss ratio must be acknowledged.

An advanced metric that encapsulates both profitability and risk is the **Sharpe ratio**. This measures the average return earned in excess of the risk-free rate per unit of volatility or total risk, thereby providing a risk-adjusted performance metric. Formally, it is calculated as:

$$\text{Sharpe Ratio} = \frac{\overline{R} - R_f}{\sigma_R} \tag{11.2}$$

where $\overline{R}$ is the average return of the portfolio, R_f is the risk-free rate of return, and σ_R is the standard deviation of the portfolio's excess return.

The Sharpe ratio is particularly useful for market makers, as it accounts for the volatility inherent in extremely frequent trading activities. It allows for a balanced view of performance where not just returns, but the variability of those returns, are measured against a benchmark risk-free investment. A higher Sharpe ratio is indicative of a more favorable risk-adjusted return.

Another important performance metric is the **maximum drawdown**, which quantifies the largest peak-to-trough decline in a portfolio's value within a specific period, illustrating the potential risk of significant losses. Understanding the maximum drawdown is crucial for market makers as it informs about the strategy's resilience to prolonged adverse market conditions.

For instance, if a market-making strategy experiences a maximum drawdown of 10%, this denotes the most pronounced drop in portfolio value from its peak, a scenario that must be anticipated and mitigated through risk management strategies such as stop-loss orders or dynamic hedging.

The **Information Ratio** (IR) is another metric that assesses a strategy's ability to generate excess returns relative to a benchmark while considering tracking errors. It is calculated as:

$$\text{Information Ratio} = \frac{\alpha}{\omega} \tag{11.3}$$

where α is the portfolio's active return, and ω is its tracking error. A higher IR signifies the strategy's ability to outperform a benchmark consistently and is especially crucial for market-making strategies that often operate with tight spreads and low margins.

Effective implementation of market-making strategies involves maintaining **liquidity metrics** such as market depth, order book imbalance, and time to execution. These indicators, while often overlooked, are vital in evaluating a strategy's capability to provide liquidity without unduly affecting market prices. Market depth gauges the volume of buy and sell orders at various prices, which can indicate the strategy's influence on the market.

Furthermore, the **volatility of returns** is a salient metric, revealing the stability of profits over time. For market makers, high volatility may suggest excessive exposure to market movements, urging adjustments in algorithm parameters to better stabilize returns. The concept is captured by the standard deviation of daily, weekly, or monthly returns, providing a picture of profit reliability and consistency.

Lastly, ongoing performance evaluation mandates the use of **backtesting metrics**. Simulation of trading strategies using historical data allows for an empirical understanding of strategy performance under various market conditions. The success of backtesting is often judged by metrics such as total return, daily average profit, and calibration of assumptions against actual market behavior.

Indeed, accurately defining and employing these performance metrics provides invaluable insight into market-making strategies, ultimately fostering their refinement and inception. By ensuring these metrics are systematically evaluated, market participants can achieve enhanced strategic alignment and informed optimizations, contributing to better decision-making outcomes.

11.2   Analyzing Trading Performance

The task of analyzing trading performance in the context of market-making strategies involves a spectrum of techniques designed to provide insight into the efficacy, robustness, and adaptability of these strategies in diverse market environments. This analysis is a critical step, guiding traders and algorithm designers to identify successful elements of their strategies and areas where performance can be optimized or risks mitigated. This section provides a comprehensive exploration of tools and methodologies that facilitate a deeper understanding of trading performance.

A primary component of performance analysis is the **trade-by-trade analysis**, which examines each transaction's relevance within the overall strategy. This entails dissecting individual trades to evaluate entry and exit points, the rationale for execution, and the resultant profits or losses. Such granular assessment allows for the identification of patterns, such as recurring conditions under which trades consistently underperform or outperform expectations.

For example, consider a market-making algorithm operating in the equity markets. By scrutinizing trades that underperformed during periods of high volatility, the algorithm can be adjusted to either avoid trading under such conditions or adopt strategies that benefit from volatility spikes, such as volatility arbitrage. Trade-by-trade analysis can also help pinpoint the impact of transaction costs, slippages, and market impacts on performance metrics previously discussed.

Another crucial aspect is evaluating the **execution quality**, which measures how effectively trades are executed at intended prices and sizes. For market makers, the difference between the expected price and the actual price, known as slippage, can significantly impact profitability. Evaluating this aspect involves using metrics such as the volume-weighted average price (VWAP) or implementation shortfall. These metrics help assess the effectiveness of trade execution strategies, ensuring that the algorithm achieves optimal order placement without incurring excessive costs.

Moreover, execution quality is tightly coupled with the assessment of the strategy's ability to maintain market neutrality. Market makers often aim to hedge away directional exposure, focusing instead on capturing spreads between bid and ask prices across myriad trades. This non-directional stance necessitates constant evaluation to ensure market neutrality is meticulously maintained across different trading environments. Performance evaluation should address instances where execution deviations lead to unwanted market exposures.

Latency analysis forms another pillar of performance evaluation, particularly in high-frequency trading strategies deployed in market making. Identifying and managing latency issues—delays in trade execution caused by technological inefficiencies—can drastically improve performance outcomes. Latency metrics help measure the speed at which an algorithm can respond to market changes, ensuring that trades are executed with minimal delay relative to decision-making timeframes. Fast execution in itself is a competitive advantage in modern trading environments, enabling strategies to maintain efficacy in volatile markets.

To gain comprehensive insights, the full **distribution of returns** must be examined rather than solely focusing on averages or aggregate performance metrics. This includes assessing the skewness and kurtosis of return distributions, which reveal the frequency of extreme values and the tail properties of the return set. Strategies may present favorable average returns yet expose traders to significant downside risks if return distributions are heavily skewed or leptokurtic, suggesting that sporadic large losses could offset regular small gains. This analysis underpins effective risk management, cautioning traders about potential vulnerabilities.

Trading performance further benefits from **performance attribution analysis**, which breaks down the sources of portfolio returns. This allows market makers to evaluate specific factors contributing to successful trades, such as favorable market conditions, advantageous spreads, or algorithmic precision versus external influences like market sentiment or macroeconomic events. Attribution analysis not only illustrates a strategy's inherent strengths and weaknesses but also guides parameter adjustments, particularly when transitioning to new market conditions or asset classes.

Applying **sensitivity analysis** enhances performance evaluation by testing the robustness of trading strategies under varying conditions. By systematically varying key parameters such as order size limits, quote frequency, and spread thresholds, traders can understand the sensitivity of their performance to these inputs. Such testing is crucial for market-making algorithms that operate with fine margins where small deviations in input parameters can lead to disproportional impacts on profitability and risk profiles.

Additional value is derived from **stress testing**, which simulates extreme market conditions to evaluate a strategy's resilience. Typically, this involves applying hypothetical or historical market shock scenarios, such as unexpected political events, crashes, or rapid liquidity evaporation, to assess how a market-making strategy holds up under stress. Stress tests substantiate strategic adjustments aimed at ensuring robustness even during adverse market conditions that might otherwise lead to significant drawdowns or loss of capital.

Continuous performance analysis draws heavily from **technological advancements in data analytics and machine learning**. By integrating real-time analytics, strategy developers can refine algorithms based on current trading data streams, using predictive models to anticipate price movements and market dynamics. Machine learning algorithms can offer insights into complex, non-linear patterns within trade data, leading to enhanced predictive accuracy and adaptability.

The establishment of **key performance indicators (KPIs)** provides a concrete framework for ongoing performance measurement. These indicators, tailored to specific goals within the market-making domain, equip traders with a structured approach to evaluate progress and performance consistency. Common KPIs might include profitability per execution, average order life span, order success rate, and mean-reversion effectiveness visualized through dashboards and periodic reporting mechanisms.

Ultimately, the aim of analyzing trading performance is to iterate and refine market-making strategies in a cycle of ongoing optimization. The commitment to detailed performance evaluations at both micro and macro levels is indispensable for success in competitive markets. By applying meticulous analysis, traders are better positioned to sustain improvements, navigate risks, and maintain strategies that are both profitable and resilient over the long term. This exemplifies the pivotal role of comprehensive performance analysis in the sustenance and evolution of market-making as a dynamic trading strategy.

11.3 Benchmarking Against Market Standards

In the complex landscape of financial markets, benchmarking against established market standards is a fundamental practice used to measure the relative performance and viability of trading strategies, notably within the sphere of market-making. By deploying benchmarking techniques, traders and portfolio managers can place their results within the broader context of market conditions, competition, and theoretical expectations, thereby assessing their strategies not just on absolute gains, but on relative efficiency and effectiveness.

Benchmarking involves comparing a given strategy's returns, risks, and other metrics to well-recognized standards or indices that reflect the performance of a specific market segment. For market makers, these benchmarks might include indices representing broad market movements, peer group performance indices, or risk-adjusted measures such as the Sharpe or Sortino ratios.

A critical step in benchmarking is selecting an appropriate benchmark. An incorrect choice can mislead performance evaluations, as benchmarks should closely align with the asset classes, geographical focus, and trading styles of the strategy being assessed. For example, evaluating the performance of a market-making strategy active in U.S. equities might utilize the S&P 500 Index or the Wilshire 5000, offering a comprehensive view of the U.S. market. Similarly, a strategy trading in emerging markets might benchmark against the MSCI Emerging Markets Index to ensure performance comparisons are contextually relevant.

Understanding different benchmark types is essential. An **absolute benchmark** measures a strategy's returns against a specific target or required rate of return. While useful for setting performance goals, it does not reflect relative market conditions. A **market-based benchmark**, on the other hand, offers a dynamic comparison reflecting market movements. These include indices such as the aforementioned

S&P 500 or bespoke indices specifically designed for sectors or asset classes relevant to particular strategies.

Peer group benchmarks provide yet another lens, typically aggregating performances of similar strategies or funds to gauge a manager's relative success. Here, market makers need to ensure that the peer group is closely matched in terms of strategy, risk profile, and market focus. This process might involve the formulation of a custom peer composite or reliance on data from commercial services specializing in fund performance tracking.

Once the benchmark has been chosen, the task of measurement and comparison begins, often using visual tools such as **performance graphs** and **return histograms**. These aid in illustrating how closely the trading strategy aligns with or deviates from the chosen standard over time. Statistical measures, such as **tracking error**, help quantify the volatility of returns relative to the benchmark, capturing the deviation in terms of how much a strategy's returns depart from those of the benchmark.

Calculating the **tracking error** provides a sense of how consistent a strategy has been in mirroring its benchmark, and is computed as:

$$\text{Tracking Error} = \sqrt{\frac{1}{N-1} \sum_{i=1}^{N} (R_i - B_i)^2}$$

where R_i represents the return on the portfolio, B_i represents the return on the benchmark, and N is the number of return periods.

Another measure integral to benchmarking is the **Information Ratio** (IR), which was previously mentioned as a key performance metric. Within the context of benchmarking, it assesses how much excess return is being derived from the risk of deviating from a benchmark. A high IR suggests that the strategy offers a favorable return for each unit of active risk and is considered a hallmark of successful active management.

Benchmarking also involves the use of **risk-adjusted return metrics**. The Sharpe ratio remains a popular choice, providing insight into how a strategy's returns compare to a risk-free alternative while adjusting for volatility. The Sortino ratio refines this further by only accounting for downside deviation, thus offering a clearer picture of the risk profile factors most relevant to a market maker's performance goals.

Mindful of information efficiency, market makers could benefit from analyzing the **Jensen's Alpha**. It represents the average return on a portfolio over theories such as the capital asset pricing model (CAPM), effectively quantifying how much of the portfolio's return is due to the manager's skill as opposed to inherent market movements.

In practice, it is also vital to consider the **beta** of a strategy against its benchmark—a measure that reflects the sensitivity of the strategy's returns to changes in the market. For a market-making strategy, maintaining a low beta might be ideal, given the goal of optimizing spread capture rather than betting on market direction.

To enhance benchmarking accuracy and relevance, often the market conditions and periods are divided into segments, such as bull and bear phases, where different benchmarks might apply or different evaluations on volatility-adjusted performance are assessed. This **conditional benchmarking** accounts for the fact that a strategy might react differently under various market stress conditions.

Furthermore, the incorporation of **backtesting**, where historical data is used to simulate how a strategy would have performed over specific time intervals against chosen benchmarks, provides prospective insights into strategy resilience and adaptation to market volatility.

In algorithmic and systematic trading, benchmarking becomes increasingly sophisticated with **algorithm performance metrics** and **predictive analytics** offering deeper insights. Machine learning models, neural networks, and other algorithmic strategies provide benchmarks grounded in large datasets, with benchmarks often extending beyond typical index returns to incorporate factors like algorithm efficiency and latency.

It is, however, important to acknowledge the limitations and potential pitfalls of benchmarking. Rigid adherence to benchmarks might lead to **benchmark hugging**, where managers replicate benchmark portfolios, thus foregoing any opportunity for differentiated returns. Also, benchmarks may not account for taxes, management fees, or potential slippage. Hence, while benchmarking furnishes invaluable relative metrics, it necessitates careful consideration and should be complemented by comprehensive evaluation frameworks that include qualitative performance assessments.

Ultimately, mastering the art and science of benchmarking against market standards empowers market makers and strategists to contextualize their results, adapt to market changes, and refine strategies for optimized performance consistent with their objectives. This establishes benchmarking not only as a tool for evaluation but as a strategic mechanism for continuous improvement and active learning in a rapidly evolving financial landscape.

11.4   Identifying Areas for Improvement

Within the ambit of market-making strategies, identifying areas for enhancement is crucial for sustaining competitive advantages and boosting risk-adjusted returns. The inherent complexity and dynamic nature of financial markets necessitate that traders and algorithm developers continuously assess their strategies, detecting sub-optimal segments and susceptibility to risks. This section explores strategic methodologies for recognizing areas ripe for improvement and fostering a culture of continuous advancement in trading frameworks.

At the heart of identifying enhancement opportunities lies the comprehensive analysis of historic and current trading performance data. **Performance diagnostics** serve as a foundational tool in this endeavor. By scrutinizing trade records, closing positions, transaction costs, and profits relative to market conditions, areas lacking efficiency or exposing significant risk can be highlighted. Emphasis should be placed on metrics such as average profitability during low-liquidity periods, success rates of limit versus market orders, and correlations with market volatility indices.

Error analysis offers further insights, where attention is directed to negative returns and failed transactions. Investigating trade execution errors, such as those stemming from high slippage, latency, or missed opportunities due to infrastructural lags, can expose tactical deficiencies. Automated alert systems can capture and log erroneous trades or underperforming sequence patterns, funneling this data into an optimization loop where algorithms are adjusted to minimize similar future occurrences.

For example, a market-making algorithm might consistently incur losses during pronounced overnight futures market movements due to gaps in pre-market data assessments. By identifying this as a point of vulnerability, adjustments can be made to incorporate global market indicators and news sentiment analysis during decision-making processes.

Liquidity analysis is pivotal, particularly since a principal function of market-making involves providing liquidity to the market while managing inventory risks. Understanding which instruments or conditions

242

lead to unsustainable inventory positions or result in unnecessarily high spreads is vital. This may involve quantifying the potential impact of liquidity constraints on transaction costs and assessing how these affect the overall bid-ask spread capture strategy.

A practical instance involves re-evaluating the impact of different time slots on liquidity, as certain periods might exhibit reduced trading volumes leading to greater bid-ask spreads. Strategically adjusting algorithmic trading windows can ensure optimal engagement during times of heightened liquidity, streamlining performance.

Ultimately, trading strategies should be equipped with **risk management frameworks** that constantly evolve as new areas for improvement are identified. One effective approach is the establishment of automated risk threshold alerts which utilize key performance indicators such as leverage ratios, exposure limits, delta hedging efficiency, and stop-loss breach frequencies. These indicators can illuminate latent risks and preemptively diagnose structural weaknesses, providing a real-time picture of trading health. Any breaches or notices prompt a systematic review, encouraging adaptive adjustments.

As trades are assessed, **sentiment and behavioral analytics**, too, offer a window into understanding forces behind market moves that may affect pricing or liquidity. Algorithms equipped with sentiment detectors gauging financial news, social media trends, or geopolitical developments provide an auxiliary layer of analysis which aids in preempting unfavorable market conditions and detecting opportunities for refinements.

Moreover, **scenario analysis and stress testing** play an instrumental role in assessing reactionary gaps and market-maker preparedness in the face of unforeseen events, such as economic shocks or major geopolitical uncertainties. These tools challenge the strategy by applying extreme yet plausible scenarios to test reaction times and outcome sensitivities. Identifying how a strategy holds under sudden illiquidity stretches or rapid volatility increases can aid in making necessary amendments to handling strategy adjustments during normal market operations.

Employing **machine learning enhancements** facilitates dynamic pattern recognition to foresee underperformance trends, thereby providing another layer of strategy refinement. These models can sift through vast datasets to uncover hidden correlations or predictive signals that traditional methods might overlook, adapting strategy inputs automatically based on detected patterns. Machine learning models can also support optimization of execution algorithms by recommending parameters that historically offer the highest probability of success.

Additionally, fostering a **feedback loop culture** within trading teams constitutes a vital practice for perpetuating the identification of improvement areas. Cultivating open lines of communication among traders, developers, and risk managers ensures a diversity of vantage points when evaluating strategic health and encouraging bold reevaluations of established norms without fear of punitive repercussions.

Regular **post-mortem evaluations** following significant trades or market shifts enhance long-term strategy performance. Conducting thorough reviews that dissect performance drivers, deviations between predicted versus actual outcomes, and identifying lessons learned fosters progressive enhancements.

In practice, consider a market-making operation frequently facing capital drawdowns during macroeconomic announcement times. A post-mortem might reveal that latency in the reaction to new data was a recurring trait, prompting audits of response algorithms to ensure timelier adjustments when such signals are released.

Finally, embracing a **multidisciplinary approach** encourages a holistic optimization process, integrating insights from financial engineering, statistical analysis, and behavioral budget insights. This broad-scope methodology ensures no opportunity for honing strategy proficiency is overlooked.

Overall, despite the inherent complexities and unknowns of trading arenas, viewing them through a lens of continuous improvement positions market makers to convert challenges into strategic advantages. By diligently identifying areas for enhancement, market makers align themselves with the pursuit of excellence and adaptability within constantly shifting financial tides.

11.5   Algorithm Optimization Techniques

Optimization of market-making algorithms is a crucial pursuit for traders and investors seeking to refine performance and edge over their competitors. In the ever-evolving financial markets, market-making algorithms must continuously adapt through optimization techniques that hone their predictive capabilities, execution efficiency, and risk management frameworks. This section provides a comprehensive overview of the methods employed to improve algorithmic trading systems, focusing on parameter tuning, machine learning enhancements, optimization frameworks, and scenario simulations.

At the heart of algorithm optimization lies **parameter tuning**, a fundamental approach that involves adjusting the input parameters to optimize performance metrics such as return-to-risk ratios, slippage, or fill rates. Parameters such as bid-ask spread thresholds, order size limits, and position entry or exit conditions must be constantly refined to align with prevailing market trends and objectives.

For instance, a market-making algorithm aiming at maintaining tight spreads might adjust its order placement frequency based on observed changes in market liquidity. During periods of heightened activity, it might allow narrower spreads, seeking to capture rapid price movements with increased volume, while in quieter periods, adjusting spreads further apart to mitigate the risk of exposure.

One effective method for parameter optimization is the **grid search**, where multiple sets of parameters are tested systematically over historical data to identify the most effective combinations. While grid search is exhaustive, it can become time-intensive with more parameters. To address this, a **random search** technique could be used, where random combinations are tested, making it computationally lighter.

Moreover, extending beyond basic optimization, sophisticated **metaheuristic algorithms** such as genetic algorithms and simulated annealing offer advanced solutions. These iterative approaches mimic natural processes to explore parameter space in search of optimal configurations. A genetic algorithm, for instance, will evolve parameter sets based on their relative success, mimicking biological evolution principles like selection and mutation, thus iteratively refining strategy assumptions.

Machine learning enhancements constitute another powerful avenue for optimization, offering adaptive learning and predictive success from historical data patterns. Machine learning models, particularly those capable of real-time learning, can adjust algorithmic parameters dynamically. Methods such as decision trees, reinforcement learning, or ensemble models, assist traders by processing vast datasets to forecast market trends, thus optimizing order executions based on an enhanced predictive capability.

Consider a support vector machine (SVM) implemented for identifying optimal times to execute trades, avoiding periods of heightened risk.

By feeding it data through regularly updated datasets encompassing market signals, trading history, and macroeconomic trends, an SVM model can evaluate and score scenarios, adapting algorithmic strategies to exploit or mitigate expected market movements.

To work effectively, machine learning models must be calibrated using thorough **cross-validation** techniques, ensuring model robustness and avoiding overfitting by validating performance on independent data samples. Additionally, employing **feature engineering** enhances algorithmic models by selecting and constructing relevant input features, thereby ensuring they capture the correct market signals for optimization purposes.

Another facet of optimization techniques involves employing **simulation environments**, where traders can experiment with market scenarios and assess the resultant impacts on trading strategies. Simulations provide a sandbox for testing potential optimization decisions without real-world risk, allowing for strategic interventions to be trialed and assessed in suggesting improved practices.

Scenario simulations entail scripting various market behaviors such as sudden spikes in volatility, liquidity crunches, or long-range market drifts. Algorithms can then be assessed for flexibility and responsiveness, leading to tailored modifications for real-world application. For instance, stress-testing against historical market crashes helps identify scenarios where strategies fail to meet expected outcomes, spotlighting key areas for risk-hedging improvements or strategic revisions.

The integration of **backtesting** within simulation frameworks further extends algorithmic optimization by recreating historical trading scenarios calibrated to identified benchmarks. Backtesting evaluates trading assumptions and parameters, furnishing insights on what responses yielded the best returns and encapsulating invaluable empirical evidence for strategy refinements.

Utilizing **adaptive algorithms** enhances optimization by allowing systems to self-modify based on changes in market conditions. These algorithms dynamically adjust to new data flows and changing environmental variables without requiring manual recalibration, thus maintaining optimal performance amidst market shifts.

Another groundbreaking strategy involves the introduction of **hybrid models**, combining deterministic algorithms with probabilistic components or machine learning-driven insights. Such combinations capitalize on the strengths of traditional models for reliability and predictability with the adaptability and nuanced decision-making of AI tools. Hybrid models leverage the advantages of both worlds, optimizing solutions for unpredictable and multifaceted market environments.

Real-time monitoring and feedback systems serve as integral components of the optimization process, offering insights into how algorithms perform in live trading environments. Critical factors such as latency, execution time, and data throughput are meticulously monitored, disclosing areas where technical augmentations can yield substantial efficiency gains. The deployment of monitoring dashboards provides a visual and analytic perspective on algorithmic health, serving as a decision-making aid for ongoing calibrations.

Implementing a culture of **continuous learning** within trading teams ensures optimization remains a priority across all operational aspects. Regular reviews and iterative cycles of feedback synthesis, strategy testing, adjustment, and redeployment foster a regime where optimization is a naturally ongoing process. This proactive approach aligns algorithmic evolution with emerging market realities and technological advances.

Employing algorithm optimization techniques is central to the effective and robust operation of market-making systems, granting traders sharper insights, finely-tuned strategies, and a competitive edge. With methods spanning parameter tuning, machine learning enhancements, simulations, and real-time feedback loops, traders can substantially uplift their trading capabilities, ensuring continued alignment with dynamic financial landscapes and evolving technological paradigms. By systematically adopting these optimization tools, market makers navigate new opportunities while mitigating traditional challenges associated with high-volume, high-speed trading environments.

11.6   Risk-Adjusted Performance Evaluation

Evaluating trading performance through the lens of risk adjustment is crucial for market makers intent on achieving sustainable profitability while conscientiously managing exposure to losses. By focusing on risk-adjusted metrics, traders can gain insights into not only the returns achieved but also the corresponding risks undertaken to earn those returns. This dual-nature assessment provides a comprehensive view that balances reward with risk and ensures that strategic decisions contribute positively to long-term objectives. This section delves into the processes and tools required for risk-adjusted performance evaluation, empowering market participants to embrace a holistic understanding of trading efficacy.

The core of risk-adjusted performance evaluation involves establishing metrics that encapsulate the interplay between returns and risk and guide strategic improvements. These include popular metrics such as the Sharpe ratio, Sortino ratio, and the Treynor ratio, each offering unique perspectives on how well returns are achieved relative to specific risk factors.

The **Sharpe ratio**, an established staple of performance metrics, calculates the average return earned in excess of the risk-free rate per unit of volatility. By normalizing returns by their standard deviation (a proxy for risk), the Sharpe ratio offers a clear portrayal of how effectively a strategy converts risk into reward:

$$\text{Sharpe Ratio} = \frac{\overline{R} - R_f}{\sigma_R}$$

where $\overline{R}$ is the average portfolio return, R_f is the risk-free rate, and σ_R is the standard deviation of the portfolio's return.

However, reliance on the Sharpe ratio alone can be misleading, especially in environments where returns are not normally distributed or exhibit heavy tails. As such, the **Sortino ratio** provides a more nuanced approach by adjusting returns relative to downside risk rather than total volatility. This distinction makes it suitable for asymmetrical return distributions where the primary concern is the mitigation of negative returns:

$$\text{Sortino Ratio} = \frac{\overline{R} - R_f}{\sigma_{\text{downside}}}$$

where σ_{downside} represents the standard deviation of negative returns, better capturing risk by focusing purely on deviations detrimental to traders.

The **Treynor ratio** extends the risk-adjusted performance framework further by evaluating returns in relation to systematic risk. It inherently captures the idea that not all risks are equal, distinguishing between diversifiable and non-diversifiable risks typical of a market-related beta factor:

$$\text{Treynor Ratio} = \frac{\overline{R} - R_f}{\beta}$$

where β represents the sensitivity of the portfolio's excess returns relative to market movements. The Treynor ratio's focus on systematically linked risks aligns well with strategies sensitive to broader market conditions, such as those actively hedging or aligned with index movements.

Beyond these core metrics, examining **Value-at-Risk (VaR)** models allows for a probabilistic estimation of potential maximum losses within a set confidence interval, thereby providing a tangible yardstick for potential risk exposure over a specified time horizon. VaR quantifies the tail risk in a probability distribution, informing decisions by helping strategists contemplate worst-case scenarios:

$$\text{VaR}_p = -\inf\{x \mid P(X \leq x) \leq p\}$$

where $P(X \leq x)$ gives the cumulative distribution function (CDF) at probability threshold p.

Similarly, **Conditional Value-at-Risk (CVaR)** extends VaR analysis by focusing on tail-end risks, offering insights into the magnitude of loss beyond the VaR cut-off point and thus providing an even deeper appreciation for tail risk:

$$\text{CVaR}_p = E[X|X \leq \text{VaR}_p]$$

Through CVaR, traders refine risk assessments by considering the average loss under adverse conditions, informing strategic adjustments to risk management practices.

Wrapped around quantitative measures, **probabilistic scenario analysis** deepens understanding by simulating environments of heightened risk or stress, such as macroeconomic disturbances or geopolitical conflicts. Scenario testing gauges actual agile responses to variability in market conditions, allowing strategies to be benchmarked not just for normal behaviors but resilience against extreme deviations.

Furthermore, incorporating approaches like **momentum or maximum drawdown analysis** can assess those extended periods of performance pressure wherein portfolios face substantial downturns. Identifying drawdowns through quantitative series analysis sharpens the focus on liquidity risk and temporal drainage of capital:

$$\text{Maximum Drawdown} = \frac{Trough - Peak}{Peak}$$

This is key in evaluating risk-adjusted returns for market makers, whose strategies may undertake frequent trading at low margins potentially susceptible to episodic liquidity constraints.

The introduction of **automated and dynamic hedging strategies** enable market makers to effectively manage risk by diversifying trading strategies, adjusting portfolio exposures, and hedging against unwelcome movements, thereby reducing volatility or marking unwanted correlation biases. Strategies like delta-neutral portfolios or options trading can mitigate exposure by capturing risks through inverse market indicators.

Sophisticated **machine learning models** can further enhance risk-adjusted evaluations by predicting transactional risk, flagging unusual volatilities, and detecting patterns suggesting shifts in systemic risk levels. By constructing quantile-based decision frameworks, these models leverage indices or sentiment indicators likely to signal heightened exposure scenarios, acting as early risk warning mechanisms.

Moreover, implementing **capital at risk (CAR)** monitoring and real-time risk dashboards enables traders to constantly visualize their risk exposure profiles relative to dashboards of acceptable limits. Such functionality allows immediate contemplation of strategic revisions in alignment with capital assessment checkpoints, reallocating exposure dynamically to areas that perpetually affirm balanced reward-to-risk outcomes.

Moreover, fostering a risk management culture across trading teams ensures that identifying and responding to risk-adjusted insights remain a priority backed through evaluation programs and contingency protocols. By instituting a blend of academic and empirical insights with contingency strategies, market makers intrinsically acknowledge the centrality of risk integrals alongside performances.

In summary, risk-adjusted performance evaluation remains an indispensable constituency of strategic success, equipping traders with insightful metrics and analyses that transcend straightforward returns. By aligning trading activities with finely tuned risk parameters, market makers pivot towards enduring returns that inherently acknowledge their operating rules enhanced by relentless pursuit of optimized returns at bounded risks, rooted within comprehensive frameworks of empirical scrutiny and continuous adaptation.

11.7   Continuous Improvement and Adaptation

In the fast-paced and ever-changing environment of financial markets, continuous improvement and adaptation are vital components of successful market-making strategies. As the dynamics of trading evolve with technological advances, regulatory shifts, and macroeconomic changes, traders and algorithm designers must cultivate a proactive approach to refining strategies, embracing new tools, and adapting to market shifts. This section explores the methods and philosophies underpinning continuous improvement and adaptation within market-making, emphasizing strategic foresight and innovation as a pathway to sustained success.

At the forefront of this process is the principle of **adaptive evolution**, where market participants must regularly assess and recalibrate strategies to remain competitive. This involves perpetually integrating feedback and data insights to iterate upon existing models, ensuring that adjustments account for both recent performance evaluations and anticipated market developments.

A key strategy for achieving continuous improvement is leveraging **feedback loops**, which involve collecting real-time performance data and reviewing the outcomes against specific benchmarks or key performance indicators (KPIs). By utilizing well-structured feedback mechanisms, traders gain timely insights into strategic shortcomings, allowing for informed revisions and improvements. Feedback loops are especially effective when implemented through automated systems that provide immediate, data-driven insights. For example, an algorithm might automatically capture deviations in expected versus actual spreads, enabling prompt modifications to mitigate emerging risks.

Performance audits further contribute by rigorously evaluating past trades, seeking hidden inefficiencies or missed opportunities. These audits, both automated and manual, help identify blind spots where strategies might lag, either due to outdated assumptions, unseen market shifts, or latency in response mechanisms. An effective audit often spans components such as algorithmic logic, parameter selections, and even transaction cost analyses, thus ensuring a comprehensive understanding of trading efficacy.

Regular **post-trade analysis** fosters a baseline for continuity, examining trades not only in isolation but as part of strategic systems. This analysis aggregates learnings from trade timings, market responses, and fulfillment rates while contemplating the informational flow that influenced execution decisions. By equipping market makers with a wealth of empirical evidence regarding trade outcomes, strategic disruptions can be identified early, and iterative improvements applied both tactically and structurally.

To facilitate adaptation, traders should maintain agility in their operational frameworks, embracing a **culture of innovation** and flexibility. Continuous education and skill enhancement among trading teams ensure familiarity with cutting-edge tools, methodologies, and theoretical advancements, while an openness to trialing novel strategies encourages experimentation within safe, controlled environments.

Market makers benefit from fostering cross-functional collaboration, leveraging interdisciplinary insights from financial analysts, quant developers, and risk managers. Collectively, these teams can ideate on adaptive techniques and strategic paradigms that outperform traditional silos, instilling a company-wide ethos of perpetual advancement.

Incorporating **scenario planning** and **stress testing** remains indispensable, promoting resilience against volatility and unforeseen market contingencies. By crafting prospective situations covering macroeconomic crises or market downturns, traders devise robustness strategies, anticipating potential disruptions while optimizing response behaviors across algorithmic systems. This ensures that adaptive strategies include contingencies built into modeling frameworks, supporting dynamic engagements with the volatile elements of financial markets.

Employing **machine learning and artificial intelligence** amplifies adaptive capabilities starkly, as these technologies can automatically identify patterns, adjust behaviors, and enhance predictive accuracy. Machine learning models, particularly those structured around reinforcement learning paradigms, are adept at continuously updating their assumptions and strategies based on recursive data input, effectively adapting autonomously to market changes over time.

Machine learning's efficacy is further augmented by **real-time data analytics**, wherein algorithms leverage live data streams to adjust trading strategies on the fly, reflecting instantaneous market realities. The continuous ingestion and processing of data empower algorithms to venture beyond static strategy sets and foster dynamic adaptability, conforming to evolving market demands without the need for extensive manual recalibrations.

To ground continuous improvement, developing a **robust risk management framework** is critical. Proactively identifying, evaluating, and mitigating risks ensures that strategies remain durable amid unpredictability, aligning well-considered risk appetites with adaptive ambitions. Through the deployment of real-time risk dashboards, traders achieve clarity on their exposure profiles, sustaining a balanced pursuit between operational agility and commercial prudence.

Emphasizing **agility in decision-making** cements continuous improvement, wherein decentralized decision authority empowers market makers to respond expeditiously to opportunities and threats. By entrusting algorithm adjustments and adaptive strategies to those closest to data and market developments, firms circumvent bureaucratic lag, gaining a competitive advantage.

Moreover, sustaining long-term adaptation requires fostering a **learning organization mentality** that prioritizes shared knowledge dissemination. By documenting key learnings and strategy evolutions, market makers cultivate repositories of institutional knowledge, preventing the repetition of past errors while nurturing a collective mastery in market adaptations.

Lastly, maintaining adaptability means engaging with **external influences and emerging trends**, including regulatory amendments, technological innovations, and investor sentiment shifts. Building a strategic anticipation of external trends complements internal strategy optimality, permitting the timely adoption of best practices poised to shape immediate and future market milieus.

Continuous improvement and adaptation are integral to mastering the challenges of modern market-making. Through disciplined execution, insightful technology-driven enhancements, and a thriving culture of innovation, traders sustain relevance and excellence within an increasingly interconnected and complex financial landscape. By harnessing adaptive thinking and evolving strategies, market makers not only thrive in current market conditions but also pioneer paths for future achievements and advantages.

Chapter 12

Technological Infrastructure for Market Making

This chapter examines the technological backbone necessary for effective market making. It highlights high-performance computing solutions crucial for executing strategies efficiently, along with robust data management systems to handle vast datasets. Network and connectivity solutions for low-latency communication are discussed, alongside the role of cloud computing in providing scalable resources. The importance of cybersecurity measures in safeguarding trading systems is underscored. Trading platforms and software integral to algorithm development are explored, complemented by insights into maintenance practices and technical support for ensuring system reliability and continuity.

12.1 High-Performance Computing for Trading

High-performance computing (HPC) forms the cornerstone of modern trading infrastructures, particularly in the domain of market making. In the arena of high-speed trading, such as algorithmic and high-frequency trading, speed equates to opportunity. The ability to execute trades with minimal latency can result in significant profitability, as even the slightest delay can lead to missed trading opportunities or financial losses.

At the heart of HPC for trading is the capacity to process complex mathematical models quickly and efficiently. Traders and financial analysts utilise these models to analyse vast amounts of market data, identify trends, and predict future movements. This requires systems capable of performing trillions of calculations per second, far exceeding the capabilities of standard computing systems.

One common application of HPC in trading is risk modeling. Complex risk models that consider a multitude of factors, such as market volatility, interest rates, and macroeconomic indicators, must be computed rapidly to inform trading decisions. For instance, the Value at Risk (VaR) model, which estimates the potential loss in value of a portfolio over a defined period, benefits greatly from the speed and power of HPC.

In the context of high-frequency trading, where firms might execute thousands of trades within milliseconds, the computational demands are even more extreme. Here, HPC systems are not just a competitive advantage but a necessity. They allow for the processing of real-time data feeds, the execution of algorithmic strategies, and immediate responses to market events, all in the blink of an eye.

Increased computational power also facilitates back-testing and optimization of trading algorithms. Traders need to validate their strategies against historical data before deploying them in real-time trading. HPC enables comprehensive back-testing, which involves running the algorithms against large datasets to assess their performance and refine parameters for optimal outcomes. This process, which would be prohibitively time-consuming on lesser systems, can be significantly accelerated through HPC.

Innovations such as parallel processing and distributed computing have pushed the boundaries of HPC further. Parallel processing allows multiple computations to be carried out simultaneously. For trading firms, this means that tasks such as analyzing multiple securities or executing various strategies can be done concurrently, greatly enhancing efficiency and throughput.

A pertinent example of HPC in action can be observed in the utilization of graphics processing units (GPUs). Historically used for rendering video games, GPUs are adept at handling parallel tasks due to their architecture. Many trading firms now employ GPUs to handle specific computational tasks that benefit from the parallel processing capabilities of these units, such as option pricing and Monte Carlo simulations.

Clusters of interconnected computers form another integral aspect of HPC, allowing firms to distribute computational tasks across multiple systems, thereby enhancing the overall processing power available for trading operations. The synergy between these clustered systems leads to improved resilience and performance, enabling financial institutions to meet the rigorous demands of modern trading environments.

As the complexity of financial markets evolves, so too must the computational models that drive decision-making processes. Machine learning and artificial intelligence (AI) are becoming increasingly prevalent in trading, enabling models to adapt and evolve based on the ever-changing market dynamics. HPC systems support these advanced models by providing the necessary computing power to train machine learning algorithms on massive datasets, leading to more precise predictions and strategies.

Another critical component of HPC is data storage and retrieval. The sheer volume of financial data produced each day necessitates vast and efficient storage solutions. High-speed, solid-state drives (SSDs) are often employed within HPC frameworks to ensure rapid access to this data, minimizing latency and maximizing the speed of computation.

However, the deployment of HPC within trading frameworks is not without challenges. The cost of building and maintaining these complex systems can be substantial, necessitating significant investment in both hardware and skilled personnel. Furthermore, the rapid pace of technological advancement requires ongoing upgrades and updates to maintain competitive parity.

To manage these challenges, firms often engage in partnerships with technology providers who can offer infrastructure and support tailored to the specific needs of high-frequency trading. These collaborations allow trading firms to leverage cutting-edge technology without bearing the full brunt of development costs.

Moreover, the integration of cloud-based HPC solutions provides a flexible alternative to traditional on-premises setups. Cloud providers offer dynamic scalability, allowing firms to adjust their computing resources in response to market conditions. This elasticity can be particularly advantageous in volatile markets, where computational needs may spike unpredictably.

Security also remains a paramount concern for HPC deployments in trading. The sensitive nature of financial data, combined with the high stakes of trading operations, requires robust cybersecurity measures. Encryption, secure access controls, and real-time threat monitoring are essential components of a secure HPC environment.

To conclude, high-performance computing is indispensable in the realm of trading, serving as the engine that powers rapid decision-making, complex analytics, and real-time execution. As markets become increasingly fast-paced and data-driven, the role of HPC will only grow, continually redefining the landscape of electronic trading. For market makers, the investment in HPC technologies promises not only increased efficiency and accuracy but also a significant competitive edge in an ever-evolving financial world.

12.2   Data Management Systems

In trading, data management systems play an instrumental role in ensuring the accuracy, efficiency, and reliability of financial operations. The sheer volume of data generated by financial markets daily is astounding. Effective data management systems must not only handle vast quantities of data but also process it swiftly to derive actionable insights and inform strategic decisions. This section delves into the intricacies of data management systems in trading, exploring their architecture, functions, and significance.

At the heart of data management in trading are robust database systems that store, organize, and facilitate access to massive datasets. These systems comprise complex architectures capable of handling real-time data influx from multiple sources, including market feeds, trading platforms, and news services. Database management systems (DBMS) like SQL, NoSQL, and NewSQL, among others, are often utilized to support these diverse operational needs.

In the context of market making, where milliseconds can equate to substantial monetary gains or losses, the speed of data retrieval and processing is paramount. In-memory databases offer a compelling solution by storing data primarily in the system's main memory rather than on traditional disk storage. This reduces latency significantly, enabling fast retrieval and processing of data. For example, high-frequency trading firms often leverage in-memory database technology to keep abreast of rapid market changes, ensuring their strategies remain responsive and timely.

Furthermore, the advent of big data technologies has ushered in a new era of data management. Technologies such as Apache Hadoop and Apache Spark are structured to manage and process large-scale datasets efficiently. They employ distributed computing models that divide tasks across clusters of computers, enhancing computing power and enabling parallel data processing. These tools are particularly useful for executing complex analytics and deriving insights from historical market data.

The ability to handle both structured data, such as numerical stock prices, and unstructured data, such as text news reports, is another crucial feature of modern data management systems. By utilizing machine learning and natural language processing, trading firms can synthesize unstructured data into their databases, enhancing decision-making processes. For instance, sentiment analysis can be applied to parse news articles and social media content, determining the market sentiment towards specific stocks and informing trading strategies.

Data management systems must also ensure data integrity and accuracy. The reliability of trading models hinges on precise and consistent data inputs. As such, these systems implement rigorous validation and cleansing processes to filter out anomalies or inaccuracies before data is used in decision-making. Data provenance, which tracks the origin and history of data, is additionally essential for compliance with financial regulations and auditing requirements. It allows firms to demonstrate the veracity and lineage of data used in trading strategies, providing transparency and trust in automated processes.

Scalability represents another critical facet of data management systems in trading. As financial markets expand and trading floors digitize, data management systems must adapt and grow accordingly. Cloud-based solutions offer a scalable infrastructure tailored to dynamic financial environments. Cloud systems provide the flexibility to scale up during periods of high market activity and scale down when demands are lower, optimizing both performance and cost-efficiency.

Security within data management systems cannot be overstated. Given the sensitive nature of financial data, securing these systems against cyber threats is vital. Encryption, robust authentication methods, and continuous monitoring protect data from unauthorized access or breaches. Moreover, the implementation of blockchain technology in data management offers enhanced security features, such as immutability and decentralized validation, further safeguarding against data tampering.

Disaster recovery and data redundancy protocols further underpin the reliability of data management systems. In the event of system failures or data loss, such protocols ensure swift recovery and continuity of operations, securing ongoing trading activities. By maintaining redundant data copies and employing automated recovery mechanisms, trading firms can minimize downtime and associated losses.

The rise of real-time analytics within data management systems empowers traders with immediate insights into market conditions. Utilizing event stream processing, these systems can ingest real-time data streams and perform instant analytics, identifying trends and anomalies as they occur. This capability is invaluable in fast-paced market environments where decisions must be made instantaneously.

Data management systems also support quantitative research and development through sophisticated data querying and storage capabilities. By providing researchers with access to comprehensive data archives, these systems facilitate the testing and refinement of quantitative models, instrumental in the evolution of algorithmic strategies. Historical data analysis remains a cornerstone of quantitative trading, informing model calibration and strategy back-testing.

The integration of artificial intelligence into data management systems further enhances their functionality. AI-driven algorithms can autonomously manage data sorting, classification, and predictive analytics, offering advanced insights and reducing the manual burden on data scientists. Predictive models powered by AI can anticipate market movements, giving traders a strategic advantage in preemptively adjusting their portfolios.

To wrap up, data management systems are the backbone of effective trading operations. They offer the infrastructure required to store, process, and analyze the copious amounts of data generated by modern financial markets. By implementing leading-edge technologies and maintaining unwavering focus on security, scalability, and reliability, trading firms can harness data management systems to bolster their competitive edge and drive innovation in trading strategies. The continued evolution of these systems promises to further revolutionize the financial trading landscape, ensuring that traders can make informed, data-driven decisions with precision and confidence.

12.3 Network and Connectivity Solutions

In the domain of market making and high-frequency trading, network and connectivity solutions are vital components of the technological infrastructure. The speed and reliability of data transmission across networks directly impact the efficiency and success of trading operations. In such a fast-paced environment, even a millisecond delay in data transfer can lead to missed opportunities or financial losses. As such, firms dedicate substantial resources to optimizing their network and connectivity solutions to ensure swift and accurate execution of trades.

At the core of network solutions for trading is low-latency connectivity. Low latency refers to the minimal delay in the transmission of data between a firm's systems and financial exchanges. It is achieved through a combination of cutting-edge technology, optimized routing paths, and high-speed data links. To attain the lowest possible latency, trading firms often invest in direct fiber optic connections to exchanges, co-location services, and advanced network hardware that includes high-performance routers and switches.

Co-location services are a prominent approach to minimizing latency in trading. By placing trading servers physically close to exchange data centers, firms can reduce the distance data must travel, thereby decreasing latency. This proximity allows for the fastest possible execution speeds, a crucial factor in algorithmic and high-frequency trading strategies. The benefits of co-location are particularly evident in trading environments where every nanosecond counts, enabling firms to act on market opportunities with unparalleled speed.

Moreover, the adoption of dark fiber networks has revolutionized connectivity solutions in trading. Dark fiber refers to unused fiber optic cables that firms can lease or purchase to establish dedicated communication lines free from external traffic. This exclusivity minimizes congestion, ensuring uninterrupted and rapid data flows. Trading firms leverage dark fiber for their core market data and order routing, creating a private and secure network environment that maximizes speed and reliability.

Advanced data compression techniques further enhance network efficiency by reducing the size of data packets transmitted over networks. This compression allows more data to travel within the same bandwidth, accelerating data delivery without sacrificing integrity. For example, proprietary algorithms can compress ticker feeds and market data, decreasing delivery time and enhancing real-time analytics capabilities crucial for making prompt trading decisions.

In addition to speed, resiliency is a cornerstone of effective connectivity solutions. Network redundancy, achieved through multiple, geographically diverse communication paths, is imperative for maintaining uninterrupted operations in the face of network failures or outages. By implementing redundant paths, firms can reroute data traffic dynamically, minimizing disruptions and safeguarding against potential financial losses. This resilience is particularly crucial during periods of market volatility, where any lapse in connectivity could result in substantial financial risks.

Further enhancing network resilience is the deployment of intelligent routing protocols. These protocols determine the most efficient pathways for data transmission, dynamically adjusting routes based on current network conditions to prevent bottlenecks and congestion. The deployment of technologies such as Software-Defined Networking (SDN) allows firms to maintain real-time control over network behaviors, optimizing routing paths and allocating bandwidth as required. SDN provides traders with a flexible and agile networking framework, easily adapted to fluctuating market demands.

As the global financial markets continue to evolve, international connectivity has become critical for multi-asset trading strategies. The ability to seamlessly connect to multiple exchanges across continents requires robust global network solutions capable of high-speed, high-capacity data transfers. Assume the need for trading firms to execute cross-border arbitrage strategies that demand instantaneous access to foreign markets. These require expansive, high-bandwidth networks connecting major financial hubs worldwide.

The role of cloud technology in augmenting connectivity solutions has also become increasingly significant. Cloud platforms provide scalable infrastructure that enhances the flexibility of connectivity arrangements. With cloud-based network solutions, trading firms can rapidly deploy trading environments in various geographical locations, adjusting resources dynamically to accommodate changes in market activity or strategy. This scalability is particularly advantageous for firms aiming to expand their operations globally without the need for extensive physical infrastructure investment.

Security within network solutions is paramount to protect sensitive financial data and trading algorithms. Implementing robust cybersecurity measures, such as encryption, secure tunneling protocols, and virtual private networks (VPNs), ensures that data remains confidential and tamper-proof during transmission. Additionally, real-time monitoring systems track network traffic to detect anomalies or potential breaches, promptly addressing security threats to maintain data integrity.

Emerging technologies like quantum networking, with its promises of ultra-low latency and high security via quantum encryption, present exciting possibilities for future network solutions in trading. While still largely in development, the potential of quantum networking for creating virtually instantaneous data links with unparalleled security features offers a glimpse into the next frontier of connectivity solutions for trading.

Ultimately, network and connectivity solutions are indispensable for ensuring the competitiveness and operational efficiency of modern trading systems. By harnessing the latest technologies and infrastructure, trading firms can achieve the high-speed, reliable, and secure data transmission required to thrive in today's electronic markets. As markets become increasingly complex and integrated globally, the continuous evolution of network and connectivity solutions will remain foundational to the success of market-making operations, driving innovation and facilitating seamless global trading activities.

12.4 Cloud Computing and Virtualization

The integration of cloud computing and virtualization into trading infrastructure has revolutionized the landscape of financial markets. These technologies offer unprecedented flexibility, scalability, and efficiency, making them indispensable to modern market-making operations. As financial firms strive to remain agile and competitive, cloud computing and virtualization provide the means to swiftly adapt to market changes, optimize resources, and enhance the robustness of trading platforms.

At its core, cloud computing enables firms to leverage a shared pool of configurable computing resources, including networks, servers, storage, and applications, which can be rapidly provisioned and released with minimal management effort. By transitioning to cloud infrastructure, trading firms can reduce the burden of maintaining complex on-premises systems, shifting instead to scalable, pay-as-you-go models offered by leading cloud providers such as Amazon Web Services (AWS), Microsoft Azure, and Google Cloud Platform (GCP).

One of the most significant advantages of cloud computing in trading is its ability to offer elastic computing resources. Elasticity allows firms to scale their computing power up or down based on real-time demands, making it particularly beneficial during periods of high market volatility or unpredictable trading volumes. For instance, during significant market events or black swan occurrences, the ability to instantly accommodate increased data processing and storage requirements ensures uninterrupted operations and optimal performance.

Moreover, cloud services contribute to cost optimization by eliminating the capital expenditures associated with acquiring and maintaining physical hardware. Instead, firms incur operational expenses that are in direct proportion to their usage, allowing for better resource management and financial planning. This economic advantage is particularly salient for smaller trading firms that may lack the resources to invest in extensive infrastructure but can nonetheless compete with larger entities by leveraging cloud capabilities.

Virtualization complements cloud computing by abstracting physical resources into virtual instances, enabling multiple operating systems and applications to run concurrently on a single physical server. This abstraction leads to improved resource utilization, reduced overhead, and greater operational flexibility. Through virtualization, trading firms can efficiently manage workloads, streamline deployment processes, and enhance system redundancy and recovery operations.

The rapid deployment of virtual machines (VMs) within a cloud environment facilitates agile development and testing of trading algorithms and platforms. Developers can quickly spin up instances of trading applications in isolated environments for testing without interfering with live trading operations. Such agility accelerates the innovation cycle, allowing firms to respond swiftly to market demands with new features or strategies.

Additionally, virtualization supports high availability and disaster recovery capabilities, key concerns in trading infrastructure. By creating redundant virtual instances across multiple data centers, firms can ensure continuity of operations in the case of localized failures. Advanced load balancing and failover mechanisms automatically redirect traffic to healthy instances, minimizing downtime and preserving trading activities during disruptions.

For trading firms that operate across multiple jurisdictions, cloud computing provides a unified platform to manage global operations cohesively. The ability to deploy applications and data across various geographic regions minimizes latency by bringing computation closer to the point of execution. This geographic diversity ensures that traders have consistent and reliable access to markets, regardless of their physical location, enhancing the speed and reliability of cross-border trading strategies.

Security and compliance are paramount in trading operations, and cloud providers have made significant strides in fortifying their platforms against cyber threats. Trading firms benefit from the comprehensive security frameworks implemented by major cloud providers, including intrusion detection systems, encryption protocols, and identity management services. In addition, rigorous compliance certifications such as ISO/IEC 27001, SOC 2, and GDPR compliance ensure that cloud platforms meet industry standards and regulatory requirements.

Cloud-native technologies like containers and microservices have become increasingly prevalent in the trading sector, offering enhanced flexibility and maintainability. Containers enable applications to run consistently across different computing environments by encapsulating all necessary dependencies, simplifying deployment, and reducing compatibility issues. Microservices architecture further decouples applications into smaller, independent components that can be developed, deployed, and scaled independently, fostering a more agile and resilient development process.

A practical application of cloud computing and virtualization in trading can be observed through the implementation of machine learning (ML) and artificial intelligence (AI) models. These technologies demand immense computational power and storage for data training and inference, which cloud platforms readily provide. Trading firms can harness cloud-based ML services to develop sophisticated predictive models that analyze patterns, forecast trends, and automate decision-making processes.

Furthermore, cloud solutions facilitate collaborative research and development efforts within and across firms. By offering centralized repositories and standardized tools, cloud platforms enable seamless collaboration among geographically dispersed teams, speeding up the development of trading strategies and analytics. This collaborative advantage is vital for firms aiming to leverage diverse expertise and drive innovation in an increasingly competitive market.

As financial ecosystems become increasingly interconnected, the emphasis on interoperability has grown. Cloud platforms offer robust APIs and integration capabilities that facilitate seamless connectivity between disparate systems, enhancing information flow and operational cohesion. By standardizing data exchange protocols, trading firms can achieve greater efficiency and agility in their interactions with partners, clients, and regulatory bodies.

In closing, cloud computing and virtualization stand as pillars of modern trading infrastructure, empowering firms with the agility and resilience necessary to navigate complex and dynamic markets. By leveraging these technologies, trading firms can improve operational efficiency, foster innovation, and maintain a competitive edge. As cloud computing continues to evolve, the trading sector is poised to benefit from ongoing advancements, setting the stage for a new era of efficient, secure, and innovative market-making operations.

12.5   Security and Cyber-Resilience

In the digital age, where financial data and trading systems are predominantly electronic, ensuring security and cyber-resilience is paramount for trading firms. The potential impact of cyber threats on financial markets is profound, with successful attacks posing risks not only to individual firms but also to broader market stability. Consequently, a comprehensive approach to cybersecurity and resilience is essential to protect sensitive data, maintain operational integrity, and preserve the trust of stakeholders.

At the forefront of securing trading infrastructures are robust encryption protocols. Encryption protects data in transit and at rest, ensuring that even if intercepted, the data remains indecipherable to unauthorized parties. Modern cryptographic techniques, such as $AES\text{-}256$ encryption, provide a strong defense against cyber intrusions, securing communications between trading platforms, data centers, and external networks. The implementation of end-to-end encryption ensures that sensitive information, such as trade orders and client data, remains confidential and secure throughout its journey.

Another critical component of cybersecurity is the establishment of a multi-layered defense strategy. This approach employs multiple independent security controls, such as firewalls, intrusion detection systems (IDS), and intrusion prevention systems (IPS), to create a robust barrier against potential attacks. Firewalls regulate incoming and outgoing network traffic based on predetermined security rules, effectively blocking malicious traffic and unauthorized access attempts.

Intrusion detection and prevention systems play a proactive role in identifying and mitigating threats. By monitoring network traffic and analyzing system behaviors, these systems can detect anomalies, recognize patterns indicative of cyber threats, and trigger automated responses to neutralize them. The deployment of advanced IDS/IPS systems that leverage machine learning enhances their ability to adapt to evolving threats, ensuring ongoing protection against sophisticated cyber-attacks.

Access control mechanisms are another vital element of trading system security. Implementing strong authentication protocols, such as multi-factor authentication (MFA), ensures that only authorized personnel can access sensitive systems and data. MFA combines something the user knows (such as a password) with something the user has (such as a hardware token or smartphone app), significantly reducing the risk of unauthorized access through compromised credentials.

Additionally, the principle of least privilege should be adhered to, granting users the minimum level of access necessary to perform their job functions. This minimizes the potential damage from insider threats or compromised accounts, containing breaches and limiting the exposure of critical assets.

Regular security audits and vulnerability assessments are imperative to identify and rectify weaknesses within trading infrastructures. Conducting thorough evaluations of systems, networks, and applications helps firms uncover potential vulnerabilities, misconfigurations, and security gaps that could be exploited by attackers. By proactively addressing these issues, firms can strengthen their defenses and prevent future incidents.

Cyber resilience goes beyond preventive measures, encompassing the ability to effectively respond to and recover from cyber incidents. A comprehensive incident response plan outlines the procedures and responsibilities for detecting, containing, and recovering from security breaches. This plan should include protocols for communication, investigation, and remediation, ensuring a coordinated and efficient response to minimize the impact of incidents.

To enhance resilience, trading firms should invest in disaster recovery and business continuity strategies. These plans ensure that critical trading systems can be quickly restored or re-routed in the event of an outage or attack, maintaining operational continuity. By employing redundant infrastructure, diverse data backup solutions, and failover mechanisms, firms can reduce downtime and mitigate financial and reputational damage.

The adoption of security information and event management (SIEM) systems provides trading firms with a centralized platform to aggregate and analyze security data from across their infrastructure. SIEMs enable real-time monitoring and correlation of security events, facilitating the early detection of potential threats and streamlining incident response efforts. Advanced SIEM solutions use artificial intelligence to enhance threat intelligence, predicting and identifying complex attack vectors before they can cause harm.

Collaboration and information sharing are also critical components of a comprehensive cybersecurity strategy. Engaging in partnerships with industry peers, government agencies, and cybersecurity organizations allows trading firms to stay informed about emerging threats and best practices. Information-sharing initiatives such as Financial Services Information Sharing and Analysis Centers (FS-ISAC) contribute to the collective defense of the financial sector by promoting the exchange of threat intelligence and mitigation strategies.

Security training and awareness programs are essential for fostering a culture of cybersecurity within trading firms. By educating employees on security best practices, potential threats, and safe online behavior, firms can reduce the risk of human error, which remains one of the leading causes of security breaches. Regular training sessions, simulated phishing exercises, and cybersecurity workshops help reinforce the importance of vigilance and adherence to security protocols.

As the threat landscape continues to evolve, trading firms must remain adaptive and forward-thinking in their cybersecurity approach. Emerging technologies such as blockchain offer innovative security advantages through their inherent immutability and decentralized nature. By implementing blockchain-based solutions for transaction verification and data management, firms can enhance transparency and reduce the risk of data tampering.

The advent of quantum computing presents both challenges and opportunities for future security strategies. While quantum computing has the potential to break current cryptographic standards, it also offers the prospect of developing new, quantum-resistant encryption methods. Trading firms must stay abreast of advancements in this field, preparing to incorporate quantum-proof security measures as technology evolves.

Ultimately, ensuring security and cyber-resilience is an ongoing and dynamic process, requiring continuous investment, vigilance, and adaptation. By prioritizing cybersecurity and resilience, trading firms can protect their critical systems and data, maintain market confidence, and contribute to the stability and integrity of the financial ecosystem.

12.6 Algorithmic Trading Platforms

Algorithmic trading platforms are at the heart of modern financial markets, enabling the execution of complex trading strategies with speed, precision, and efficiency. These platforms have transformed the trading landscape, allowing for automated decision-making processes that capitalize on market inefficiencies and opportunities unobservable to the human eye. In this section, we explore the multifaceted components of algorithmic trading platforms, their functionalities, and their profound impact on trading practices.

Algorithmic trading platforms serve as the interface that connects trading algorithms with financial markets. They provide the necessary infrastructure for developing, testing, deploying, and managing trading strategies according to predetermined rules and parameters. The effectiveness of these platforms hinges on their ability to support high-frequency, low-latency trading environments where decisions must be made in microseconds.

A pivotal component of algorithmic trading platforms is the support for a broad array of financial instruments, including equities, futures, options, currencies, and commodities. This diversity enables traders to formulate strategies that capitalize on arbitrage opportunities across multiple asset classes. For instance, a stat-arb algorithm might simultaneously trade pairs of correlated stocks to exploit short-term pricing anomalies, an opportunity that relies on the platform's ability to handle various instruments seamlessly.

Numerous languages and environments are used for coding trading algorithms on these platforms. While traditional languages like C++ and Java are often utilized for their execution speed and efficiency, the rise of newer, versatile languages such as Python has gained traction due to ease of use and a robust ecosystem of libraries. Python, with its extensive libraries for data analysis and machine learning, such as pandas, NumPy, and TensorFlow, provides an excellent framework for developing data-driven trading algorithms.

To support the rapid development cycle demanded by algorithmic trading, platforms often integrate integrated development environments (IDEs) and debugging tools. IDEs facilitate code writing, testing, and monitoring, offering real-time feedback to enhance the iterative development process of complex trading algorithms. Debugging tools are vital for identifying logic errors or performance bottlenecks, ensuring that algorithms operate as intended under different market conditions.

Back-testing and simulation capabilities are essential features of algorithmic trading platforms. These functionalities enable developers to validate the effectiveness of trading algorithms against historical data, providing insights into potential profitability and risk exposure. High-quality back-testing engines consider transaction costs, slippage, and liquidity constraints, allowing for realistic evaluations of algorithm performance. This rigorous testing process minimizes the risk of deploying unprofitable or flawed strategies in live trading environments.

Algorithmic trading platforms also offer sophisticated risk management tools. These tools are crucial for defining and enforcing risk parameters such as stop-loss limits, position sizing, and portfolio diversification. By automating risk controls, platforms ensure that trading strategies consistently adhere to pre-established risk thresholds, safeguarding capital and optimizing returns. Moreover, real-time monitoring of market conditions informs dynamic adjustments to risk parameters, enhancing adaptability and resilience in volatile markets.

The real-time data-feed integration is another critical element of algorithmic trading platforms. These platforms ingest vast amounts of market data, including price quotes, trade executions, technical indicators, and news events, to inform algorithmic decisions. The ability to process and analyze data streams in real time is paramount to executing trades at optimal moments, a prerequisite for high-frequency and event-driven trading strategies. Leveraging big data technologies, platforms can efficiently handle and process these data streams, enabling insights-driven trading operations.

For successful algorithmic trading, platforms must integrate seamlessly with various exchange APIs, brokers, and execution venues. This connectivity facilitates the rapid transmission of trade orders and the receipt of market data to and from financial exchanges. Advanced direct market access (DMA) capabilities allow trading platforms to bypass traditional intermediary layers, reducing latency and improving execution speeds. By establishing low-latency connections with exchanges, platforms provide the competitive edge needed in high-frequency trading contexts.

Another emerging trend in algorithmic trading platforms is the integration of machine learning and artificial intelligence. These technologies enhance the sophistication of trading algorithms, enabling them to adapt and iterate strategies based on evolving market conditions. By applying techniques such as supervised learning, reinforcement learning, and natural language processing, AI-driven algorithms can uncover patterns and trends beyond human capabilities, achieving higher predictive accuracy and strategic innovation.

A practical example of algorithmic trading can be observed in trend-following strategies, wherein algorithms identify and capitalize on momentum signals. Platforms enable the development of these strategies by incorporating technical indicators such as moving averages, relative strength indices, or Bollinger Bands. By continuously analyzing trading signals, algorithms can place buy or sell orders when predefined thresholds are breached, effectively harnessing market trends for profit.

To ensure reliability and uptime, algorithmic trading platforms are designed with high availability architecture. Robust infrastructure, including failover mechanisms, load balancing, and replication services, minimizes the risk of downtime and data loss, ensuring uninterrupted access to markets. This resilience is particularly critical in volatile market scenarios where timely trading responses can mitigate potential losses or capture lucrative opportunities.

Security within algorithmic trading platforms is of paramount concern to protect sensitive data and trading strategies from unauthorized access. Implementing encryption protocols, multi-factor authentication, and rigorous access control measures reinforce platform security. Regular security audits and penetration testing practices further ensure that platforms remain robust against emerging threats, maintaining the confidentiality and integrity of trading operations.

To conclude, algorithmic trading platforms represent the technological backbone of contemporary trading solutions, enabling the automation and optimization of trading strategies with unprecedented efficiency. Through their comprehensive tools and features, these platforms empower traders to harness data-driven insights, implement sophisticated strategies, and compete in a highly dynamic market environment. As technological advancements continue to shape the trading landscape, algorithmic trading platforms will play an integral role in driving innovation, efficiency, and profitability in the financial markets.

12.7 Maintenance and Technical Support

Effective maintenance and comprehensive technical support are critical components of sustainable trading infrastructure, ensuring the continuous operation and reliability of trading systems. In the high-stakes environment of financial markets, even minor disruptions can lead to significant financial repercussions. Thus, robust maintenance strategies and responsive technical assistance underpin the performance, security, and longevity of trading platforms.

The foundation of a solid maintenance regime lies in preventive maintenance practices. These involve regular inspections and servicing of hardware and software systems to preemptively address potential issues before they manifest as failures. By implementing a proactive maintenance schedule, trading firms can avoid unplanned downtimes and ensure that all components of their trading infrastructure are operating optimally. Regular updates to software applications, firmware, and drivers fall under preventive maintenance, as do routine hardware checks to assess the health and performance of physical components such as servers, storage devices, and network equipment.

Moreover, predictive maintenance methodologies have emerged as an innovative approach, utilizing data analytics and machine learning to forecast potential system failures. By analyzing historical performance data and system logs, predictive maintenance models can identify patterns indicative of impending failures, allowing firms to take corrective action in advance. This data-driven approach enhances the reliability of trading systems, reducing unexpected breakdowns and minimizing maintenance costs over time.

Technical support teams play a pivotal role in managing the complexities of trading systems, providing expertise and assistance to resolve technical issues swiftly and efficiently. These support teams are often categorized into multiple levels to address issues of varying complexity. Level 1 support handles basic troubleshooting and user queries, while Level 2 and Level 3 support involves more specialized expertise to tackle complex technical problems, including system configuration, network issues, and software bugs.

A well-structured ticketing and incident management system is integral to efficient technical support operations. Upon encountering an issue, users can report it through the ticketing system, which prioritizes incidents based on severity and impact. This systematic approach not only streamlines the process of issue resolution but also ensures accountability and transparency. By maintaining detailed records of incidents and resolutions, trading firms can identify recurring issues, assess system health, and refine their support strategies over time.

One critical aspect of technical support is ensuring system integration and compatibility. Trading infrastructures often comprise diverse systems and applications developed by various vendors. Ensuring seamless interoperability and compatibility between these components is vital to maintaining efficient operations. Technical support teams are responsible for managing integration challenges, coordinating with vendors to resolve compatibility issues, and ensuring that system updates or changes do not negatively impact other components.

Disaster recovery and business continuity are integral elements of maintenance and technical support. A comprehensive disaster recovery plan outlines procedures for restoring system functionality in the event of catastrophic failures, such as power outages, cyber-attacks, or natural disasters. This plan should include detailed strategies for data backup and restoration, system reconfiguration, and alternate site provisioning. Regular testing and refinement of the disaster recovery plan are essential to ensure readiness and effectiveness.

Technical support extends beyond reactive measures, encompassing proactive efforts to educate users and enhance their understanding of trading systems. Comprehensive training programs and documentation empower users to utilize trading platforms effectively, minimizing user-induced errors and enhancing overall efficiency. Training sessions can cover a broad range of topics, from basic system navigation to advanced algorithm development and risk management techniques.

For many trading firms, particularly those operating at scale, outsourcing maintenance and technical support to managed service providers (MSPs) offers a practical solution. MSPs bring specialized expertise and resources, managing day-to-day operations, security, and maintenance tasks while allowing firms to focus on core trading activities. These providers offer tailored support services, including 24/7 monitoring, incident response, and regular performance assessments, ensuring high levels of system availability and reliability.

The role of cloud service providers in streamlining maintenance and support should not be overlooked. By adopting cloud infrastructure, trading firms can leverage the advanced support services offered by providers, including automated updates, patches, and scalability. Cloud platforms also provide redundancy and failover capabilities built into their services, enhancing system resilience and simplifying disaster

273

recovery processes.

Furthermore, feedback loops between maintenance teams, technical support, and system users are essential for continuous improvement. By actively soliciting user feedback and analyzing system performance metrics, firms can identify areas for enhancement and optimize their support strategies. This iterative process fosters a culture of innovation and responsiveness, ensuring that trading platforms continue to meet evolving user needs and market demands.

Emerging technologies, such as artificial intelligence and automation, are set to redefine maintenance and technical support paradigms. AI-driven support solutions can rapidly diagnose and resolve issues by autonomously analyzing system logs and user interactions. Auto-mated maintenance tasks, such as routine software updates and health checks, reduce the manual burden on support teams, allowing them to focus on higher-impact activities.

Lastly, confidentiality and security must remain at the forefront of main-tenance and support practices. Given the sensitive nature of financial data, all maintenance activities and support interactions must adhere to strict security protocols. Access controls, encryption, and secure com-munication channels help safeguard data integrity and prevent unau-thorized access during maintenance procedures.

A comprehensive approach to maintenance and technical support is essential for sustaining the robust performance and security of trading systems. By combining preventive and predictive maintenance strate-gies, efficient technical support services, and leveraging cutting-edge technologies, trading firms can ensure operational continuity and re-silience. As the trading environment continues to evolve, maintenance and technical support will remain critical to achieving long-term success and competitiveness in the financial markets.

Chapter 13

Case Studies and Real-World Applications

This chapter explores real-world applications and case studies to illustrate the practical implementation of market making strategies. It examines successful market making models and analyzes notable failures to draw critical lessons. Innovative strategies in emerging markets are highlighted, along with the ethical challenges encountered in live trading scenarios. The impact of technological advancements on market making practices is evaluated, providing insights into the transformative role of AI and automation. The chapter concludes with a discussion on future trends in market making, informed by current developments and regulatory changes in the industry.

13.1 Historical Market Making Successes

In examining the history of financial markets, market making has played an indispensable role for centuries, serving as the backbone for ensuring liquidity and price discovery. Successful market making strategies have not only facilitated smoother transactions but have also helped markets maintain orderliness. This section delves into several remarkable historical market making successes, analyzing the strategic choices that contributed to their effectiveness in various financial settings and exploring the lessons these cases offer to contemporary practitioners.

Market making involves continuously quoting both buy and sell prices to profit from the spread, thereby providing liquidity to the market. This activity requires efficient capital deployment, managing inventory risks, and predicting short-term price movements accurately. Notable historical cases have illustrated the brilliance in combining these elements.

One of the earliest forms of market making can be traced back to the Amsterdam Stock Exchange in the 17th century, where Dutch traders known as *jobbers* maintained orderly markets by committing to buy and sell large quantities of assets. These jobbers navigated the complexities of a burgeoning global trade network by applying robust inventory management techniques and forging critical intelligence networks to anticipate market movements. The success of these strategies laid the groundwork for the future of market making operations across the globe.

Transitioning to the 20th century, the New York Stock Exchange's specialist system represents a pivotal success in market making history. Specialists, specific members of the exchange, were tasked with maintaining liquid and orderly markets for certain securities. Their success derived largely from their specialized knowledge, enabling them to correct imbalances by buying or selling against temporary market anomalies. By efficiently managing their inventory and applying advanced trade execution techniques, specialists were able to stabilize markets especially during times of significant volatility. The profound impact of the specialist system was evident during the market crash of 1987, where specialists played a crucial role in the recovery by maintaining equilibrium amidst widespread panic.

In more recent times, one cannot overlook the impact of the electronic market making revolution, epitomized by companies such as Optiver and Virtu Financial. Optiver, founded in 1986, rose to prominence by deploying automated trading systems to optimize their market making operations. The firm's proprietary trading algorithms enabled them to react in nanoseconds to market signals, managing risks with unprecedented precision. Such technological advancements allowed these firms to quote tighter spreads and handle larger volumes, ultimately enhancing liquidity across multiple global exchanges.

Virtu Financial, on the other hand, has become synonymous with market making success in the electronic age. The firm's business model revolves around high-frequency trading strategies aimed at capturing spreads efficiently while minimizing risks through sophisticated statistical models. Virtu's resilience was particularly noteworthy during the "Flash Crash" of 2010, where despite the market's abrupt descent, the firm's risk management algorithms and diversification strategies ensured continuous operation without significant losses. This highlighted the importance of technology-enabled risk management in safeguarding against extraordinary market events.

An insightful case study involves the London Stock Exchange's transition from floor trading to the electronic trading system known as SEAQ in 1986. During this transition, market makers like Smith New Court pioneered in adopting screen-based trading which led to increased efficiencies and reduced transaction costs. By leveraging technological advancements, Smith New Court was able to consolidate its market position and handle larger trade volumes with lower spreads.

Moreover, the effectiveness of market making in futures and options markets, as demonstrated by firms such as DRW Trading, underscores the adaptability and success of these strategies. DRW Trading has successfully utilized sophisticated quantitative models to engage in market making across various complex derivatives markets. Their approach involves not only basic bid-ask spread capturing but also taking informed positions based on implied volatility dynamics and interest rate projections. This proactive approach has allowed them to better anticipate market movements and adjust their trading strategies accordingly.

Analyzing these historical successes reveals several key tenets of effective market making:

- **Strategic Risk Management**: An essential component involves managing inventory and exposure to market volatility. This is achieved through a keen understanding of market microstructure and the implementation of dynamic hedging techniques.

- **Technological Integration**: Successful market makers have consistently been at the forefront of adopting and developing cutting-edge technology. The ability to process vast amounts of data in real-time and execute trades at high speed is a defining advantage.

- **Liquidity Provision**: Constantly providing liquidity across market conditions establishes credibility and trust, leading to increased market share and competitive advantage.

- **Adapting to Market Evolution**: The successful transitions from physical trading floors to electronic systems demonstrate adaptability as a critical success factor. Thorough knowledge of market regulatory changes and their implications is crucial.

- **Client and Counterparty Trust**: Building deep relationships with counterparties and clients ensures continual flow and reduces information asymmetry. Successful market makers maintain transparency and integrity in their dealings.

These principles, derived from historical case studies, highlight that the future of market making will likely center on further integrating artificial intelligence and machine learning to foresee cross-asset correlation and other complex market dynamics. The successes of the past provide a template but also pose questions about the ongoing evolution of market making as technologies and regulations continue to evolve.

As we reflect on these historical insights, market participants are equipped to enhance their strategies, ensuring that liquidity provision remains robust, adaptable, and innovative. These historical market making successes serve not only as a testament to the ingenuity of past market makers but also as a guide for the future, inspiring the continuous evolution and sophistication of market making practices.

13.2   Algorithmic Trading Firms and Their Models

Algorithmic trading represents a remarkable evolution in financial markets, reshaping how trading is executed by leveraging complex artificial intelligence and statistical models to make rapid trading decisions. This section delves into the intricacies of algorithmic trading firms, exploring their model architectures, adaptation to shifting market environments, and the distinct advantages these models have conferred. We also examine specific case studies of prominent firms that have succeeded through algorithmic trading, which has become a pivotal component of modern market making.

At the heart of algorithmic trading is the concept of executing trades using pre-programmed instructions accounting for variables such as timing, price, and volume. This approach capitalizes on the ability to execute orders at speeds and frequencies far beyond human capabilities, thus capturing opportunities for profit in milliseconds. High-frequency trading (HFT), a subset of algorithmic trading, focuses on high-speed transactions and often serves as a feeder to market making strategies by providing continuous and instantaneous liquidity.

A prototypical model within algorithmic trading firms is the statistical arbitrage model, which exploits pricing inefficiencies between securities. This model relies extensively on quantitative methods, engaging in strategies such as pairs trading, in which models predict the convergence of two correlated securities' prices. A classic example is the pair trading strategy executed by Renaissance Technologies, a renowned firm in algorithmic trading history. Renaissance's Medallion Fund, spearheaded by Jim Simons, utilized sophisticated mathematical models to predict broader price movements, achieving consistent returns over decades—even in volatile markets—with minimal drawdown.

Moreover, machine learning models have become increasingly prevalent in recent years, as firms like Two Sigma Investments have evidenced. Two Sigma employs machine learning to analyze vast datasets and discover patterns that are not immediately apparent through traditional statistical methods. By incorporating news sentiment analysis and alternative data sources such as satellite imagery and social media trends, Two Sigma enhances their predictive capabilities, realizing a competitive edge through information asymmetry.

Another hallmark example is Citadel Securities, recognized as one of the world's leading market makers and providers of liquidity. Citadel has pioneered the use of high-frequency trading models that leverage predictive analytics to consistently capture market inefficiencies. Their models incorporate advanced risk management tools, allowing for instantaneous recalibration in the face of fluctuating market conditions. Citadel's adaptive algo-architecture has enabled it to maintain resilience during periods of intense market stress, such as the market fluctuations observed during the COVID-19 pandemic.

Algorithmic trading firms utilize several model layers to enhance their trading strategies:

- **Signal Generation Models**: These models identify potential trades by predicting future price movements based on historical and current market data. Techniques such as time series analysis, regression models, and deep learning networks are frequently employed.

- **Execution Algorithms**: Once a trading signal is generated, execution algorithms determine the optimal way to execute the trades, minimizing market impact and execution costs. Algorithms like VWAP (Volume Weighted Average Price) and TWAP (Time Weighted Average Price) are widely used to ensure trades are carried out efficiently.

- **Risk Management Models**: Integral to any trading strategy is the implementation of robust risk management models. Techniques such as Value-at-Risk (VaR), scenario analysis, and Monte Carlo simulations help algorithmic trading firms manage exposure to adverse market movements.

- **Portfolio Optimization Models**: These models assist in aligning trading strategies with broader investment goals, optimizing positions based on risk/return trade-offs. Techniques from operations research and linear programming are typically utilized.

An integrated approach towards these model components ensures that algorithmic firms are not only efficient in execution but also attuned to broader market dynamics. Firms like Getco (now part of Virtu Financial) exemplify this integrated approach by combining cutting-edge technology with strategic insights, traversing multiple asset classes and geographies, thus driving liquidity and trading efficiency across the board.

An often underrated but critical component of successful algorithmic trading is the infrastructure. Co-location with exchanges to minimize latency, the deployment of state-of-the-art data processing capabilities, and the continuous refinement of code are all intrinsic to the maintenance of competitive advantage. As with DRW Trading, the relentless emphasis on keeping infrastructure at the forefront of technological innovation has allowed algorithmic firms to maintain pace with the rapid evolution of financial markets.

Challenges, however, remain inherent in algorithmic trading. Regulatory scrutiny has increased, with global regulatory bodies examining the systemic risks posed by high-frequency trading and its potential to amplify market disturbances. Firms must adapt to regulatory changes around transparency and reporting, such as the EU's MiFID II directive, which emphasizes transaction reporting and compliance adherence.

Adaptive algorithm design, coupled with a deep dedication to understanding market mechanics, positions these trading firms for sustained success, even as market structures evolve. The vanguard of algorithmic trading continues to push the boundaries by integrating advanced AI-driven techniques, utilizing innovative datasets, and maintaining rigorous compliance with evolving regulations.

Future trends indicate a growing role for quantum computing and blockchain technologies, potentially revolutionizing algorithmic models and further optimizing trade executions and risk management frameworks. Trusted names like QuantLab Financial and Tower Research Capital continue to innovate, emphasizing adaptive learning systems that refine strategies in real time. As the frontier of technology advances, so will the models driving algorithmic trading, setting the stage for an increasingly complex and competitive landscape.

The success stories and models outlined underscore a profound shift in trading paradigms, where speed, precision, and innovation coalesce to define the forefront of financial markets. Algorithmic trading firms have not only transformed traditional trading spaces but also shaped the modern perception of market liquidity—a significant achievement that continues to influence trading strategies worldwide.

13.3   Failures and Lessons Learned

While the landscape of market making and algorithmic trading boasts numerous success stories, it is equally important to acknowledge the failures that have shaped the evolution of these strategies. Understanding what went wrong in past incidents provides critical insights for improving future trading practices and risk management protocols. This section examines significant failures in market making, unearthing the lessons they offer and providing a framework for learning from these high-stakes missteps.

The story of Long-Term Capital Management (LTCM) stands as one of the most spectacular failures in the financial industry and is a cautionary tale about the dangers of over-leveraging and insufficient accounting for market risk. Founded by Nobel laureates and esteemed Wall Street traders, LTCM employed sophisticated quantitative models for market making and arbitrage, intending to capture spreads with minimal risk. Despite the intellectual rigor and advanced modeling, LTCM's overreliance on financial leverage proved catastrophic. The firm's models inadequately accounted for extreme market events, such as the 1997 Asian financial crisis and the 1998 Russian debt default, leading to a liquidity crisis that necessitated a Federal Reserve-led bail-out. The core lesson from LTCM's collapse is the paramount importance of stress testing models under extreme conditions and maintaining adequate liquidity reserves to withstand unexpected market shocks.

Another instructive case is Knight Capital's trading fiasco in 2012, which underscores the vulnerabilities inherent in technological errors in algorithmic trading. Knight Capital, a major player in market making, suffered a technological error that led to a trading debacle, burning through approximately $440 million in 45 minutes due to erroneous algorithm deployment. A software malfunction activated an obsolete trading algorithm, executing millions of trades at hefty losses. This failure highlighted the critical need for robust testing, verification procedures, and contingency protocols to manage technological risks. Consequently, the concept of continuous integration and rigorous code testing has become industry best practice, ensuring algorithmic stability and reliability under all market conditions.

Further insights can be garnered from the "Flash Crash" of May 6, 2010, a stark illustration of the cascading effects that algorithmic trading strategies can unleash in financial markets. The crash was initiated by the rapid execution of a large sell order, which interacted with high-frequency trading algorithms, prompting a liquidity drain and the subsequent plummet of the U.S. stock market. This incident underlines the necessity for circuit breakers and other safeguards to halt trading during periods of excessive volatility. Moreover, it highlights the importance of understanding algorithm interactions and ensuring that models are designed to account for, and adjust to, emergent systemic risks.

The experiences of numerous market makers during the 2008 financial crisis further emphasize the need for proactive risk management strategies. Many firms found themselves over-leveraged and ill-prepared for the precipitous drop in asset values, leading to significant losses and, in some instances, bankruptcy. This scenario emphasizes the importance of diversification and constant reevaluation of market positions to ensure alignment with financial health and objectives.

Additionally, the downfall of Barings Bank in 1995 due to rogue trading activities by Nick Leeson reveals a critical lapse in risk management and internal controls. Leeson's speculative trading, hidden in unauthorized accounts, eventually culminated in comprehensive losses that crippled the bank. The Barings case reiterates the necessity for transparent trading operations, diligent monitoring, and adequate oversight mechanisms to mitigate the risk of unauthorized trading activities.

From these historical failures, several overarching lessons emerge:

- Comprehensive Risk Management: The significance of incorporating robust risk management practices is repeatedly underscored. Not only should firms establish limits on leverage and exposure, but they should also engage in continuous risk assessment to quickly adapt to changing market conditions.

- Robust Model Testing and Validation: Ensuring the accuracy and functionality of trading algorithms through exhaustive testing and validation is crucial. Employing simulations and back-testing can identify potential vulnerabilities and improve the reliability of trading models.

- Structural and Technological Redundancies: Establishing structural and technical redundancies helps safeguard against system failures and operational disruptions. This includes maintaining backup systems and establishing protocols for rapid resolution of technological issues.

- Regulatory and Compliance Adherence: Staying abreast of regulatory changes and maintaining stringent compliance ensures that trading activities do not inadvertently breach legal or ethical boundaries, which could result in severe financial penalties or reputational damage.

- Effective Communication and Transparency: Maintaining open channels for communication and transparency within trading operations can prevent systemic abuses and facilitate the early identification of potential issues.

- Adaptive Learning and Continuous Improvement: The ability to learn from past mistakes and continually improve reflects a commitment to excellence. Incorporating lessons learned and adapting strategies to account for new information strengthens trading frameworks.

As the trading landscape continues to evolve, firms that internalize these lessons will be better positioned to capitalize on opportunities while mitigating potential threats. In a dynamic market environment, the ability to be agile, forward-thinking, and risk-aware distinguishes successful market makers from those susceptible to past pitfalls. By instilling practices grounded in these lessons, firms can embark on a more resilient trajectory, ensuring sustained success and stability in market making and algorithmic trading.

13.4   Innovative Strategies in Emerging Markets

Emerging markets represent a frontier of opportunities and challenges for market makers and trading firms seeking to exploit new avenues for growth. Characterized by dynamic economic landscapes and rapid industrialization, these markets offer unique conditions that necessitate innovative strategies to capture potential high yields while managing associated risks. This section explores various innovative market making and trading strategies that firms have employed successfully in emerging markets, highlighting the inherent challenges and exceptional opportunities these markets present.

Emerging markets, such as those in Southeast Asia, Latin America, and Africa, are often marked by lower levels of liquidity and less mature financial infrastructures. These characteristics pose distinct challenges; however, they also present opportunities for market makers to establish themselves as crucial providers of liquidity and to benefit from potentially larger spreads and market inefficiencies.

One prominent strategy employed in such markets is *local partnership and knowledge integration*. By collaborating with local financial institutions and stakeholders, international market makers can gain invaluable insights into regional market dynamics, regulatory environments, and cultural nuances that stand as pivotal elements for successful operation. For example, in China's rapidly evolving financial markets, firms such as Goldman Sachs have forged joint ventures with local companies to navigate complex regulatory mandates and tap into domestic expertise, allowing them to tailor trading strategies that align with local market conditions and consumer behavior.

Another strategy revolves around *leveraging technological advancements and mobile integration*. Fintech innovations have dramatically reshaped financial landscapes, particularly in regions where traditional banking infrastructure is limited. Mobile-based trading applications have gained traction in places like Africa, where firms capitalize on high mobile penetration rates to offer easily accessible trading platforms. For instance, the success of M-Pesa in Kenya illustrates the role of mobile platforms in expanding financial inclusion. By creating algorithms designed to work seamlessly across mobile platforms and cater to local user interfaces, market makers can engage a previously untapped demographic, increasing liquidity and market activity.

Tailored financial products also play a critical role in capturing opportunities in emerging markets. Customizing financial products to meet the specific needs of local investors can significantly enhance trading volumes. In India, the introduction of commodity derivatives tailored to local agricultural products, such as guar seed and castor oil, by firms such as NCDEX has allowed traders to hedge against price volatility specific to regional commodities. Such tailored instruments not only provide risk management solutions to local producers and traders but also increase liquidity as global investors seek exposure to these unique assets.

Recognizing the *evolving regulatory environments* within emerging markets is another vital component. Regulations in these regions are often subject to rapid changes as governments strive to develop robust financial systems. Understanding these regulatory trajectories allows market makers to preemptively adjust their strategies. For example, after South Africa's enhancements in foreign exchange management to encourage transparency and capital flow, firms like JP Morgan revised their forex trading strategies to align with new compliance standards, thus capitalizing on deregulation benefits.

The concept of *cross-market arbitrage* has also found a firm footing in emerging markets. Due to market segmentation and varying levels of market development, arbitrage opportunities—where traders can exploit price differences between different markets or regions— often arise. Sophisticated platforms capable of executing cross-border trades in real-time are essential, requiring robust technological infrastructure and comprehensive market data analysis to identify and act upon transient inefficiencies.

Furthermore, *local currency stability strategies* form a significant part of dealing with emerging markets, as currency volatility poses substantial risks. Innovatively designed hedging models, which might leverage options and forward contracts tailored to the specific currency risks endemic to a particular region, have become essential. Firms have also employed machine learning algorithms to forecast currency movement patterns, enhancing their ability to hedge effectively and safeguard against adverse market conditions.

In studying these strategies, several critical lessons and best practices emerge:

- **Emphasis on Local Insights**: Understanding cultural, regulatory, and economic nuances through local expertise is paramount for developing effective strategies and maintaining compliance.

- **Technological Adaptation and Innovation**: Creating flexible trading platforms suited to the technological realities and limitations of specific regions is vital. Leveraging AI and machine learning to process diverse datasets can offer significant predictive advantages.

- **Risk Management Strategies**: Crafting risk management protocols that consider the volatility and regulatory unpredictability specific to emerging markets ensures resilience against unforeseen adverse conditions.

- **Community Engagement**: Building and maintaining trust with local communities and stakeholders can enhance brand loyalty and lead to sustained market presence. Market makers should aim to establish a reputation for reliability and integrity within local ecosystems.

- **Diverse Product Offerings**: Innovating and diversifying financial products to meet local needs while educating market participants about their use can expand a firm's reach and facilitate broader market participation.

By deploying these innovative strategies, market makers and traders can take advantage of the vast potential of emerging markets, positioning themselves as indispensable components of these economies' financial systems. As the global economic landscape diversifies, emerging markets will continue to play an increasingly influential role, with their success intimately linked to the ability of market participants to adapt and innovate.

The experience of successful market makers in emerging markets underscores the significance of an adaptive approach that respects regional diversity, leverages technology, and prioritizes cultural and regulatory alignment. Firms that boldly embrace these strategies not only enhance their prospects within these dynamic environments but also contribute to the stabilization and development of financial markets worldwide, reinforcing the broader agenda of economic inclusivity and global integration.

13.5 Ethical Challenges in Real-World Scenarios

The rapid advancement of technology and its integration into financial markets have dramatically reshaped the landscape of trading and market making. While these developments have brought about increased efficiency and liquidity, they have also given rise to complex ethical challenges that market participants must navigate. In this section, we explore ethical dilemmas encountered in real-world scenarios, analyzing the implications of these challenges and suggesting strategies to mitigate them while maintaining the integrity of financial markets.

One of the primary ethical challenges in modern trading involves the use of algorithmic and high-frequency trading (HFT) strategies. These techniques, designed to execute trades at speeds beyond human capability, can sometimes lead to market manipulation concerns. A notable instance is the "quote stuffing" controversy, where traders flood the market with false orders to obscure competitors' view of true market supply and demand levels. Such practices, though not outright illegal, tread a fine line between clever strategy and unethical manipulation. The challenge here is maintaining transparency and fairness in markets, ensuring that HFT does not unfairly disadvantage slower or less technologically-equipped participants.

Market abuse, including insider trading and front running, remains a perennial ethical issue. In algorithmic trading, the use of vast amounts of data and machine learning models to predict market trends can lead to unintended breaches of privacy or misuse of privileged information. A case highlighting this is the enforcement action taken against certain hedge funds using satellite imagery to analyze parking lot traffic at retail chains, raising questions about the ethical boundaries of data usage. While such innovative data strategies are within legal boundaries, they provoke debate about what constitutes fair competition versus exploitation of asymmetric information.

Another ethical consideration involves the deployment of autonomous trading systems. With AI systems making decisions without direct human intervention, accountability becomes a gray area. For instance, if a trading algorithm inadvertently causes a "flash crash" or executes trades that violate regulations, determining liability can be challenging. Questions about the extent of human oversight and the potential for these systems to exacerbate market instability provoke significant eth-

287

ical discussions in the trading community.

Conflict of interest is another area of concern, especially in the realm of market making. Brokerage firms that engage in proprietary trading might prioritize their trades over those of their clients. The Securities and Exchange Commission (SEC) has enacted strict regulations to mitigate these issues, yet ensuring full compliance remains a persistent ethical hurdle. The well-documented case of Goldman Sachs' "Abacus deal," where it allegedly bet against its clients' investment products while simultaneously selling them, exemplifies the ethical conflicts that can arise in such scenarios.

The ethical use of artificial intelligence (AI) in trading also presents significant challenges. AI's potential for harvesting data to generate insights conflicts with privacy and consent norms. Furthermore, AI systems may inadvertently reinforce biases present in training datasets, leading to unfair or discriminatory trading decisions. Addressing these biases requires traders and technologists to develop rigorous auditing and adjustment protocols to ensure that algorithmic decision-making processes adhere to ethical standards.

Aside from technology-driven concerns, environmental ethics has gained prominence in the trading domain. The substantial energy consumption associated with cryptocurrency trading, particularly the blockchain's proof-of-work mechanisms, poses ethical questions about ecological sustainability. With environmental impact becoming a crucial consideration for investors, market participants are increasingly pressured to balance profitability with ecological responsibility.

In navigating these ethical challenges, several strategies and frameworks can be implemented:

- Developing Comprehensive Ethical Guidelines: Creating an overarching ethical framework that encompasses all trading activities ensures adherence to moral and legal standards. This includes clear guidelines on data usage, conflict of interest management, and AI deployment.

- Enhancing Transparency and Accountability: Implementing transparent algorithms and audit trails fosters trust and accountability. Ensuring that stakeholders understand how decisions are made allows for greater oversight.

- Balancing Innovation with Regulation: While innovation drives market efficiency, it must be balanced with robust regulatory oversight. Collaborating with regulators to develop forward-thinking policies that anticipate future ethical challenges is paramount.

- Strengthening Oversight and Governance: Institutions should establish strong governance structures to ensure that ethical considerations are integrated into decision-making processes. This includes regular ethical reviews and audits of trading activities.

- Promoting Ethical Education and Culture: Cultivating an organizational culture that prioritizes ethics is crucial. Continuous education and training can ensure that ethical considerations are top of mind for all trading professionals.

- Utilizing Impact Assessments: Conducting environmental and social impact assessments for trading activities can guide traders in understanding and mitigating their broader implications.

These strategies emphasize that ethical considerations are not merely ancillary to trading activities but integral to sustainable financial practices. As markets and technologies continue to evolve, a proactive ethical stance will be indispensable for ensuring that market making and trading serve the interests of the broader economy and society at large.

Ultimately, addressing ethical challenges in real-world trading scenarios is a multidimensional effort that requires cooperation among market participants, regulators, and technology developers. By fostering an environment of transparency, accountability, and education, the financial industry can navigate its ethical landscape, setting standards that reflect the value of integrity and fairness in an increasingly complex and interconnected world. As we move toward future innovations, maintaining a vigilant and adaptive ethical outlook will be key to cultivating trust and stability within global financial markets.

13.6   Technology-Driven Transformations

Technology stands as the driving force behind transformative changes in financial markets, particularly in the realms of trading and market making. From the early days of electronic trading systems to the current advancements in artificial intelligence and quantum computing, technology has continuously redefined how market participants interact, make decisions, and derive value. This section explores the profound impact of technological innovations on market making practices, examining specific examples of breakthroughs, their implications for market dynamics, and the future trends looming on the horizon.

The evolution of electronic trading platforms marks one of the most significant technological transformations in financial markets. The transition from traditional floor trading to electronic systems has streamlined processes, reduced transaction costs, and increased transparency. Notably, the introduction of NASDAQ in 1971 as the first electronic stock market heralded a new era, leading to a proliferation of electronic communications networks (ECNs) that facilitate direct trading between two parties. This innovation laid the groundwork for modern algorithmic trading strategies that dominate the markets today.

Algorithmic trading, which relies extensively on technology, has seen exponential growth due to its ability to execute trades at lightning speeds based on pre-set criteria. Algorithms analyze vast datasets, identify patterns, and implement trades within milliseconds, maximizing profit potential and enhancing liquidity. A quintessential example of this is the success of firms like Renaissance Technologies, whose Medallion Fund employs complex mathematical models to generate consistently high returns. This trajectory underscores how technological prowess can yield formidable competitive advantages.

High-frequency trading (HFT), a subset of algorithmic trading, epitomizes the zenith of technology-driven trading. HFT firms utilize state-of-the-art hardware and co-locate servers with exchanges to minimize latency, thus executing trades during fleeting market discrepancies. The advent of HFT has vastly improved market liquidity and tightened bid-ask spreads. However, it has also sparked debates about market stability and fairness, leading to regulatory scrutiny aimed at curbing potential systemic risks.

The integration of artificial intelligence and machine learning into trading strategies has further amplified the technological transformation. AI systems can process and interpret vast datasets in real-time, delivering insights that were previously inaccessible through manual analysis. Two Sigma Investments exemplifies the integration of AI, utilizing advanced machine learning models to parse alternative datasets—such as social media feeds, satellite imagery, and economic indicators—to inform trading decisions. This approach not only enhances decision-making accuracy but also enables traders to respond dynamically to market shifts.

Blockchain technology represents another frontier of technological transformation, particularly in enhancing transparency and reducing fraud. Its decentralized ledger system ensures secure, immutable records of transactions, presenting compelling applications in areas such as clearing and settlement processes. The rise of decentralized finance (DeFi) platforms powered by blockchain has introduced a paradigm shift, enabling peer-to-peer trading and lending without traditional intermediaries. These developments foster greater inclusivity and innovation within markets, albeit raising regulatory and security concerns that necessitate careful consideration.

Quantum computing holds promise for the future of market making and trading. Although still in its nascent stages, quantum computing's ability to solve complex problems exponentially faster than classical computers could revolutionize tasks such as option pricing, risk assessment, and portfolio optimization. Firms investing in quantum technologies, such as IBM and Google, are actively exploring financial applications, envisioning an era where quantum algorithms could drastically enhance efficiency and predictive accuracy in trading systems.

As we examine these technology-driven transformations, several impacts and trends become apparent:

- **Enhanced Market Efficiency**: Technology has dramatically increased trading speed and efficiency, reducing friction and lowering costs across the trading process. This evolution supports more liquid and accessible markets, benefiting traders and investors globally.

- **Data-Driven Decision Making**: The ability to harness big data has transformed market analytics. Advanced data processing tools enable traders to glean actionable insights and develop more informed strategies, taking advantage of market anomalies and trends.

- **Regulatory Challenges**: The pace of technological change has outstripped existing regulatory frameworks, compelling regulators to adapt quickly to manage new risks while fostering innovation. Effective oversight will be crucial in ensuring technology serves the broader market interest.

- **Cybersecurity Concerns**: With greater reliance on technology comes heightened vulnerability to cyber threats. Ensuring robust cybersecurity measures and incident response strategies is essential to protect market integrity and investor confidence.

- **Automation and Human Collaboration**: While automation expedites many processes, the synthesis of human intuition and machine efficiency offers the most strategic advantage. As such, training market participants to operate alongside advanced technologies remains a critical focus.

- **Sustainability Considerations**: The environmental footprint of technology, particularly in sectors such as cryptocurrency mining and data centers, prompts a reevaluation of technological implementations aligned with sustainable practices.

Looking ahead, the trajectory of technology-driven transformations suggests a continued acceleration towards more complex, automated, and intelligent systems within trading and market making. The convergence of AI, blockchain, and quantum computing heralds unprecedented opportunities and challenges, requiring market participants to not only innovate but also carefully navigate the ethical and regulatory landscape that accompanies these advancements.

Technology-driven transformations continue to redefine the boundaries of possibility within financial markets. As the interplay between humans and machines becomes increasingly sophisticated, the emphasis on maintaining transparency, security, and fairness will be paramount. Embracing change with a mindful approach will enable firms to leverage technology for strategic gain, fostering a robust and forward-thinking market environment that caters to diverse global stakeholders.

13.7   Future Trends and Developments

As financial markets continue their rapid evolution, understanding future trends and developments is crucial for market makers, investors, and policymakers. The trajectory of financial innovation is influenced by technological advancements, regulatory shifts, and global economic trends, all of which shape how markets will function in the coming decades. This section explores anticipated trends and examines their potential implications for market dynamics, investment strategies, and regulatory frameworks.

One of the most significant future trends in financial markets is the increasing use of artificial intelligence and machine learning. These technologies will likely continue to revolutionize how trading decisions are made, enabling more precise and efficient market operations. AI-driven algorithms can process large and varied datasets in real time, providing insights into market trends and identifying opportunities and risks with unprecedented accuracy. As these technologies become more advanced, we can expect increased adoption across asset classes, with AI systems evolving to recommend optimized trading strategies, real-time risk adjustments, and personalized investment portfolios tailored to individual investor goals.

In tandem with AI, the rise of *quantum computing* promises to open new frontiers in market analytics. Quantum computing, with its ability to perform complex calculations at previously unimaginable speeds, could dramatically enhance financial modeling, particularly in areas such as derivatives pricing, risk management, and high-frequency trading. Quantum algorithms are expected to provide deeper insights into market patterns and correlations, giving traders a competitive edge. Companies such as IBM and Google are investing heavily in quantum research, and their breakthroughs could redefine market efficiency in the not-so-distant future.

Moreover, the role of *blockchain technology* in transforming financial markets is undeniable. Blockchain's decentralized and secure infrastructure offers significant potential benefits for improving transaction transparency and reducing settlement times. The rise of decentralized finance (DeFi) platforms exemplifies a broader trend towards disintermediation, where traditional financial intermediaries are bypassed in favor of peer-to-peer transactions. This shift could democratize access to financial services, allowing individuals worldwide to engage directly in trade and investment activities without the need for traditional banking infrastructure. However, it also presents challenges, as it requires new regulatory frameworks to safeguard against fraud and ensure consumer protection.

Another trend shaping the future is the *growing importance of environmental, social, and governance (ESG) factors* in investment decisions. Investors are increasingly prioritizing sustainability and ethical considerations, driving demand for securities that align with these values. Market participants are integrating ESG metrics into their evaluation processes, with technologies like AI aiding in the analysis of companies' ESG performance. In response, we can anticipate the development of innovative financial products, such as green bonds and sustainability-linked derivatives, which cater to the ESG-focused market landscape.

As markets become more interconnected, the *globalization of financial services* will continue to expand. Cross-border trading and investment activities are expected to rise, facilitated by advanced technology and harmonized regulatory standards. However, this interconnectedness also raises the potential for systemic risks and market contagion, necessitating robust global regulatory coordination. Institutions like the Financial Stability Board (FSB) play a crucial role in maintaining stability in an increasingly complex global market environment.

The proliferation of *digital currencies*, including state-backed central bank digital currencies (CBDCs), represents another significant development. CBDCs, being explored by various governments, have the potential to alter traditional banking and payment systems. They could enhance efficiency, reduce transaction costs, and promote financial inclusion by providing a secure and accessible means of digital payment. Nonetheless, the introduction of CBDCs will need careful consideration of privacy, cybersecurity, and monetary policy implications to ensure they complement existing financial systems effectively.

Additionally, the concept of *personalized finance* is gaining traction. As consumer data becomes more accessible, financial services are increasingly tailored to individual preferences and life circumstances. Through advanced data analytics and AI, firms can create customized investment solutions and financial planning advice, enhancing customer engagement and satisfaction. This trend towards personalization reflects a broader shift in consumer expectations, emphasizing convenience, transparency, and real-time access to financial services.

An essential factor driving these future trends is the *evolving regulatory landscape*. Regulators are challenged to keep pace with financial innovations, ensuring that stability and integrity are maintained without stifling innovation. Regulatory technology (RegTech), employing AI and data analytics, is emerging as a powerful tool for improving regulatory compliance and oversight. As financial systems grow more complex, efficient regulatory responses will be vital to address issues such as data privacy, market manipulation, and systemic risk.

In exploring these future trends, the following strategic considerations emerge:

- Technology Engagement: Market participants must remain at the forefront of technological advancements, integrating new tools and methodologies to enhance operations and remain competitive in a rapidly evolving market.

- Risk Management Adaptation: Adapting risk management frameworks to incorporate emerging technologies and address new risk dimensions, such as cyber threats and geopolitical risks, is essential.

- Emphasis on Sustainability: Proactively incorporating sustainability considerations into investment decisions will become increasingly important in attracting capital and aligning with stakeholder values.

- Regulatory Compliance: Engaging in constructive dialogue with regulators and staying informed of evolving regulatory requirements will ensure compliance and mitigate risks associated with innovation.

- Consumer-Centric Approach: Emphasizing personalized, transparent, and customer-focused services can enhance customer loyalty and provide a competitive advantage in the marketplace.

The financial markets of the future promise unprecedented opportunities for growth and innovation, but they also present new challenges that require thoughtful navigation. By embracing technological advancements, prioritizing sustainable practices, and adapting regulatory frameworks, market participants can capitalize on these trends, driving market evolution and contributing to a resilient and inclusive financial ecosystem. As we look to the future, collaboration between industry, regulators, and technology providers will be paramount in shaping a financial marketplace that is robust, equitable, and prepared for the unforeseen challenges of tomorrow.